Sociological Impressionism

A Reassessment of Georg Simmel's Social Theory

Sociological Impressionism

A Reassessment of
Georg Simmel's Social Theory

David Frisby

HEINEMANN · LONDON

Heinemann Educational Books Ltd
22 Bedford Square, London WC1B 3HH

LONDON EDINBURGH MELBOURNE AUCKLAND
HONG KONG SINGAPORE KUALA LUMPUR NEW DELHI
IBADAN NAIROBI JOHANNESBURG
EXETER (NH) KINGSTON PORT OF SPAIN

ISBN 0 435 82320 5

Typeset by The Castlefield Press of Northampton
in 10/12pt Journal Roman, and printed in Great Britain by
Biddles Ltd, Guildford, Surrey

Contents

Acknowledgements

The material for this study was assembled from a number of libraries and I am very grateful to the staff of the following for their assistance: the University of Glasgow Library, the British Library, the Universitäts- bibliothek Heidelberg, the library of the Institut für Soziologie und Ethnologie der Universität Heidelberg, and the Universitätsbibliothek Wien. In particular, I wish to thank Dr Karsten Witte (Berlin) and the staff of the Deutsche Literaturarchiv, Marbach/Neckar for permission to consult the largely unpublished manuscript by Siegfried Kracauer, *Georg Simmel: Ein Beitrag zur Deutung des geistigen Lebens unserer Zeit.* My thanks go to Siegfried Unseld and Suhrkamp Verlag for per- mission to quote from this manuscript. Duncker & Humblot, publishers of *Buch des Dankes an Georg Simmel* very kindly gave me permission to quote from this book, for which I am very grateful.

The research for this book was carried out in the summer of 1978 at the University of Heidelberg. I am very grateful for the generous financial support of the British Academy who awarded me a fellowship to study at Heidelberg. Further research in the summer of 1979 at the University of Vienna was supported by a bursary from the Republik Österreich Bundesministerium für Wissenschaft und Forschung to whom I wish to acknowledge my thanks.

My research in Heidelberg was facilitated by the hospitality of Wolfgang Schluchter who provided me with a study in the Institut für Soziologie. I also wish to thank Horst Baier (Konstanz) for his assistance. Finally I wish to thank Pru Larsen for typing the manuscript.

Responsibility for the interpretation of Simmel's work contained in these pages must, of course, remain my own.

David Frisby
Glasgow

Preface

The following study of Simmel's social theory grew out of a number of factors. As an undergraduate, I had read some of Simmel's work with great interest but had broadly concurred with the label then attached to him, namely that of a 'formal' sociologist. With no clear indication of the context within which Simmel had attracted this label, I could see that his sociology was surprisingly ahistorical and therefore might attract the label 'formal'. Because of other connotations, I also equated formal sociology with boring sociology. Along with many other 'classical' sociologists, Simmel remained *'museal'* or museum-like, as one of several objects 'to which the observer no longer has a vital relationship and which are in the process of dying. They owe their preservation more to historical respect than to the needs of the present' (Adorno, *Prisms*, p. 175). It is no easy task to resuscitate near fossilised figures from the sociological mausoleum. At that time, I had no wish to do so and even today would be content to leave many of these figures to whom I was introduced where they are.

Many years later, I was asked to complete a translation of Simmel's *Philosophie des Geldes* with which I had, by then, become acquainted at second hand. In the course of this work which I originally undertook largely for reasons of financial gain — in the supermarket of knowledge, this proved to be an illusion — I became interested once more in Simmel's work, but this time in a Simmel that I hardly recognised. This prompted me to investigate the context of The Philosophy of Money. Not only was I confronted with an author whose object of study he sought 'to illuminate with a firework rather than a study lamp' (Schmoller) but also a work whose analysis of the spirit of capitalism was 'simply brilliant' (Max Weber) and which 'forms a very interesting correlate to Marx's *Capital*' (Goldsheid). To some of his students the author himself was seen as 'a philosophical Monet' (Lukács) who had 'the finest mind amongst all his contemporaries' (Ernst Bloch). Yet not only was Simmel's work unacknowledged in terms of his professional position (he only received a chair of philosophy in 1914 and then only in the marginal University of Strasbourg) but even within a decade after his death his work had ceased to find much resonance within Germany. In the United States, however, Simmel's sociology was taken up by the Chicago School, and later in the 1950s and early 1960s after the publication of English translations of some of his work. But even here I was surprised to find that the only book written on Simmel's social theory in English by Spykman was published as long ago as 1925.

Spykman's study was largely expository. The present work does not pretend to be a comprehensive exposition of Simmel's work. Since more of his works have now appeared in translation – notably *The Problems of the Philosophy of History* (1977) and *The Philosophy of Money* (1978) as well as more recent collections of extracts from his other works – another such expository study of Simmel's social theory appears less pressing. Instead, the present study attempts to reconstruct some of the central themes in Simmel's work largely through the original texts themselves as well as contemporary commentaries. It will soon become apparent that there is no shortage of Simmel texts nor, for that matter, contemporary commentaries upon his work. By re-examining them I hope to be able to confront the paradox of Simmel's work, namely the enthusiasm with which it was greeted by many of his contemporaries and its relative neglect today. Through this reconstruction I hope to rescue Simmel from the time warp within which he seems to be trapped. I would argue that this can only be done by entering that world which now seems so closed off to us. This hermeneutic intention is, however, combined with an ideological–critical one that seeks to question the tradition within which Simmel's work is located.

If my interpretation of Simmel is somewhat different from that which is usually offered to us, namely as a 'formal', 'systematic' sociologist, then this is, in part, due to this reconstruction of the central motifs in Simmel's work. However, my major debt in the task of reinterpreting Simmel's writings must be to a number of very disparate sources. The first is, of course, Simmel's own texts and in particular the astonishing range of articles that he wrote, many of which have not even been considered in the German reception of his work. The second is the numerous accounts of Simmel by his contemporaries some of which, like Lukács' article of 1918, are significant for the interpretation of Simmel presented here. In particular, the unpublished study by Siegfried Kracauer, *Georg Simmel: Ein Beitrag zur Deutung des geistigen Lebens unserer Zeit* (the first chapter of which did appear in *Logos* in 1920) has provided me with the most sensitive assessment of Simmel's work by any of his students.

In the course of working on this book, I have been influenced by two other works both of which seem, at first sight, to be as far removed from Georg Simmel as possible. The first of these is Walter Benjamin's *Charles Baudelaire* — a collection from his *Passagenarbeit* on nineteenth century Paris that remained incomplete and largely unpublished during his lifetime. This study of Baudelaire and the accompanying fragments on nineteenth century Paris do seem to have little in common with a reassessment of Simmel's work. But this initial impression is deceptive. Not only did Benjamin read Simmel's *Philosophy of Money* in the course of working on the *Passagenarbeit* and occasionally quote his other writings, but, more importantly, he extracts a number of central motifs in Baudelaire's work, some of which at least suggest stimulating comparisons with Simmel's approach. Specifically, Benjamin discusses the role of the *flâneur* as a key to understanding Baudelaire's work. Although Simmel is writing within a very different context, it is possible to see him as a sociological *flâneur* who not necessarily 'goes botanising on the asphalt' but certainly assembles a whole array of fleeting glimpses of diverse aspects of social life. Like the earlier physiologies which Benjamin describes, Simmel's impressions leave the world undisturbed. From the opposite direction, too, it is possible to see how Benjamin, like Simmel, is also fascinated by apparently insignificant objects, though the realm of significance differs greatly for the two writers. However, this is hardly the place to follow through the inspirations and parallels that can be derived from Benjamin's text.

The second apparently unconnected text which has stimulated a series of questions and possible insights into Simmel's work is Robert Musil's *Der Mann ohne Eigenschaften* — again an incomplete work. Without placing too much emphasis upon the relationship, it is known that Musil attended Simmel's lectures in his period of study at Berlin between 1903 and 1910. *The Man without Qualities* contains one of the most devastating attacks upon historicism and *Lebensphilosophie* (the latter assumes considerable importance in Simmel's later writings) as well as a critical response to the George circle with which Simmel was associated though not a full member. More generally, the novel's 'hero' Ulrich shares with Simmel an interest in phenomena without a commitment to them, a conscious essayism, a rootlessness, an aestheticisation of reality, a perspectivism and many other attributes. Again, however, one should guard against immediately transcribing these features onto Simmel's life without taking due account of the different contexts within which the two are located.

In the light of these and other influences, I have chosen to examine a somewhat limited range of themes in Simmel's work. Yet I hope that they are both significant enough to illuminate other areas of his work that I do not necessarily cover and stimulating enough to restore an interest in his writings.

The first chapter examines some of the problems associated with any assessment of Simmel's sociological work and confronts the seemingly fragmentary nature of his work. Some attempt is also made to provide an outline of Simmel's life and milieux derived largely from contemporary sources. In chapter two Simmel's attempt to lay the foundations of sociology and the study of social interaction is critically examined. This can only be fully understood in the light of demarcations with other disciplines, especially psychology and history. This is also the place to investigate why Simmel's sociology has attracted the label 'formal'.

Following on from this assessment of Simmel's success in founding sociology as an independent discipline, the third chapter takes up Simmel's approach to his subject matter. For many other sociologists, this would consist of an explication of their 'method'. If, however, we free ourselves from the confines of the causal–analytical paradigm for rewriting the history of sociology, then it can be readily shown that Simmel's approach to his object of study cannot be easily assimilable into this framework. Indeed, it can only lead to a gross distortion of much of his work. Instead, the provocative description of Simmel as a 'sociological *flâneur*' points to a fundamentally different approach to his 'method' which highlights the aesthetic dimension of his sociology.

In terms of the orthodox reception of Simmel's work, the fourth chapter, which deals with his analysis of various forms of social interaction drawn from his essays as well as his *Philosophy of Money*, will appear even more problematic. The title of the chapter 'Snapshots *sub specie aeternitatis*' – literally 'Snapshots under the aspect of eternity' – is intended to be neither esoteric nor misleading. It is, in fact, Simmel's own title for seven short pieces which he published in the key Munich *Jugendstil* journal *Jugend* between 1900 and 1903. As so often in Simmel's work, the clues to a genuine understanding of his texts lie within the texts themselves in the specific sense that he often captures his mode of experiencing reality without stating that he himself subscribes to it. Another example would be the related description of aesthetic distance from the world that is found in his *Philosophy of Money* which also pinpoints his own approach, as I argue in the previous chapter and elsewhere. The reader of Simmel's essays on social phenomena must be struck by the distinctive impression gained from them.

It is, indeed, that of a snapshot or a fleeting glimpse of some social phenomenon which is, at the same time, also seen to have universal significance or, at least, is taken as an instance of a more general essential form. Some of these essential 'forms' of interaction are therefore examined in this chapter.

Simmel's tendency not to reveal his own person or his own views upon specific issues has already been alluded to. In his major works, this is particularly apparent for his attitude towards political and economic events and tendencies. It is very easy to gain the impression that Simmel was totally uninterested in contemporary socio-political and economic developments from a reading of his major works – even, ironically, from *The Philosophy of Money* which ostensibly, at least, contains a potential critique of a capitalist money economy – and from those sociological essays within which an aesthetic distance is preserved. But this would be misleading. It is not even that a political dimension, for instance, is totally absent from Simmel's works. There are, in fact, a whole range of articles and comments upon social and political movements – upon the women's movement and trade unions, for instance – which, for us, are buried away in newspaper articles and journals. In the light of this, we can plausibly argue that a political dimension is present in Simmel's work but that it seldom constitutes an integral part of his major analyses of social phenomena. This socio-political and economic dimension of Simmel's work – including some of his wartime writings which initially exhibited considerable enthusiasm for the First World War – is dealt with in the final chapter of this study.

This brief outline of the contents of the study is not intended to give the impression that the central themes of Simmel's sociology – sociation (*Vergesellschaftung*), form, social differentiation, interaction (*Wechselwirkung*), totality and the notion of the fundamental interrelatedness (*Wesenszusammengehörigkeit*) of phenomena, etc. – have been ignored or are dealt with only tangentially. Rather, my intention has been to relate them to the wider context of Simmel's life and work as a whole in order to avoid that degree of abstraction of the discussion of concepts which acts as a barrier to the understanding of Simmel's work.

1 Georg Simmel: A Kind of Introduction to a Man Without Qualities?

'He is a man without qualities!'
'What is that?' asked Clarisse sniggering.
'Nothing. It's absolutely nothing!'

Robert Musil, *Der Mann ohne Eigenschaften*

This philosophy is not the world view of a person motivated by powerful ideas but rather the incursion of a self-less person into the world.

Siegfried Kracauer, *Georg Simmel*

I

Any attempt at a reassessment of the sociological work of Georg Simmel is confronted with a series of difficulties, some of which are faced by any critical reconstruction and interpretation of social scientific and other texts, and others that are peculiar to Simmel's work. Like any of the 'founding fathers' now trapped within the sociological museum, Simmel's contribution to the development of sociology has already been assessed within various traditions. American sociology, for instance, upon which Simmel exerted his greatest influence, has passed through a series of phases of interpretation of his work. In a recent study of Simmel's work, Schnabel convincingly shows that American commentators have tended to respond to his work as 'enclosed miniature theories' of aspects of social life rather than to see specific themes and analysis in Simmel's work as part of a whole.[1] Secondly, the American sociological traditions have ignored those parts of Simmel's work (his *Philosophy of Money*, for instance) that could be seen as part of his own reception of Marxism. Further, textbook histories of sociology have taken Simmel's work as providing evidence of the steady thematic accumulation of our knowledge of the social world

whilst, associated with this textbook misinterpretation of the development of any science, generations of 'honest positivists' have found in
his work a near inexhaustible fund of fruitful hypotheses. The earliest
interpretations of Simmel's sociology in American sociology by Spykman[2] and Abel[3] both in their differing ways established a reading of
his sociology in terms of a functional and formal theoretical practice —
labels that have persisted for decades despite the increasing recognition of the ambiguities of both 'form' and 'function'.[4] Although
Spykman does offer a more comprehensive treatment of Simmel's
work than Abel, who concentrates his attention upon Simmel's *Soziologie*, both commentators separate out Simmel's philosophical and
metaphysical intentions from his practical empirical aims in a manner
that prevents a comprehensive understanding of Simmel's work and
serves to make his sociology more 'formal' than it actually is. However this separation does facilitate the reception of Simmel's sociology
within an empiricist tradition since potential hypotheses can be extracted from their original context and cleansed of any philosophical
contamination. The Chicago School (Small and, especially, Park and his
followers) offers, as Schnabel points out, one of the few instances in
American sociology of the interaction between Simmel's work and
empirical sociology prior to the Second World War.[5] The publication
of Kurt Wolff's selections from Simmel's work in 1950[6] stimulated
a renewed interest in his work and heralded the continued examination
of hypotheses from his work both at the micro level as in Mills' studies[7]
and at the macro level of Caplow's *Two Against One*[8] and Coser's
Functions of Social Conflict.[9]

Whilst these developments lead in the direction of a scientistic reduction of Simmel's sociology to a corpus of testable hypotheses, the later
collection of essays upon facets of Simmel's work edited by Kurt Wolff
in 1958[10] together with Coser's subsequent collection[11] and Wein-
garten's study of Simmel's philosophy of history[12] might conceivably
have served to infuse a hermeneutic intention into the study of Simmel's
work or at least begun to comprehend the significance of his work as a
whole, in contrast to an excessive emphasis upon his *Soziologie* and the
undue commitment to the stereotype of Simmel's sociology as 'pure'
and 'formal'. But this did not take place. Nonetheless, the recent
translation of Simmel's *Philosophy of Money*[13] and *Problems of the
Philosophy of History*[14] should at least enable a broader assessment of
his 'sociology' to be made.

However, a central problem faced by an attempt to re-examine Simmel's work remains its incorporation into false traditions and stereotypes,

the most persistent of which is clearly the categorisation of his sociology as 'formal'. Aside from some exceptions such as the work of Tenbruck,[15] which seeks to analyse this categorisation in some detail as well as provide a more generous assessment of Simmel's sociology, the label 'formal sociology' has been consistently and almost universally attached to his work. Aron, for instance, who provided an early critical account of Simmel's philosophy of history,[16] merely repeats the by then standard judgment of his sociology when he states that 'Simmel is rightly regarded as the founder of formal sociology which he conceived as a *geometry of the social world.'*[17] This typical stereotype of Simmel's sociology must be examined in detail later. For the moment, it is sufficient to note that such judgments seldom appear alongside an account of *why* Simmel's sociology is formal aside from his interest in social 'forms'. Schnabel correctly points out that Aron's classification of Simmel as a founder of a formal systematic school of sociology contradicts Simmel's own intentions. It is also one of the many judgments of Simmel's work that leaves out of account those contributions to sociology that lie outside his *Soziologie*.

The continued encapsulation of Simmel's work within unexamined stereotypes is hardly conducive to an attempt to comprehend the author's sociological corpus as a whole. But it is not merely in the fact that various interpreters have repeated such categorisations of Simmel's work that the problem lies. In almost all accounts of the development of sociology as a discipline, Simmel's contribution has been clearly overshadowed by that of his contemporary, Max Weber. The development of an academic Max Weber growth industry — often for social and political reasons just as much as academic ones — has not only meant that Simmel's contribution to the development of sociology has been reduced to that of a precursor of Weber but also that most commentaries on the relationship between the two writers have usually come from those primarily interested in the development of Weber's work rather than that of Simmel.[18] Again, to take Aron's influential study, Simmel is confined to a few pages in an overview of the development of German sociology which is seen to culminate in the work of Max Weber. More surprisingly, but even more influential, is the absence of any discussion of Simmel's work in Parsons' *Structure of Social Action* — though Parsons did sketch out a chapter on Simmel which was never included in the final published version.[19] This is worth mentioning, not merely for its effect upon an assessment of 'sociological classics' by generations of American sociologists, but also because Simmel does have a quite elaborate if not systematic theory of social action that, for instance, includes and predates Weber's concept of purposive—rational action. Perhaps, too, the sheer volume of research on Max Weber's originality has not only led to the neglect of Simmel as a social theorist in his own right — as opposed to one forerunner, amongst others, of Weber — but has contributed to the absence of any detailed study of the relationship between the two writers.

If one were to compare the works of Simmel and Weber, then even a cursory glance would reveal the very different nature of the texts one would be confronted with. Simmel's sociological and philosophical texts are strikingly different from those of Max Weber. They could not easily be assimilated into a causal—analytical tradition as has been done — equally mistakenly, one could argue — with critical rationalism's reception of Weber's work. At the expense of distorting Simmel's work as a whole, one can, of course, attempt this since, according to a recent commentator, 'it is not difficult to derive straightforward relationship-between-phenomena propositions from Simmel's writings, and where the subject matter is less grandiose . . . such propositions may well be candidates for operationalisation in the fuller sense.'[20] This mode of assimilating Simmel's work into the mainstream of neo-positivist sociology has certainly taken place but at the expense of ignoring the nature of the texts from which propositions are extracted. How, then, would one characterise Simmel's sociological texts?

It is strange that the Anglo-American reception of Simmel's work should have relied so heavily upon extracts from his *Soziologie* which is one of his apparently most unsystematic works.[21] When first published in 1908 it signified, in fact, the end of Simmel's major preoccupation with sociology. The only subsequent exception in terms of an explicitly sociological work — aside from occasional essays — was his slender volume on the *Grundfragen der Soziologie* published in 1917.[22] The *Soziologie* itself consists of either reprinted or reworked essays that had already appeared in the previous fifteen years. An undue concentration upon this work as exemplifying Simmel's major contribution to sociology could only reinforce the unsystematic impression of his work that one might easily derive from glancing over his long list of sociological essays. More significantly, it contradicts both the epithet of 'systematic' sociology that has so often been applied to Simmel's work as well as his own intention — which is apparent even from his guarded and modest claims in the foreword to the *Soziologie*.[23] Furthermore, this emphasis upon a single collection ignores the ostensibly more systematic works by Simmel that are broadly located within the sphere of sociology — his *Über sociale Differenzierung* (1890),[24] *Die Probleme der Geschichtsphilosophie* (1892)[25] and *Philosophie des Geldes* (1900).[26] However, the more systematic nature of these earlier studies should not be overemphasised since the most substantial of them — *The Philosophy of Money* — also emerged out of a whole series of essays published by Simmel in the preceding eleven years.

If we turn to the reception of Simmel's work by his contemporaries, we find that they too had considerable difficulty in locating it within some recognisable tradition and framework. This was not merely because Simmel was, as we shall see, one of the first sociologists in Germany to attempt to lay the foundations for the discipline, although the absence of an established sociological tradition would make it difficult to locate 'sociological' discourse as something distinct from philosophical, psychological or historical discourse. Rather, it was the nature of Simmel's work itself that presented his contemporaries with problems of interpretation, and especially with comprehending his work as a whole. Max Adler, for instance, who greatly admired Simmel's work, echoed the doubts of many of his contemporaries in relation to understanding Simmel's bewildering range of interests when he suggested that

> What certainly makes a deeper understanding of Simmel more diffi-
> cult is not merely the . . . problems of style but also the largely
> merely fragmentary assessment of his work for which he himself
> was in large part to blame. Because he wrote upon the philosophy
> of history at one time, at another upon money and then again upon
> Schopenhauer and Nietzsche as well as upon Rembrandt without an
> apparently recognisable system, it might appear as if his frame of
> mind exhibited the same erratic jumps of thought as the immediacy
> of the diversity of objects with which he concerned himself.[27]

Adler went on to suggest that there was, in fact, a unity discernible in Simmel's life work. But for the moment we might usefully remain with the overall impression of diversity and fragmentation associated with Simmel's work. At first sight, then, Simmel, with his studies of music, philosophers, artists, a money economy, psychology, education, social differentiation, religion and a myriad of accounts of all aspects of social life, might appear as an unsystematic polymath. Such a judgment might also be reinforced by a study of any of Simmel's major works which often combine philosophy with sociology, psychology and sometimes, as in *The Philosophy of Money*, economics. Thus, it is not merely the diversity of different studies that presents the reader with the problem of grasping Simmel's work as a whole but the apparent diversity of theme and perspective within each of his works. Yet this too cannot be the reason why we have difficulty in perceiving the unity of his work.

Siegfried Kracauer, one of Simmel's students and one of the most astute commentators upon his work, commences his assessment of Simmel with the problem of locating Simmel's object of study. Kracauer suggests that one can readily exclude a number of areas that Simmel is not concerned with. One can exclude a central metaphysical concept such as preoccupied Spinoza or Schopenhauer as a focus of his work, a fundamental interpretation of history, the natural sciences, biology (unlike Bergson) and experimental psychology. Instead, Simmel's interests lie elsewhere:

> The raw material of his reflections comprises the inexhaustible plurality of intellectual situations, psychological events and forms of existence that exist equally within communal life just as much as intimate personal life. Indeed, the facts upon which the philosopher hangs his reflections have their origins in countless instances of the empirical and experiential realm of the highly differentiated individual. The human being as the agent of culture and thoroughly matured intellectual essence, in full possession of their intellectual energies . . . bound together with their fellow human beings through common actions and feelings always remains the central focus.[28]

Kracauer expands upon this general characterisation by pointing to three areas of concern in Simmel's work — social formations and relationships, the individual ('The psychological in any form fascinates this thinker, his writings are a genuine mine for the psychologist') and 'the realm of objective values and human achievements within this realm' (especially in the spheres of ethics, aesthetics and religion). Yet even this narrowing down of the focus of Simmel's concerns does not provide us with the key to his work as a whole, even though it might reduce the apparently fragmentary and bewildering array of themes.

However, if instead of seeking the distinctive features of Simmel's work in the content of what he deals with, we turn to his approach to his subject matter and his manner of ordering it we may come closer to understanding the uniqueness of Simmel's texts. But even here one should guard against a reading of Simmel that seeks to incorporate his approach to his object of study within an elaborate systematic social scientific 'method'. Whilst Simmel's last sociological work *Grundfragen der Soziologie* (1917) is more systematic in terms of distinctions and demarcations than his earlier works (i.e. those written during the high point of Simmel's interest in sociology — 1890—1908) and whilst he speaks in this late work of 'these studies carried out according to a sociological method', in terms of the majority of Simmel's writings, as Becher has pointed out, 'expressions such as "mode of observation", "viewpoint", "standpoint", "research tendency" would be more accurate here. This would also correspond with Simmel's perspectivism. The concept of "method", taken in its strict sense, is false.'[29] Indeed, those readings of Simmel's work which try to reinterpret his intentions in the light of the subsequent predominance of causal–analytical social sciences are likely to completely obscure what is distinctive about his approach to his object of study.

In his *Philosophy of Money*, Simmel speaks of 'the possibility . . . of finding in each of life's details the totality of its meaning'.[30] Whilst Simmel is sometimes able to hold together these 'details' within a broader encompassing phenomenon such as the money economy, his persistent essayism suggests that this was always achieved with difficulty. Much more typical of his work is the presentation of impressions of one of 'life's details' within the context of some generalities concerning social interaction. Taken together, Simmel's essays – given the extent to which his major works are reconstituted essays, they form the majority of his work – do appear to meander through the most diverse aspects of social life. Further, within a single essay or larger work we are usually confronted with the most unlikely connections and analogies between the 'details' of our social life. For this reason, Kracauer on several occasions described Simmel as 'a guest, a wanderer' who possesses 'the capacity for association, the gift of seeing the connectedness and meaningful unification of arbitrary phenomena. Simmel is an eternal wanderer between things; an unlimited capacity for combination allows him to step out in any direction from any single point.'[31] The positive side of this capacity for freely moving between the most diverse phenomena and highlighting connections between them lies in Simmel's ability to illuminate in a stimulating manner almost any phenomenon within the social and cultural sphere. What unifies even his major works is a relationism that seeks to constitute the totality of social life. As Kracauer argues with reference to *The Philosophy of Money*,

> the inexhaustible multitude of interspersed analogies refer back time and time again to the unifying core conception of the whole work which may be briefly expressed as follows: from any point of the totality one can arrive at any other, each phenomenon bears and supports the other, there is nothing absolute that exists unconnected to other phenomena and that possesses validity in and for itself.[32]

But as many of his contemporaries pointed out, this could only leave the reader with the impression of the totally unsystematic nature of

Simmel's thought: 'The associating nature of Simmel's phantasy, its ease of penetration into countless life processes of the most diverse form is necessarily connected with something negative: with the thinker's lack of a central idea.'[33] When we search for a key concept even in Simmel's sociological work we can find only the concept of interaction or reciprocal effect (*Wechselwirkung*) and, associated with it, that of the essential interrelatedness (*Wesenszusammengehörigkeit*) of social phenomena. The reader is likely, on the one hand, to be stimulated by the most unusual insights whilst, on the other, to feel completely lost since 'this wandering from relationship to relationship, this extension into the far and near, this intermeshing secures no nesting place for the mind which seeks to grasp a totality: it loses itself in infinity.'[34]

Kracauer was one of the first commentators to point out that one cannot be guided by central concepts in Simmel's work since 'one almost never finds constant meaning attached to concepts'. One instance of this is, of course, the ambiguity and elusiveness of the concept of form which has played such a crucial role in labelling Simmel's work 'formal sociology'.[35] Hence, the epithet 'systematic sociology' also appears completely inadequate as a characterisation of Simmel's work, especially as he himself explicitly rejected any concept of system. Rather than a systematic body of thought, we are confronted in reading his work with a plurality of experiences and concepts and, as we shall see, with a deep-rooted relativism. It is not merely when we glance over the bewildering array of essays on disparate themes that we are struck by this diversity and pluralism. Even within an individual work we are often struck by an apparently chaotic ordering of phenomena. As Kracauer argues, Simmel

> in his *Soziologie* highlights an array of essential qualities of social life without, however, encompassing them in their totality, without subsequently asking whether they perhaps connect with one another and can be mastered according to some basic principle 'or other. Forms stand alongside forms, types against types in unending sequence and no law orders their diversity.[36]

Hence, nothing could be further from Simmel's intentions than a taxonomy of social forms organised according to some hierarchical principles or laws.

If we focus more closely upon Simmel's texts we find that they possess other distinctive features. What is striking about Simmel's work is the extent to which it is dominated by a consistent essayism. Not only was Simmel 'the master of the philosophical essay', as Köhler pointed out, but also 'in the last resort, all his writings, even those of the first period are either actual essays or collections of them'.[37] These are essays without footnotes and references. They are not, by and large, 'academic' articles of the kind that Max Weber wrote. Even a work as substantial as *The Philosophy of Money* is written entirely without references and footnotes. In the *Soziologie*, too, there are very few footnotes. Whatever the sources of Simmel's insights and illuminating instances, we have no easy access to them. It is as if they are deliberately obscured from the reader's view in order that the author may preserve his incognito. As essays they possess considerable aesthetic attractiveness but this aesthetic appeal seldom, if ever, encourages our engagement. Most often we remain interested without being committed to them or disturbed by them. Therefore, it is very difficult to subsume Simmel's work under the rubric of systematic 'analysis' of the social world. Instead, Simmel provides us with countless 'impressions' of the most diverse aspects of social relationships and institutions and maintains an aesthetic distance from his object of study. This more general 'approach' to his subject matter or 'perspective' is probably the key to understanding Simmel's 'method', rather than assuming that, since many testable hypotheses can be extracted from his work, we can subsume it under some contemporary notion of causal—analytical social science.

However, this does not mean that Simmel neglects the epistemological foundations of sociology. In his essays on 'The problem of sociology',[38] 'How is society possible?'[39] and 'On the methodology of social science'[40] as well as in the more substantial *Problems of the Philosophy of History* and elsewhere, Simmel does address himself to such issues. On the other hand, this does not prevent us from concurring with contemporary reviewers of, say, his *Soziologie* who, like Masaryk, complained that the first two of the above-mentioned essays hardly constituted a sufficient foundation for a whole volume (of 573 pages) of essays on aspects of social life.[41] Be that as it may, one of the objects of the present study must be to re-examine Simmel's attempt to establish sociology as an independent discipline.

If it is not at all clear that Simmel subscribed to some rigorous 'method', this does not mean that we should not investigate his mode of dealing with his subject matter, especially since his views changed in the course of developing a sociological perspective. His early work on social differentiation approaches its object in a different manner from his study of the effects of a money economy. If the period around the turn of the century constitutes the high point of Simmel's interest in sociology then an examination of the many studies and essays of this period does reveal an impressionism, a distancing from reality, an aestheticisation of reality that is worthy of study. It will be argued that here is the key to Simmel's 'methodology'.

Similarly, it has often been pointed out that from his major writings we know very little of Simmel's own responses and attitudes to the contemporary social, economic and political events of his time. In some way, the author always appears absent from the text and we are left to guess at his own evaluations. It would not be difficult to relate this reticence to an aestheticisation of the world, to that distance from reality which Simmel himself so aptly describes. But this does not mean that his work is totally void of comment upon contemporary issues. Rather, they must be sought not in his major writings but buried away in newspaper and journal articles and, occasionally, in some of the little correspondence that has so far been located. Even then, the comments remain fragments. We might draw a contrast with Max Weber at this point. It is inconceivable that we would find in Simmel's work the kind of bold proclamation that is contained in Weber's inaugural lecture at Freiburg in 1895 where he announces 'I am a member of the bourgeois classes, I feel myself to be a member and am educated in their world-views and ideals.'[42] Nor is it easy to conceive of Simmel confidently pronouncing on the vital issues of the day in the same manner as Weber did, as Mommsen's work has shown.

Indeed, this relative paucity of comment upon the issues of the day, this confinement of his own views to passing comments and references in his main works is again part of the overall sense of fragmentary knowledge that we possess in relation to Simmel's work and life. No biography of Simmel has yet been attempted and any such attempt would have to rely upon scanty and scattered sources. Significantly, a brief outline of Simmel's life by Landmann containing interesting primary material is entitled 'Building blocks towards a biography'.[43] The whole edifice has hardly been outlined.

II

This is not the place to attempt a biography of Georg Simmel, however timely such a project might be. It has already been argued that we know relatively little of Simmel's life as a whole. Instead, we have a number of sketches and fragments that might provide some basis for building up a picture of Simmel. Indeed, because anyone searching for an overview of Simmel's life is confronted with a whole range of frag-ments and assessments of his work and since Simmel himself consciously developed a fragmentary essayism that pervades so much of his work, it is perhaps fitting that we should seek a view of Simmel through these fragments — in fact, in the spirit of his own work. Such an un-orthodox biographical outline is supported by Simmel himself since, according to Margarete Susman,

> Biographical raw material is, according to him, without value for the presentation of philosophy. And yet nonetheless the biographical plays a significant role in Simmel's work too. Not only the time but also the place of his birth in the heart of the then already metropolitan, lively, restless Berlin on the corner of Leipziger- and Friedrichstrasse was decisive for his life and thought.[44]

Perhaps this is nowhere more obvious than in his preoccupation with city life in many of his essays and with the features of modern urban life found in his *Philosophy of Money*. The latter prompted one of his reviewers — the fellow impressionist philosopher, Karl Joël — to suggest that it 'could only be written in these times and in Berlin'.[45]

The period within which Simmel wrote his major works and his countless essays and which ostensibly receives so little attention in these works is not easy to reconstruct. Margarete Susman refers to this period around the turn of the century as

> a time that has become unintelligible to present day people who are externally fundamentally transformed. It was a time that no longer and never again knew what reality was because it possessed no real problem vis-à-vis this reality. The concrete reality of life for the intellectual members of the upper strata, as long as they were not stirred by socialism, ran its course unproblematically.[46]

This historicist image of the period would have to be challenged in any reconstruction of these 'times', but Susman points to an essential feature of Simmel's work which prompts a number of fundamental questions. Was the social, political and economic reality of Wilhelmian Germany unproblematic for Simmel? Was he ever 'stirred by socialism' or did he always maintain an aesthetic distance from reality? What was Simmel's relationship to the upper strata of Berlin society? In more general terms, what is the nature of the reality that Simmel presents to us in his work? No simple biographical sketch would answer these questions but since they relate centrally to both Simmel's approach to his subject matter and to the neglected political dimension of his thought they will be discussed in later chapters.

The paradox of Simmel's life was not only that his work was often so quickly forgotten but also that since he appeared to be at the centre of Berlin intellectual life we should now know so little about him. This centrality is emphasised most forcefully by Landmann in the course of pointing to the paradox of Simmel's popularity and subsequent neglect when he states that, with regard to the period prior to the First World War,

> Together with Dilthey, Husserl and Bergson, Simmel is one of the most striking representatives of this period, that perhaps did not find such a worldly and clear expression as in him. In Simmel, who confronted the new problems in their pure immediacy, one could feel the pulse-beat of the times most forcefully. His audience at the University of Berlin was the largest and most select. He had connections not only with the foremost philosophers and academics of his time, with Bergson, Troeltsch and Max Weber but also with artists and poets, with Rodin, George and Rilke. He was the centre of the intellectual elite.[47]

Again, this passage points to the paradox of Simmel's life and work. Simmel's closeness to 'the pulse-beat of the times' surely cannot mean that he analysed the socio-political and economic transformation of Wilhelmian Germany like no other writer. Rather, it must refer to Simmel's impressionism, his capacity for grasping the atmosphere of his times as viewed from the perspective of 'the intellectual elite'. Simmel might comment upon trade union freedom, socialised medicine, the women's movement, and university politics in articles and, presumably, in his lectures whilst at the same time maintaining a perspective that distanced himself from these movements and events.[48] In his major works we seldom have any idea of Simmel's own evaluation of a contemporary problem.

And yet Simmel was a central focus of an intellectual elite in Berlin and he did attract more students to his lectures than anyone else, much to the annoyance of the Prussian ministry of education who often considered them to be the wrong kind of students. With regard to Simmel's popularity, the following opening lines of an article in the Berlin journal *Die Zukunft* for October 1914 testify to his following:

> When the calendar of lectures for the summer semester at the University of Berlin appeared some months ago, we took it up somewhat nervously, sought at once the decisive indication and already discovered that Georg Simmel was no longer in it. We will no longer be able to hear him in Berlin, we will no longer see him: and that is sad because (and this is the most remarkable thing about him) one first fully comprehends him not when one reads him but when one hears and sees him.[49]

In 1914 Simmel took up the chair of philosophy at the University of Strasbourg — the first that had been offered to him — which he held until his death in 1918. In the present context, one could hardly conceive of any other contemporary figure exciting such a response to their departure from Berlin. But once more, the paradox presents itself in the contrast between this passage and the negative judgment of one of his contemporaries, Ernst Troeltsch who, at the close of an assessment of Simmel's work, suggests that 'his influence remained . . . one upon the general atmosphere and affected, above all, the higher levels of journalism.'[50] This damning judgment is certainly not the most accurate of Troeltsch's assessments but it does point to the contrast between Simmel's popularity during his lifetime and his relative neglect so soon after his death in 1918. But the year of Simmel's death is itself significant since it marks the end of a whole social order, however much many of its ruling strata might dream of its continuation in Weimar Germany. In any case, Simmel's major influence was without doubt during his years in Berlin down to 1914. Simmel himself certainly felt cut off from his natural milieux in Strasbourg. In turn, many of his students and younger contemporaries felt cut off from Simmel's work when they came to assess it after his death. Even Siegfried Kracauer — some of whose work would certainly qualify for Troeltsch's category of 'the higher levels of journalism' and who has left us one of the most sensitive appreciations of Simmel's work — concluded that by 1919–20 (the probable date of Kracauer's unpublished manuscript), after the experience of the war, his generation was already remote from the world of Simmel's works and especially his philosophy of life (*Lebensphilosophie*): 'We feel irrevocably separated from an epoch that took life emptied of meaning as the ultimate driving force of human existence and that, rootless as it was, possessed no goal and no reason [*kein Wohin, kein Wozu*]'.[51] If this deep separation from Simmel's world was true for Kracauer, who had studied with Simmel, then it is even more true for present-day readers of his work. But despite the difficulties involved, some attempt must be made to locate Simmel's work within the context of his own milieux. Wherever possible, this will be carried out by reference to contemporary accounts.

The bare biographical details of Simmel's life and education are well summarised by Kurt Wolff and might readily serve as the basis for their subsequent elaboration. Wolff writes:

> Georg (Friedrich Eduard) Simmel was born in Berlin on March 1, 1858, of Jewish parents, both of whom had early converted — his father to Catholicism, his mother to Protestantism. He was baptised

a Protestant but left the church during World War I, without, however, embracing Judaism. After graduating from the gymnasium he studied at the University of Berlin, beginning with history under Theodor Mommsen, moving to psychology, especially *Völkerpsychologie* (Moritz Lazarus), then to ethnology (Adolf Bastian), and at last to philosophy (Eduard Zeller, Friedrich Harms); he minored in Italian, specializing in Petrarch. . . .

As his dissertation he submitted a paper on 'Psychological–Ethnographic Studies on the Beginnings of Music' . . . it was rejected; he obtained his doctorate instead (in 1881) with an essay for which he had received an academic prize two years before, *Description and Assessment of Kant's Various Views on the Nature of Matter*. On the basis of a second essay (again on Kant) and a 'test' lecture, 'On the Theory of the Association of Ideas' . . . he was appointed *Privatdozent* in 1885 at the University of Berlin, a post he held for the unusually long period of 15 years, after which he was promoted to *ausserordentlicher Professor*. In 1914, almost as long again, he became an *Ordinarius* at the University of Strasbourg, four years before he died (September 26, 1918).[52]

In order to fill out this outline of Simmel's life, one must have recourse to the material collected by Landmann, especially on Simmel's academic career, that part of Simmel's correspondence which has survived and accounts by his contemporaries of aspects of his life.

Little is known either of Simmel's family background or his early life. According to his son Hans,[53] Simmel 'had no interest, in fact even an aversion, in concerning himself with the history of his predecessors'. From the same source we learn that he 'did not experience his childhood as predominantly happy; only very occasionally did he speak much of his early remembrances'. Somewhat surprisingly, in view of Simmel's own wide ranging interests, Simmel 'always insisted that no one in his parents' house had a notion of genuine intellectual culture'. From the reminiscences of Sabine Lepsius (née Graef) — a member of the Stefan George circle and through whom George got to know Simmel — it is clear that Simmel's cultural interests were awakened either through his studies or through other contacts such as her own family; in any case, away from 'his jealous mother who tyrannised him with her love'.[54] His family also kept him reluctantly in Berlin since, according to Hans Simmel, upon enquiring why his father had never studied anywhere other than in Berlin, Simmel replied 'I might just as well have told my mother that I wanted to be a missionary amongst the Botocudo indians as study elsewhere'.[55]

In the second half of the 1880s, when Simmel had already completed his *Habilitationschrift* and was lecturing in Berlin University as a *Privatdozent*, he met his future wife Gertrud Kinel in Sabine Graef's house. They were married in July 1890, the year of publication of Simmel's first major work in social theory, *Über sociale Differenzierung*. Though this work signifies the start of Simmel's most productive period of publications in the social sciences down to his *Soziologie* of 1908, the early phase of Simmel's work is not only largely unresearched but also — perhaps for this reason — untypical of our image of Simmel. As Landmann suggests:

> The *young Simmel* starts out from pragmatism, social Darwinism, Spencerian evolutionism and the principle of differentiation. Fechner's atomism and Spencer's 'determinate differentiation' lead him . . . to the problem of the individual. Through his teachers Lazarus and Steinthal . . . however, Simmel already early on became acquainted with the 'objective spirit'. The fact that, in this first phase, Simmel exercised little influence and that he himself turned away from it has hardly been investigated at all.[56]

Yet Simmel's interest in the social sciences and sociology had already commenced by 1890. In May 1889, Simmel gave a paper on the psychology of money — published in the same year — that was to form the early basis for the substantial study on *The Philosophy of Money*.[57] In 1887, he had published his first article on pessimism — a theme that concerned Simmel for more than a decade.[58] In 1890 he published the first of several articles on women — this early one was entitled 'On the psychology of women'.[59] Although this early phase of Simmel's work is characterised by a continued interest in philosophy, his lectures and seminars in Berlin also testified to a growing concern with social issues.[60] In the summer semester of 1887 Simmel was lecturing on 'Ethics with special reference to sociological problems', in the winter semester of 1888/9 upon 'Selected aspects of social science', in the summer semester of 1890 upon 'The main theories of psychology and their application to ethical and social problems'. In the succeeding two decades, Simmel was to regularly lecture and give seminars upon sociology as an independent discipline without it necessarily being appended to ethics or psychology.

The only major reviewer of Simmel's *On Social Differentiation: Sociological and Psychological Investigations*, Ferdinand Tönnies,[61] recognised in his book the worth of someone who had only just started to grapple with sociological problems. In Simmel's study,

> there remains sometimes something uncertain and also, in fact, unfinished. One does not always notice that the subject matter of six chapters are connected by the concept of differentiation and one would indeed do better to see each one as independent of the others.

The introductory chapter, concerned with the methods of the social sciences, does not seem to me to be the strongest one.[62]

In keeping with this uncertain feeling, Tönnies felt that, on the one hand, he 'came across psychological comments of great sensitivity' whereas, on the other, 'social problems are handled with a crude fist and are first of all moulded in the simplest form in order, from the greatest distance in which the thinker remains from life, to penetrate into the appropriate depths of knowledge'. Tönnies also questions Simmel's argument that 'one cannot . . . speak of laws of social development' — a thesis which Simmel consistently maintained throughout his work. There are also other themes in this study which recur in Simmel's later works. Social differentiation is again dealt with, for instance, in the context of the consequences of a money economy in his *Philosophy of Money* in 1900.

But if we survey Simmel's subsequent development, we are confronted with an increasing preoccupation with sociological themes that are treated in a different manner. The 'comments of great sensitivity' come more to the fore, particularly in Simmel's essays. At the same time, however, it is not always easy to see a consistency in Simmel's intellectual development. Some substantial works — notably the *Einleitung in die Moralphilosophie* of 1892/3[63] are neglected in Simmel's later works. Other themes are taken up and then often dropped again. Kracauer argued that whereas there are writers who have an ultimate goal which one can see unfolding in their work and which appears to give it considerable consistency, there are others who lack this central focus:

> The other type, to which Simmel belongs, does not remain totally spellbound by an ultimate notion that encompasses the diverse stages of its development. Rather, his thoughts steadily transform themselves, partly as a result of their immanent consistency, partly as a result of experiences which haunt and beset him during the different periods of his development.[64]

If we accept Kracauer's interpretation, then it goes some way towards accounting for the diversity of Simmel's writings.

In the decade after Simmel's marriage and the publication of his first major work, we can see the diversity of his interests in his prolific writings in this period and in his teaching. The first edition of *Probleme der Geschichtsphilosophie* appeared in 1892 and was followed by the *Einleitung in der Moralphilosophie* in 1892—3. At the turn of the century Simmel published the first edition of his *Philosophy of Money*. From 1893 onwards, Simmel lectured or gave seminars on sociology every year, though not necessarily every semester, until 1908 — the year of publication of his *Soziologie*. In the 1890s, he continued to lecture fairly consistently upon Kantian philosophy, the history of philosophy and ethics and, somewhat intriguingly, in 1895, 1897, 1898 and 1899 upon 'Social psychology with reference to socialism'.[65]

But both the range of Simmel's interests and the extent to which he outlined parts of his major sociological writings can best be seen from the increasing numbers of journal and newspaper articles that formed earlier versions and sections of *The Philosophy of Money*.[66] Chapters one ('The problem of sociology') and eight ('The self-preservation of the social group') of his *Soziologie* appeared as articles in 1894 and 1898 respectively.[67] Without listing the increasing number of articles which Simmel published in this decade, it is possible to give some impression of the range of his work. His brief political commentaries often appeared in newspaper or journal articles and ranged from such themes as trade union rights and peasant liberation to 'Militarism and the position of women' and 'The Women's Congress and Social Democracy'.[68] From 1897 to 1904 Simmel also published a number of brief articles — sometimes satirical — poems and aphorisms in the influential Munich *Jugendstil* journal *Jugend*.[69] Of course, Simmel was also continuing to publish articles on psychology and philosophy at the same time as reviews of recent works by Gustav le Bon, Stefan George and Paul Ernst.[70]

The breadth of his interests probably also accounted, in part, for the popularity of his lectures in Berlin. Simmel, Landmann argues, 'soon also belonged to the points of attraction of Berlin University through his resolute striving towards modernity'.[71] By the end of the 1890s he was lecturing in the largest lecture theatre in the university. In a letter to Heinrich Rickert in 1898, Simmel himself expressed concern for student numbers. He writes to Rickert that he is

> rather proud of the fact that I have over 70 students in a private seminar on social psychology. This is a lot for such a remote and unpractical area . . . I am also satisfied with the major logic lecture since, in competition with the Ordinarius and at a very inconvenient time I still have over 60 students.[72]

Later in the same year, Simmel mentioned to Rickert that of his students

> a large portion of them are foreigners and women. I cannot say that I was very happy with the large percentage of female students: they disturb the unity of the auditorium for me. Since, in fact, I don't

speak to the audience but to myself I prefer it when the auditorium
is as colourless and indifferent as possible. The dual form of appearance and the bright clothes disturb me.[73]

But the large student numbers and his popularity did not serve to advance his academic career. Aside from the jealousy of his colleagues at
his popularity. Simmel had to reckon with the anti-Semitism of powerful members of his faculty as well as mistrust of the new discipline
of sociology.

Simmel's first official attempt at promotion in 1898 to *Ausserordentlicher Professor* — which would still not permit him to have doctoral
candidates — was unsuccessful. In their letter to the ministry of education in support of Simmel's case, the professoriat of the philosophy
faculty — including Wilhelm Dilthey and Gustav Schmoller — pointed
to the popularity of his lectures and the extent of his publications.
Their view of Simmel's theoretical position and of sociology is significant. In their letter of 3 June they write:

> His standpoint is Spencer's theory of evolution. The task that he has
> set himself in the so-called sociology in particular lies in the analysis
> of psychological forms, dominant processes and structures which are
> produced and are effective in society. His efforts in folk psychology
> are related to this. Thus he pursues the effectiveness of the principle
> of saving energy in the psychological sphere, he analyses the process
> of social differentiation psychologically, he deals with the psycho-
> logical side of such social facts as competition or money. In his most
> comprehensive work, too, the two volume introduction to moral
> philosophy, he is inclined to focus upon sociological and evolution-
> ary derivation for the basic elements of moral consciousness.[74]

This application was rejected by the ministry. Two years later in 1900
we find the professoriat of the faculty once more submitting an application for the same position on Simmel's behalf. Again, their caution
vis-à-vis sociology is even more apparent. In arguing that sociology is
an extremely fruitful line of study for philosophers and political
scientists, they clearly have reservations about its status:

> For this area of study, like no other, is certainly a hotbed of pseudo-
> science [*ein Tummelplatz der Halbwissenschaft*]. But precisely be-
> cause Dr Simmel has extracted a nexus of useful investigations from
> the indeterminate collective concept of sociology and has worked
> upon it with scientific exactitude he has distinguished himself from
> other sociologists.[75]

It is worth mentioning in passing that Dilthey, one of the signatories
to Simmel's application, excluded Simmel's sociology from the general
critique of sociology that is made in his work. Be that as it may, the

title of *Extraordinarius* was granted by the Prussian ministry to Simmel in 1901.

In the meantime, Simmel had been working on other projects. In a letter to Rickert in 1896, he anticipates that 'In the course of the decade I hope to present you with a "Theory of Relativism" in which everything with which I fundamentally agree and disagree with you will be set down. In the meantime, other things have been commenced.'[76] Not unconnected with a 'theory of relativism', one of the projects upon which Simmel was already working was his *Philosophy of Money*. Two years later, Simmel was complaining to Rickert of the difficulties he was having in developing a theory of value in this study. In particular, he wished to retain a relativist theory of value but recognises that he can 'only maintain my relativism if it is capable, as it were, of solving all the problems that are presented by absolutist theories'.[77] Later in the same year, Simmel was still complaining of 'the difficulties in the theory of value': 'I am groaning over and doubting my theory of value. Even the most elementary point up to now provides me with insurmountable difficulties.'[78] Despite these problems, *The Philosophy of Money* was well received when it appeared in 1900 and prompted many reviews that were often more favourable and enthusiastic than for his later *Soziologie* in 1908.[79]

The Philosophy of Money was a work which, according to his friend and reviewer Karl Joël, 'could only be written in these times and in Berlin' and captured the atmosphere of the period like no other of his studies. Simmel himself identified his fate with that of Berlin and, according to his son Hans, saw his own development linked with that of the city. Hans Simmel recalls his father expressing himself in roughly the following manner: 'Berlin's development from a city to a metropolis in the years around and after the turn of the century coincides with my own strongest and broadest development.'[80] In a similar vein, Simmel remarked that 'Perhaps I could have achieved something that was also valuable in another city; but this specific achievement, that I have in fact brought to fruition in these decades, is undoubtedly bound up with the Berlin milieu.'[81] What was Simmel's 'Berlin milieu' around the turn of the century?

Aside from the large audiences for his lectures — reputedly even larger after 1900 — Simmel also held another 'audience' in his home. When Leopold von Wiese somewhat disparagingly referred to Simmel's sociology as 'a sociology for the literary salon' he not only highlighted the strong aesthetic aspect of many of Simmel's sociological essays but also unwittingly pointed to the social location of some of his

reflections. Simmel's sociology was created by someone who regularly ran a 'salon' at his home. Perhaps it is the heightened degree
of reflection necessitated by the salon and its relative distance from
social reality that makes Simmel's social location as social observer
different from that of the *flâneur*. Or perhaps the *flâneur* element
in Simmel's work is the result of a retreat into more abstract typi-
fications of the social world than are described in Benjamin's characterisation. This distinction must be the object of further study in a later
chapter.[82]

Accounts of Simmel's private seminars are provided by a number of
participants. Margarete Susman in a memoir suggests that Simmel and
his home environment embodied the refined culture of this period.

> It was the culture of the beginning of the century, that Simmel . . .
> embodied and which only a decade later was to be destroyed in the
> First World War. The large high study on the ground floor with the
> view into the garden was covered with valuable old Persian carpets.
> Pictures by the great masters, many original drawings by Rodin
> hung on the walls. Everywhere, in cupboards or in the open stood
> vases, bowls from the far east, exquisite Buddha figures. . . . Not
> quite in the middle of the room stood a large, black grand piano . . .
> that almost dominated the room.[83]

Simmel worked mornings and evenings and entertained in his home in
the afternoons. Again, Margarete Susman described the atmosphere of
these 'salons':

> I will never forget the distinctive fragrance which one encountered
> upon entering Simmel's house: a mixture of the smell of hand-picked
> apples and very expensive cigarettes. The receptions in the Simmel
> household, the weekly '*jours*' were conceived entirely in the spirit of
> their common culture. They were a sociological creation in minia-
> ture: that of a sociability whose significance was the cultivation of
> the highest individuals. Here conversation took on a form . . . which
> floated in an atmosphere of intellectuality, affability and tact
> detached from the ultimate burden of the personal element. Simmel
> certainly obtained the masterly chapter of his 'Little Sociology' on
> conversation [the reference here is to the chapter on sociability in
> *Grundfragen der Soziologie* — D.F.] from the experience of this
> select society. Only exceptional people, distinguished by intellect
> or even by beauty, took part in these social events.[84]

Simmel's '*jour*' 'at which one always met interesting people' certainly
has all the characteristics of a salon society. The atmosphere is confirmed by Edith Landmann who, in 1901, participated in Simmel's
private seminar on aesthetics at which

The participants sat around a huge table at whose narrow upper side sat Simmel, at the other his wife. . . . Some of them, myself included, read out their papers yet I did not have the impression that Simmel exhibited great interest in them; his interest seemed rather in holding forth upon his own new aesthetic reflections — particularly upon Japanese art of which he was a collector — in small circles of people. Not everyone was by any means in agreement with him, as one could confirm on the journey home. But there always remained the impression of a select society, an impression that was possibly even stronger in the *jour* which took place on the first Sunday of the month. . . . One evening there appeared amongst the few late guests to the *jour* a grand figure dressed in black who had obviously not expected to meet the other guests and before whom one immediately took one's leave. It was George.[85]

The reference here to the poet Stefan George is symptomatic of Simmel's relationship to a whole range of artistic figures who were then at the centre of the cultural scene in Germany and elsewhere. Simmel corresponded with Rilke and was a friend of the dramatist Paul Ernst. He corresponded with Rodin and later met him in Paris.

But what is particularly significant at the turn of the century is Simmel's close relationship to the George circle. Walter Benjamin detected this influence — presumably the aestheticism — in *The Philosophy of Money* when he suggested that 'not without reason does it emerge out of the period in which Simmel sought to "approach" the George circle'.[86] In 1898 and 1901 Simmel wrote two appreciative articles upon George's poetry.[87] Simmel's relationship to the group around Stefan George was facilitated by his close friendship with Sabine and Reinhold Lepsius and his even closer liaison with Gertrud Kantorowicz (who had a child by him). Gertrud Kantorowicz was frequently in attendance at the *jours* and was close to Stefan George himself. Although never formally a member of the George circle, there is little doubt that there was a two-way relationship between Simmel and George in terms of influence. As one contemporary says of Simmel,

The way in which he stood and spoke and listened, the way in which he was moved by his own thoughts, even the way he dressed was of simple distinction and it was not only in his lectures on aesthetics that there was around him an aura of a world of rare and great things. I am not in any doubt that this was something that radiated from Stefan George. Since the second half of the 1890s . . . the period around the middle of his life, Simmel belonged to the small group of artists and intellectuals who in Berlin hoped to see in the poet of 'Jahr der Seele' the emergence of an intellectual social life in Germany.[88]

If we accept Singer's view of the impression made by George upon Simmel — and this can be confirmed not only in Simmel's three essays on George but also in their frequent meetings — then it is also quite plausible to argue that Simmel played an important role in reinforcing some of the central tenets of the George circle.[89] Thus, for instance, Simmel dedicated the third edition of *The Problems of the Philosophy of History* (1907) to Stefan George 'poet and friend' and the first edition of *The Philosophy of Money* to George's and Simmel's close friends Reinhold and Sabine Lepsius. Conversely, Troeltsch argues that Simmel himself had a strong influence upon the George circle. In a later chapter, the intellectual constellation around this group and the aesthetic dimension of Simmel's work will be examined more fully.

If, however, we return to Simmel's development after the turn of the century we find that he sometimes appears torn in the direction in which he wishes to move. In 1901, for instance, he writes to Rickert,

> I wanted to start a very comprehensive sociology (an obligation with which I am not very sympathetic but which is unavoidable) when a second edition of my 'Moral philosophy' was necessary. This means a completely new book, a completely new foundation. . . . On the other hand, for some time now, my major interest has been in the philosophy of art and I am burning to bring together my ideas upon it.[90]

Since this 'comprehensive sociology' did not appear until 1908 as the *Soziologie*, we may reasonably assume that Simmel's interests did lie elsewhere. A glance at what he was offering in his lectures and seminars between 1901 and 1908 does, however, suggest a continued concern for sociology. Every year until the summer semester of 1908 Simmel offered courses on sociology. Thereafter they became much less frequent. In the remainder of his time in Berlin (i.e. until 1914) sociology was only offered in the winter semesters of 1909/10 and 1911/12. This would seem to confirm Troeltsch's comment upon Simmel's change of direction that 'in later years, when I brought him round to sociological questions, he rejected discussion of them; these things "no longer interested him"'.[91]

If we turn to his publications in the period 1900 to 1908, then it is apparent that Simmel's interests were also moving in the direction of philosophy. His collection of lectures on *Kant* were published in 1904,[92] the important fully rewritten second edition of *Problems of the Philosophy of History* appeared in 1905,[93] *Kant und Goethe*[94] and *Die Religion*[95] both appeared in 1906 and *Schopenhauer und Nietzsche* in 1907.[96] Kracauer is probably correct in arguing that the second edition of the volume on the philosophy of history and the study of Kant mark 'the genuine epistemological period of the thinker which roughly commenced after the completion of the *Philosophy of Money*' and also signified the end of his earlier epistemological naivety.[97] Even though this would suggest that Simmel's interest in philosophy was increasing, the absence of a rigid separation between sociology and philosophy would indicate that ostensibly 'philosophical' works might have great relevance for sociology. This is especially true of the second edition of *The Problems of the Philosophy of History*. Shortly before its publication, Simmel writes to Rickert that not only has he fundamentally changed the orientation of the study but that he has found its 'genuine purpose', namely

> Overcoming the naive realism of the historian, the proof that cognition not merely 'orders the laws' of nature but also those of history . . . one could characterise my orientation in this study as the 'transcendence of psychologism'. In fact, it is not for me a case of its transcendence but rather by taking it up in a higher methodology, through which, in diversion, I can arrive at the essence of art.[98]

This transcendence of 'naive realism' on the part of historians was crucial to the development of Max Weber's own views upon the study of historical phenomena, as any study of his methodological writings would show.[99] Moreover, the reference to the centrality of the 'essence of art' suggests that Simmel had not given up his interest in the aesthetic questions that he was 'burning to bring together'.

This interest in aesthetics is also confirmed by glancing through his essays in the years down to 1908. These include essays upon 'The picture frame', 'Rodin's sculpture and contemporary intellectual trends' (Simmel went to Prague in 1902 with Margarete Susman to see the exhibition of Rodin's work), aesthetic quantities, Venice, 'The problem of style' and several others.[100] As has already been indicated, the early part of the first decade of the century was also the period during which Simmel was contributing to *Jugend*, the Munich *Jugendstil* journal. Most of the essays on aesthetics in this period were quite short and were not collected together during Simmel's lifetime. What this suggests is that, despite his profound interest in aesthetic issues, he did not have a definite plan for a substantial work in this area.

In contrast, the period from 1903 to 1908 saw the publication of essays that were either directly taken up in the *Soziologie* of 1908 or were reworked and then included. Thus essays on 'The spatial projections of social forms', 'The sociology of competition', 'The sociology of space', 'The end of conflict', 'On the sociology of poverty', 'Gratitude', 'On the philosophy of domination', 'On the sociology of the aristocracy', 'Sociology of the senses', 'Sociology of super- and sub-ordination', 'The letter', 'Psychology of decoration' and 'On the nature of social-psychology' were all published between 1903 and 1908 and all taken up in the *Soziologie*.[101] The first chapter of the *Soziologie* 'The problem of sociology' had already appeared in a different form in 1894 and chapter seven on 'The self-preservation of social groups' had appeared in 1898. Taken together, they account for contributions to eight of the ten chapters that go to make up the *Soziologie*.[102]

After the publication of the *Soziologie* in 1908, Simmel appears to have been much less interested in sociology. His lectures and seminars on sociology were less frequent, as was the publication of essays on sociology. Does this suggest that the period within which Simmel was preoccupied with sociology can be narrowly circumscribed? Such a view is advanced most forcefully by Tenbruck who contends that Simmel's *Soziologie* appeared

> after sociological study was already left far behind him and he had definitely turned his attention towards philosophical and aesthetic questions. The sociological period, announced by the themes of a number of articles in the 1880s, commences with the study *Über sociale Differenzierung* (1890) and reaches its real high point and completion in the *Philosophie des Geldes* (1900). Between these dates there lies a large number of articles which in changed or enlarged forms, in the original formulation or translated, improved, merged with one another, are reworked and finally presented in the collection *Soziologie*. The important new edition of the philosophy of history in 1905 and several shorter articles on sociology after 1900 are only the rounding off and development of positions already definitively reached earlier, additional studies that contribute nothing essential to the total work.[103]

It should be apparent, however, that the confinement of Simmel's sociological work to virtually a single decade is an extreme judgment that leaves out of account the articles published between 1903 and 1908 which go to make up the majority of the *Soziologie*. In a modified form, that is by extending Simmel's period of sociological production from 1890 to around 1908, Tenbruck's thesis becomes more plausible. This modified thesis can be maintained even if we take into account Simmel's post-1908 sociological writings and his *Grundfragen der Soziologie* (1917). As we shall see, the events of 1908 certainly closed off possible lines of direction in Simmel's life and work.

In 1908 Simmel was considered for the second chair of philosophy at Heidelberg University. On the recommendation of Max Weber and Gothein, Rickert was placed first on the list for consideration and Simmel second. Since there was some doubt as to whether Rickert — then in Freiburg — would accept, Simmel appeared to have a good chance of securing this chair. The Heidelberg faculty argued that Simmel was both 'the most unique figure' in contemporary philosophy and a major influence upon present-day sociology. They went on to say that, 'If he can be secured for Heidelberg, then the social sciences as a whole and in all their branches — in the direction of philosophy, politics and economics — would find such a comprehensive represent-ation as exists nowhere else.'[104] In complete contrast, the Baden minister of education Böhm received a very negative reference for Simmel that was openly anti-Semitic and reactionary. This reference by Schäfer referred to Simmel as 'an Israelite through and through, in his external appearance, in his bearing and in his mode of thought . . . His lectures are well attended . . . by certain categories of students who are very numerous here in Berlin.'[105] He goes on to give his views upon Simmel's sociological orientation and refers disparagingly to sociology in general.

> Simmel owes his reputation largely to his 'sociological' activities. . . . In my view, however, sociology has yet to earn its position as a science. In my opinion, it is a dangerous error to wish to put 'society' in the place of the state and the church as the authoritative organ of human coexistence.[106]

Such judgments no doubt earned Berlin University the sarcastic reput-ation as 'His Majesty's intellectual regiment of the guards' (as it was referred to by du Bois Reymond, the scientist).

The second chair remained unfilled in 1908 and after much nego-tiation was offered in the following year to Troeltsch. Simmel himself was eager to take the chair and clearly tried to respond to some of the criticism of him from within university circles in Heidelberg and Berlin. Thus, for instance, he wrote to Max Weber in March 1908,

> In certain circles the idea exists that I am an exclusively critical, even destructive spirit, and that my lectures lead only to negation. Perhaps I don't have to tell you that this is a nasty untruth. My lectures as, for many years, all my work, tend exclusively toward the positive, toward the demonstration of a deeper insight into world and spirit, with complete renunciation of polemics and criticism in regard to divergent conditions and theories.'[107]

In the same letter, Simmel reveals his awareness of the Prussian ministry's dislike of him when he says that 'though they don't like me, they know nonetheless that I am a *great attraction* in the university and would perhaps not be happy if I received a call.'[108] This ironic comment cannot detract from the bitterness which Simmel no doubt felt in being passed over for this chair at the age of 50 and with so many publications to his name and such a high reputation amongst many of the leading intellectual figures in Germany. Writing around 1908 or 1909, Max Weber saw why Simmel would continue to be overlooked and why he

> remains deprived of the 'official' recognition that would come through conferring the rank of *Ordinarius* which he more than deserved well over a decade and a half ago. The grounds for this — banal as they are — are known for Berlin and for Prussia by anyone who wishes to know them. And outside of Prussia, experience has shown that all efforts by other faculties to recruit Simmel will remain futile for as long as the responsible agencies lack the resolve to emancipate themselves from those Prussian eminences who would feel themselves disavowed by an appointment of Simmel elsewhere.[109]

One can only speculate what effect a successful call to Heidelberg would have meant for the intellectual and, above all, the sociological development of both Simmel and Weber. As it was, there is little doubt that Simmel moved increasingly away from sociology towards philosophy — and especially the philosophy of culture and *Lebensphilosophie* — at the same time as Max Weber was moving increasingly in the direction of sociology.

Simmel's increasing orientation towards philosophy and aesthetics and away from sociology can be viewed from a number of directions. Simmel took great interest in and frequently published in a new journal for the philosophy of culture, *Logos*, established in 1909. In December of that year Simmel wrote to Rickert and to Max Weber expressing his desire to participate in this new venture, especially as a 'philosophy of culture' was to well characterise his later writings in the cultural sphere. Simmel explained to Weber that he did not wish to have his name on the title page of *Logos* as 'mere decoration' but rather to 'genuinely "co-operate"' in order to 'have an influence on both the direction and the level of the journal'. Significantly, Simmel also suggests that

> This is also the reason why I have refused and still refuse the presidency of the Sociological Association: neither my time *nor my inclination* or my knowledge is sufficient in order to really do justice to it and to direct it, and only if I did so could be so responsible for it as, in my opinion, the presidency obliges one to be.[110]

Simmel's lack of inclination to be president of the newly founded Sociological Association did not prevent him from participating in its first congress in Frankfurt in October 1910 where he gave the opening paper on 'The sociology of sociability'.[111] Apart from a contribution to the discussion of a paper by Ernst Troeltsch at the same congress — which, he complained to Weber when it appeared in the published proceedings, had become 'absolute nonsense' on account of the non-functioning of the Association's expensive stenograph[112] — there is no subsequent evidence of Simmel's active participation in the meetings of the Association.

When Simmel did continue to write upon sociological themes, he did so increasingly within the context of a philosophy of culture. This tendency became more marked in his later writings. Whereas, for instance, he had discussed the fragmentation of social life and individuals in *The Philosophy of Money* as a consequence of the division of labour, he later saw this process as part of the general human predicament. This may be seen as part of Simmel's increasing affinities with *Lebensphilosophie* and his growing interest in Bergson's philosophy. After the *Soziologie* of 1908 and until 1914 all Simmel's volumes of published work are upon philosophy and aesthetics. They comprise his *Hauptprobleme der Philosophie* (1910),[113] *Philosophische Kultur* (1911)[114] and *Goethe* (1913).[115] Aside from Simmel's address to the German Sociological Association in 1910, the only explicitly sociological essays that he published in the same period — and both were very short pieces — were 'The sociology of mealtimes' (1910)[116] and 'On tact. The sociology of sociability' (1912).[117] One might also add the essay on 'Female culture' (1911) since it did appear in the social science journal, the *Archiv für Sozialwissenschaft*.[118] In contrast, the majority of Simmel's other essays published between 1909 and 1914 are either in the field of aesthetics — 'Rodin's art', 'The seventh ring', several on Goethe, 'The philosophy of landscape', etc.; or in philosophy and ethics — 'On the essence of philosophy', 'The concept and tragedy of culture', the important article on ethics 'The individual law', etc.[119] There is little doubt that Simmel was becoming increasingly preoccupied with a philosophy of culture and with a *Lebensphilosophie* in his last years in Berlin. In 1911 he informed his friend Keyserling that this was the direction in which he saw philosophical reflection moving:

> It will interest you that for a long time now I assert in my lectures: each major intellectual epoch has had a central concept whose position has thereby determined that it characterises the highest reality and, at the same time, the highest value: for the Greeks the

concept of Being, for Christendom that of God, in the 17th and
18th centuries that of Nature, in the 19th that of society and now
that of 'Life' appears to have entered in this position.[120]

This concept of life in Simmel's later work not only becomes a corner-
stone of his metaphysics but also becomes increasingly abstract and
devoid of specific content, and especially a social content. The notion
of life as a value-creating energy coincides with Simmel's interest in
Bergson's vitalism and justifies Kracauer's comment that 'the affinity
between Simmel's doctrine and that of Bergson is unmistakeable'.[121] In
this later period Simmel was sometimes referred to as 'the German
Bergson'.

In the last years at Berlin down to 1914, Simmel's career was no
further advanced than in earlier years. In 1910, although recommended
for the post, Simmel was turned down for the chair of philosophy at
the small Prussian University of Greifswald. In a letter to Husserl in
1911, Simmel comments ironically upon this rejection in an anecdote:

> Recently, an official inquired of Elster why he had not called me to
> Greifswald where I was nominated for the first place [on the list].
> To which he replied that I certainly didn't fit into such a small
> university; but if, for example, I were to be recommended for
> Göttingen then he would call me with the greatest pleasure.[122]

Simmel's only academic honour in this period was, however, an honorary
doctorate of politics bestowed upon him in October 1911 at Freiburg
University.

Despite his persistent lack of academic recognition, Simmel continued to attract large numbers of students to his classes. In his private
lectures, according to his son Hans, 'he had 100—250, in public lectures
often double this number. Many foreigners . . . particularly Russians'
also attended his lectures.[123] Simmel, much to the annoyance of some
members of the faculty, was one of the first to permit women in his
private seminars long before they were allowed to be admitted as full
students in the winter semester of 1908/9. He continued to attract
'revolutionary' students, so much so that it was said that 'Simmel is
a focal point of revolutionary and anti-German aspirations'.[124] It was
in these later years at Berlin that Simmel attracted such figures as Georg
Lukács (one of his favourite students), Ernst Bloch (with whom he
went to Florence in the summer of 1910) and later Karl Mannheim.

But in spite of (or because of) his popularity, Simmel failed to gain
a university chair until early in 1914 when, at the age of 56, he secured
a chair of philosophy at the University of Strasbourg. It is clear that

Simmel would have preferred to remain in Berlin had he been offered a chair there. Early in January 1914, Simmel wrote to Adolf von Harnack concerning his Strasbourg offer that 'if I accept it (and I have still not decided upon it), it will not be with a light heart. For the influence upon our philosophical culture, which I can exercise in Berlin, will not be achieved so easily elsewhere.'[125] When Simmel did accept the chair in Strasbourg, he parted from Berlin with great reluctance, as Gertrud Simmel's letter to Marianne Weber testifies: 'Georg has taken his leave of the auditorium very badly — it has affected him enormously. The students were very affectionate and sympathetic, one felt a very sincere contact with him. It was a departure at the full height of life, achievement and influence.'[126] Immediately upon signing the final contract for the Strasbourg chair, Simmel was aware of the need to maintain contact with other universities in the vicinity. Thus, at the end of January 1914, Simmel was writing to Rickert with a plan for academic co-operation. He writes:

> The idea occurred to me as to whether a kind of philosophical 'cartelisation' might be possible between Heidelberg, Freiburg and Strasbourg. Perhaps a south-west German corner of philosophical culture might be created if we could possibly transfer large numbers of students between the three universities . . . In the course of time, one ought then to enlarge the concept of 'philosophical culture'.[127]

With the outbreak of war, this proved not to be feasible and Simmel at first remained unsure as to why he had moved to Strasbourg at all. In April 1914 he wrote to his friend Keyserling that 'the reason why I have risked this leap in the dark . . . will not be easily grasped and it is perhaps not possible to be grasped.'[128]

At the end of his first summer semester in Strasbourg war was declared and Simmel, much to the surprise of some of his admirers, was enthusiastically in its favour. Simmel had been fond of saying that 'a national misfortune has befallen the Germans twice: the Thirty Years War and the reign of Wilhelm II'. But he joined the majority of intellectual enthusiasts for the war. This led, for example, to the break in his friendship with Ernst Bloch who, along with Jaspers, Radbruch, Lederer and Lukács in Heidelberg, rejected the war hysteria. In Bloch's last letter to Simmel he wrote: 'For a whole lifetime you seek out the truth as if you saw it, and now you find the absolute in the trenches. No, not that!'[129] Simmel's existential enthusiasm for the war took the form of applauding the 'absolute situation' which created the ultimate existential decision for Germany. Ironically, this too is the closing comment upon the *Mann ohne Eigenschaften* when Ulrich, lacking the qualities for rational decision (*Entscheidung*) finally makes an arbitrary decision (*Dezision*) as an ultimate one — he volunteers for military service in the First World War. But Simmel was far from being as chauvinistic as many of his colleagues in philosophy who adhered to the philosophical 'Ideas of 1914' and, as the war progressed, his initial enthusiasm waned dramatically.[130]

Away from Berlin and his large student following and in a city in which he never felt at home, Simmel found it difficult to continue to write with great enthusiasm. This was, of course, compounded by the war and the atypical student body that he was confronted with as well as the hostility of many of his colleagues. According to at least one of his students, there was hardly any reference to the war in his lectures. It seems plausible to suggest that the aesthetic retreat from reality found in his earlier writings had become a real inward retreat for Simmel in Strasbourg. Not surprisingly, therefore, he was keen to consider the possibility of securing a chair in Heidelberg after the death of Windelband and Emil Lask in 1915. The candidates for the two chairs were Simmel, Rickert, Husserl, Heinrich Maier, Eduard Spranger and Ernst Cassirer. In the event, Rickert was appointed to one of the chairs and, after further machinations, Heinrich Maier was offered the second, despite Rickert's efforts to secure it for Simmel. Once more, Simmel was passed over for a chair and, in a letter to Rickert in December 1915, after thanking him for his support, complains of his false image amongst many members of university faculties and education ministers:

> Sometimes I am too one-sided, sometimes too many-sided, here 'really only a sociologist', there 'only of talmudic sagacity', mostly 'only critical and negative', etc. I have given up protesting at this nonsense. . . . To this extent you are right that I am not disappointed; but I cannot and will not deceive you that the decision is painful.[131]

Earlier that same month, Simmel informed Rickert that he had recently finished his book on Rembrandt and was now revising his *Problems of the Philosophy of History* once more,

> whose fourth edition will again be a completely new book. Recently, some new insights into 'time' in the historical sense have occurred to me. If I have the life and energy to carry it out, then I hope, in so doing, to illuminate a number of obscure areas of a fundamental kind that the theory of history has, as far as I can see, hitherto overlooked. But who today can trust in the future?![132]

In December of the following year, Simmel told Rickert that he was still working on this new edition but was faced with a large number of difficult problems such that 'completion is not at all in sight, particularly since the hours of complete concentration in these times are so few.'[133] The new edition was never completed, though some of Simmel's later reflections were published. The brief essay *The Problem of Historical Time*, for instance, was published in 1916.[134]

During his four years at Strasbourg University, Simmel's interest in sociology continued to become increasingly subordinate to philosophical and especially metaphysical aims. In lectures and seminars, sociology was only offered twice – and then only in one-hour periods – in the winter semesters of 1914/15 and 1917/18. His last sociological work, *Grundfragen der Soziologie*, was published in 1917;[135] *Rembrandt* appeared in 1916,[136] some of his wartime essays, *Der Krieg und die geistigen Entscheidungen* appeared in 1917,[137] *Der Konflikt in der modernen Kultur* (actually an extended lecture) in 1918[138] and his most metaphysical work, *Lebensanschauung. Vier metaphysische Kapitel* in the same year.[139] No sociological essays appeared in this period. The majority of published essays and articles were either on the war, aesthetics, the philosophy of culture or metaphysics. Of course, elements of his earlier sociology are again embedded in these later writings on the crisis of modern culture, for instance, but the distance that Simmel perceived between subjective and objective culture in *The Philosophy of Money* had become unbridgeable except at the level of the metaphysics of individualism.

An often resignatory pessimism in Simmel's wartime writings confirms the effect moving to Strasbourg and the war were having upon his life. Writing to his friend Hermann Keyserling in March 1918, Simmel openly reveals his exhaustion:

> I have passed the whole period of the war in Strasbourg, aside from short lecture tours within Germany for charity, on the western front for the field-grey students and briefly to Holland at the invitation of Amsterdam students. How hard these years were and still are cannot be expressed; they have had the effect of aging me twice or three times what is normal (I was 60 years old some weeks ago). The whole external life is very quiet and runs almost monotonously; thus, inner excitement did not find the corresponding reaction that its external fateful movements could have guaranteed.[140]

Four months later, Simmel expressed his feelings about his existence in Strasbourg more cryptically but in a similar vein to Marianne Weber in the following terms:

There is hardly anything to report from us. We live in the antinomy between the enormous inner emotions and tensions and a cloistered, closed-off, indifferent, desolate external existence. Academic activity is = 0, the people (with, of course, one wonderful exception) alien and inwardly distant.[141]

By this time, Simmel was ill and knew that he was dying from cancer of the liver. He died on 26 September 1918.

2 A Foundation for Sociology?

Sociology is gaining more and more ground in the universities and it is certainly only a matter of time before this fact will be officially recognised everywhere. So it is perhaps not insignificant for both the external and internal functioning of science that, as I hope and as I will attest to, I have contrived to substitute a new and sharply de-marcated complex of specific tasks for the hitherto lack of clarity and confusion surrounding the concept of sociology.

Georg Simmel, 3 March 1895

The impressionist philosopher Simmel, who must have known it to be true, once said that there are only fifteen people in the world but these fifteen move about so quickly that we believe there to be more.

Ernst Bloch

I

Simmel's confident pronouncement in 1895 to Althoff, the Prussian education minister, that not only was sociology becoming more popular and would be soon accepted officially as a valid discipline but also that he himself had already clarified the nature of sociology's aims is only partly born out by the evidence.[1] It is certainly true that Simmel's lectures were already well subscribed. In the summer semester of 1894, 152 students were enrolled for his course on sociology. In the following semester (Winter 1894/5) 269 were enrolled for a course entitled 'On pessimism' — which would have embodied at least some sociological content.[2] But it is not the case either that sociology soon came to be officially recognised as an accepted discipline or that Simmel's own work was officially rewarded, as his subsequent career testifies to. Nonetheless, since 1887 Simmel had already been lecturing on socio-logical themes even though the first course to be simply entitled 'Soci-ology' was offered in the summer of 1894. Subsequently, he offered a course on sociology every year until 1908 and thereafter only in 1909/10, 1911/12 and 1917/18.[3]

By 1895 Simmel had already published work in the field of sociology. In 1890 his book on social differentiation (*Über sociale Differenzierung*) had outlined some of the themes that were later taken up in his *Philosophy of Money* and his *Soziologie*. Though not directly located within sociology, the first edition of his *Problems of the Philosophy of History* (1892)[4] not merely formed the basis for a demarcation of sociology from history but also introduced some crucial methodological reflections on historical understanding that were later greatly modified in the 1905 edition and taken up by Max Weber.[5] Equally significant for Simmel's claim to have already clarified the tasks of sociology is the essay 'The problem of sociology' (1895)[6] which, in a revised version, was to constitute the first crucial chapter of his *Soziologie* (1908).[7] In this respect, then, Simmel may have been correct in suggesting that he had at least commenced to outline 'a new and sharply demarcated complex of specific tasks . . . surrounding the concept of sociology'. Certainly in subsequent years via his *Philosophy of Money* and down to the *Soziologie* — both of which are composed of rewritten or re-printed articles to a greater or lesser degree — Simmel had established a specific form of sociology in Germany.

If we accept Tenbruck's claim that *The Philosophy of Money* signifies the high point of Simmel's sociological period or even if we modify it to extend to and include the *Soziologie*, then we must accept his important corollary that, with regard to his sociological work, Simmel 'is thus specifically and in a strict sense not a contemporary of Max Weber's. As the latter commenced work on sociology, the former had already taken his leave of it.'[8]

Hence, it is all the more important to examine the extent to which Simmel was successful in establishing a foundation for sociology that was in part modified or rejected subsequently by Max Weber as well as establishing a sociological tradition in its own right.

What this more precise dating of Simmel's interest in sociology and indeed his sociological work as a whole implies is that the most obvious place to look for the foundation of his sociology is not the *Soziologie* of 1908 but his much earlier contributions in the previous decade. The high point of Simmel's interest in sociology thus predates any major contribution by Max Weber to sociological discourse. Even though Simmel gave the opening address to the first meeting of the German Sociological Association in 1910, he explicitly turned down a request to be its first president because he had neither the time nor the 'inclination' for such a task. Furthermore, his written work testifies to his lack of interest in the heated debates in the *Verein für Sozialpolitik*, in the *Methodenstreit* as a whole and in the subsequent *Werturteilsstreit* which so preoccupied Weber. These, then, are not the debates which animate Simmel's foundation of sociology. Simmel's attempt to ground sociology as an independent discipline involved him not merely in locating a theoretical field for sociology and possibly a distinctive 'approach' but also its differentiation from the study of psychology — which remained a persistent interest through much of his career — and the study of history.

But this is not to suggest that he totally neglected psychology or history in his subsequent work. Indeed, in the field of social psychology it is not difficult to argue that, amongst his contemporaries, Simmel was one of its greatest contributors and even plausible to suggest that he was one of its founders. In the case of historical study, the situation is more complex. On the one hand, Simmel retained an interest in the philosophy of history from the publication of the *Probleme der Geschichtsphilosophie* in 1892 through its complete revision in 1905 — which was so significant for Weber's own clarification of the notion of historical understanding — and down to the brief essay 'Vom Wesen des historischen Verstehens' in 1918. On the other hand, however, the ambiguous category 'formal' sociology so often attached to Simmel's name would suggest that a 'historical' sociology is not one of his concerns. Be that as it may, many of his contemporaries did see Simmel's sociology as lacking a historical dimension though clearly not a philosophy of history. And this is despite the fact that very early on Simmel had sought to demarcate sociology from the philosophy of history.

Therefore, the starting point for the study of Simmel's attempt at a foundation for sociology should commence with his earliest contributions and not with his seemingly more systematic later work such as the *Grundfragen der Soziologie* (1917) which distinguishes the field of sociology itself, 'general sociology', 'pure or formal sociology' and 'philosophical sociology'.[9] These apparently more systematic reflections upon the nature of sociology, although they are sometimes reworked versions of earlier pieces, are not necessarily what animates and informs the works written during the height of Simmel's interest in sociology. When the *Grundfragen* was published in 1917, Simmel had only taught a course on sociology twice since 1908. For the reader of Simmel's work in translation, the time span within which he was concerned with sociology is obscured by the fact that collections of his essays on sociology are not arranged chronologically. Therefore, his essay on

'The field of sociology' might remain unlocated historically rather than being the last essay on the nature of sociology that Simmel wrote.[10] If Tenbruck's argument is correct that the high point of Simmel's interest in sociology is around 1900, then we must turn to his early attempt to establish sociology as an independent discipline.

Although this implies an examination of a limited number of contributions, they do indeed form the basis for Simmel's subsequent elaboration of sociology as an independent discipline. They comprise the first chapter of *Über sociale Differenzierung* (1890), 'Das Problem der Soziologie' (1894), 'Zur Methodik der Socialwissenschaft' (1896), 'Die Selbsterhaltung der socialen Gruppe' (1898), and the first chapter and addendum to *Soziologie* (1908). The last named consists of 'The problem of sociology' and 'How is society possible?', the former being a reworked version of the 1894 essay.[11] In addition, there are a number of brief reviews of other works written in the 1890s which further elaborate upon Simmel's notion of society.[12] Again, what this indicates is that Simmel's attempt to ground sociology is largely completed by 1900 and definitely established by 1908. Referring to the *Soziologie*, Maria Steinhoff was thus correct in asserting that

> The major work was for him something like a farewell to socio-logical research. His interest had slowly transferred to other ques-tions, especially cultural philosophical ones. Later, he once ex-pressed to Troeltsch that actual sociological problems 'no longer interest him' and in autumn 1913 'on the grounds of other direc-tions for his studies' he left the executive of the German Sociological Association.[13]

This would seem to largely substantiate Tenbruck's claim that Simmel's concern for sociology was on the wane after 1900. Whether Simmel had by then established sociology as an independent discipline with specific demarcated tasks must be investigated by turning to the writings of this earlier period.

II

The introductory chapter of Simmel's first major sociological work *Über sociale Differenzierung* (1890) is entitled 'On the epistemology of social science'.[14] It confirms Frischeisen-Köhler's view of his early writings as 'at first much more destructive than constructive'[15] insofar as Simmel's aim is both to counter earlier conceptions of sociology and to demarcate a space for sociology out of the social sciences as a whole and away from metaphysics and the philosophy of history. At the same time, Simmel also rejects the claims of at least one already existing sociological tradition, namely that generated by Comte's positivism. Although traces of Spencer's evolutionism are present in Simmel's early work, he does not appear to accept Spencer's foundation of sociology itself.[16] As has been pointed out by Tenbruck and others,[17] Simmel clearly owed much in his early work on the foundations of sociology to Dilthey even though he never acknowledged his influence. For his part, Dilthey excepted Simmel's sociology from his strictures against what he took to be the predominant features of this new discipline.[18] It is not difficult to find passages and theories in Dilthey's own early work that are reminiscent of Simmel's later writings. If we take Dilthey's *Einleitung in die Geisteswissenschaften* (1883), then we find not merely a notion of society as 'our world' comprising the 'play of interactions' and 'the summation of interactions' but also more specific references to the concept of interaction (*Wechselwirkung*) that is so central to Simmel's notion of society as when Dilthey suggests that 'The individual . . . is an element in the interactions of society, a point of intersection of the diverse systems of these interactions who reacts in conscious intention and action upon their effects.'[19] Similarly, as we shall see, Dilthey had already in this work inveigled against the claims of a German philosophy of history and British (Spencer) and French (Comte) sociology to possess the means for knowledge of the whole of historical social reality. Although never as explicitly as Dilthey, Simmel too rejected similar claims in his early writings, and specifically in the first chapter of his book on social differentiation.

Simmel starts out by trying to discover what is distinctive about this new discipline called sociology in order to make it an independent discipline. He argues that if we commence with the content rather than the method we are confronted with a series of existing disciplines out of which a new discipline is to be defined. From this standpoint 'it is an eclectic discipline insofar as the products of other disciplines form its material'. It is thus a second order discipline that provides a new synthesis and 'a new standpoint for the observation of already known facts'.[20] Hence, what is distinctive about sociology cannot be a new subject matter but must be a new mode of observation.

It is necessary for sociology to clarify what this standpoint is. Simmel argues that 'in the last instance, there is no science whose content emerges out of mere objective facts but always entails their interpretation and ordering according to categories and norms that are

a priori for the relevant science.'[21] The social sciences possess a particularly large fund of conceptual formations that bind diverse elements
together. This might be taken to mean that we need strict definitions
of the basic concepts of sociology before we can commence an analysis
of its subject matter. Simmel takes as instances of these basic questions: 'What is a society? What is an individual? How are reciprocal
psychological effects of individuals upon each other possible?' In passing we can note that the relation between individual and society and
social interactions are among the central themes of Simmel's later
sociology. For the moment, however, we must return to his main
argument which is that such strict definitions of basic concepts are not
necessary if a demarcation of the sphere of study has already been
agreed upon. Simmel argues this is so on the grounds that in the logical
systematic construction of a science, definitions of basic concepts do
come first, but they can only be given simply and clearly for a science
that is already developed: 'The simplest result of reflection is, in fact,
not the result of the simplest reflection'.

Simmel recognises that sociology's sphere of study is ostensibly
very complex. The sheer diversity of 'latent and effective forces' in
society means that their 'reciprocal effects' (*gegenseitige Wirkungen*)
and multiple combinations are almost infinite and immeasurable.

> Hence, if it is the task of sociology to describe the forms of human
> communal existence and to find the rules according to which the
> individual, insofar as he is the member of a group, and groups relate
> to one another, then the complexity of this object has a consequence
> for our science which, with regard to its epistemological relationship,
> . . . stands alongside metaphysics and psychology.[22]

Simmel here sees the tasks of sociology as both describing the *forms* of
what he later termed sociation (*Vergesellschaftung*) and the *rules* of
sociation and interaction between individuals and groups. However, he
seldom takes up the issue of rule-governed behaviour with regard to
interaction in quite the same obvious manner in which he describes
forms of sociation.

Simmel's argument at this stage moves in a different direction. He
seeks to recognise that sociology does stand in a significant relationship
to metaphysics and psychology whilst at the same time insisting that
sociology should be demarcated from both. Neither metaphysics nor
psychology can form the basis for a sociology since both lack 'the
unambiguousness of a scientific rule'. Indeed, metaphysics is characterised by the total ambiguity of the object since 'the whole world of
which metaphysical assertions speak contain such a wealth and diversity

of individual elements'[23] that it would be false to generalise a particular truth or to draw a conclusion for the whole from particular assertions. Similarly, there exists such a 'wealth of nuances' in each psychological function that where one takes some psychological state as a cause then one is conflating a whole complex of diverse factors.

Simmel goes further and rejects the notion of causal laws in psychology and, by inference, in sociology itself. In psychology, there are so many processes and forces in operation that 'the establishment of a causal connection between simple psychological concepts . . . is always completely one-sided'.[24] Apparently causal connections in one isolated sphere are always subsequently invalidated because the psychological totality within which they are located has changed in the meantime. Hence,

> This is the reason why psychology cannot achieve any laws in the natural scientific sense: because, in view of the complexity of its phenomena, no isolated, simple action or force is to be observed in the mind. Rather, each is directed by so many supplementary phenomena that it is never possible to establish with complete certainty what in fact is thus really the cause of a given effect or the effect of a given cause.[25]

Nonetheless, Simmel argues that it would be false to reject the metaphysical and psychological standpoints since both are precursors of exact knowledge insofar as they do provide one-sided connections that must be subsequently qualified.

Sociology finds itself in a similar situation to psychology since 'the complexity of the object completely prevents its separation into simple parts and its basic forces and relationships'.[26] As with psychology, the complexity and fluidity of interactions within the object of study prevents the easy location of basic forces. This assertion was to become one of the essential elements of Simmel's theory of society, namely the fundamental interrelatedness of all social phenomena and the apparent absence of any ordering or priority within its elements. Here, however, Simmel is concerned to reject the concept of laws in sociology: 'Thus, one cannot speak of laws of social development. Undoubtedly, each element of a society moves according to natural laws; yet for the whole there exists no law; as in nature so equally here, there is no higher law above the laws that govern the movements of the smallest parts.'[27] This applies to differentiation itself even though it is the subject of Simmel's study. Again, there is already present in these early formulations a central feature of Simmel's subsequent social theory: the absence of a law of the totality of society. What changes, however, is his later rejection of the concept of law in society altogether. In 1890 Simmel was still committed to a form of residual positivism.

Simmel maintains that if we accept a notion of the ceaseless inter-action of diverse elements in society then we are confronted with a problem of the definition of society. The concept of society only seems to be meaningful as a 'collective expression' that is contrasted with the mere sum of individuals. But Simmel argues that the only genuine reality is the individuals who make up society; society itself is an ideal synthesis and not the actual object of scientific study. In other words,

> If society is merely a . . . collection of individuals who are the actual realities, then this [collection] and its behaviour also constitutes the real object of science and the concept of society evaporates . . . what palpably exists is indeed only individual human beings and their situations and activities: therefore the task can only be to under-stand them, whereas the essence of society, that emerges purely through an ideal synthesis and is never to be grasped, should not form the object of reflection directed toward the investigation of reality.[28]

Although Simmel is not explicit here as to his focus of criticism, it is reasonable to suggest that − like Dilthey earlier − he is opposed to the reliance upon a hypostatised conception of society that is to be found not merely in Comte and Spencer but in much contemporary German philosophy. In contrast, Simmel is insistent that 'To investigate the plurality as such, that already has the individual human subject in-cluded within it, is, as I believe, one of the most important precon-ditions for a rational foundation of social science.'[29] Again, Simmel is at pains to point out that we can never treat this plurality as an absolute unity since each part possesses a relative autonomy. On the other hand, he seeks to guard against a thorough-going individualistic foundation for sociology which would reduce social reality merely to isolated atoms. Actual individuals are empty without development and action and, specifically, interaction.

Simmel develops a theory of interaction which not merely sees interaction as central to sociology but also elevates it to a universal principle. With regard to the apparently infinite diversity of elements within a single whole he suggests that 'there exists only one basic factor which provides at least a relative objectivity of unification: the inter-action [*Wechselwirkung*] of the parts. We characterise any object as unified to the extent to which its parts stand in a reciprocal, dynamic relationship.'[30] At an even more universal level, Simmel explicates what is later to become a crucial feature of his conception of society when he states that 'we must accept as a regulative world principle that everything interacts in some way with everything else, that between every point in the world and every other force permanently moving relationships exist.'[31] Out of this ceaseless interaction we cannot extract one element and say that this is the crucial one. This universal principle of interaction is, however, not merely a heuristic device for Simmel since 'the dissolution of the societal soul into the sum of interactions of its participants lies in the direction of modern intellectual life as such'. Society itself is not the primary factor since 'society is not an entity fully enclosed within itself, an absolute unity, any more than is the human individual. Compared with the real interactions of the parts it is only secondary, only the result.'[32] Thus, even in this early passage Simmel insists upon what subsequently interests him, namely, social interactions. The nature and function of a whole society remains secondary throughout his work.

It is not the unity of society that ensures the existence of its parts but the part that ensures the existence of the whole society. These parts or elements are not merely individuals; they can also be whole social groups. Sociology's concern is 'with empirical atoms, with conceptions, individuals and groups that function as unities'. Hence sociology does not commence with the concept of society since it is

> only the name for the sum of these interactions . . . It is therefore not a unified, fixed concept but rather a gradual one from which more or less is also applied according to the greater number and cohesion of the existing interactions that exist between given persons. In this manner, the concept of society completely loses its mystical facet that individualistic realism wishes to see in it.[33]

If the focus is on real interactions, then Simmel must face the boundaries of his concept of society. The instance which he gives is two warring states, since the interaction between them would lead one to conceive of them together as a society on this definition. Similarly, at the opposite extreme, two interacting individuals might be seen to constitute a society. This difficulty leads Simmel to argue for the flexibility of concepts and 'the incongruence between the rounding-off of our concepts and the fluctuation of things'. Definitions must, therefore, be seen as guides to reality. Nonetheless, one can see the boundaries of what is genuinely social in those entities that exist as objective structures independently, to some extent, of the individual participants. Later, Simmel was to analyse these quasi-objective structures or social generalities as well as the most fleeting forms of interaction.

In this early attempt to establish the task and scope of sociology, Simmel was already moving away from the extreme nominalism and logical atomism of his earlier philosophical and psychological work by means of the concept of interaction. At the same time this notion of interaction is elevated to 'a regulative world principle' that seems to be substituted at this stage for a metaphysically hypostatised concept of society. As a general concept without specificity it readily becomes a pseudo-concrete totality opposed to the individual. With respect to sociology itself, it is already seen to be constituted not by any new subject matter but by a new mode of observation. As Steinhoff correctly suggests in pulling Simmel's various notions together, 'Simmel's sociology is thus based on *no new material object* but on a *formal object*, a new "mode of observation", a "standpoint", an "abstraction".'[34] Although not yet very clear about the nature of this abstraction, Simmel is already aware that all sciences rest upon abstraction from the total reality on the basis of concepts. Which concepts are crucial for the establishment of sociology as an independent discipline is explicated more fully in Simmel's next constitutive essay 'The problem of sociology' (1894).[35]

Here Simmel moves further away from what has been termed the 'speculative atomism' of his earliest work in that he announces from the outset that 'the most significant and consequential progress' in historical and human studies has been 'the transcendence of the individualistic perspective [*Anschauungsart*]'. Now, instead of viewing human phenomena as the result of human fate, 'the human sciences have become the science of human society', and no object of study can escape this new perspective.[36] As a result, the new tendency in human studies is 'to trace each individual event back to the historical situation, the needs and achievements of the totality'. But this orientation is so general that it cannot serve as the basis for a particular independent science. Thus, for instance, sociology cannot be the all-encompassing name for the whole of the modern human sciences.

In this way, Simmel returns to his central concern to ground sociology as an independent discipline by reiterating some of his earlier arguments and developing new formulations of the problem. Whereas his first attempt to discuss the foundation of the social sciences oscillated between the social sciences as a whole and sociology in particular, this essay is more specifically focused upon sociology. Simmel reformulates his opposition to sociology as a collective, encyclopaedic discipline as follows:

Sociology as the history of society and all its contents, i.e. in the sense of an explanation of all events mediated by social forces and configurations, is no more a specific science than is 'induction'. In a similar manner [to induction] . . . it is a method of acquiring knowledge [*Erkenntnismethode*] , a heuristic principle.[37]

It must exist in a more restricted sense than as 'a mere research tendency that is falsely hypostatised into a science of sociology'.

What problems are faced in this demarcation of sociology as a distinctive, independent discipline? Simmel compares sociology's situation with that of psychology since some attempts have also been made to make all sciences reducible to psychology on the grounds that they are all the products of the human mind. But this fails to distinguish the science of psychology from the functions of the psyche itself. Similarly, one might argue that everything which occurs in society should be the object of sociology. On the contrary, Simmel presents his first formulation of the aims of sociology in a restricted form when he insists that

Just as the differentiation of the specifically psychological form of objective matter produces psychology as a science, so a genuine sociology can only concern itself with what is specifically societal [*das Specifisch-Gesellschaftliche*] , the form and forms of sociation [*Vergesellschaftung*] as such as distinct from the particular interests and contents in and through which sociation is realized.[38]

These interests and contents constitute the content of other disciplines. Sociology is to be concerned specifically with 'the forms of socialisation [*die Socialisierungsformen*] '.

Again, having demarcated the object of sociology in this way, Simmel feels required to delineate what he means by society within the confines of this more narrow conception of sociology. 'Society in the broadest sense' exists 'where several individuals enter into interaction'. Since these interactions may be very diverse sociology 'must concern itself with sociation of the most diverse levels and types'. Though specific causes and goals form 'the *material* of the social process' without which sociation is not possible, it is the *form* which that material takes which, abstracted from the content, constitutes the subject matter of sociology. Forms of sociation are less diverse than their content since 'the same form, the same type of sociation can enter into the most diverse material'. Sociology is to be concerned with 'sociation as such and its forms. These forms develop out of the contact of individuals, relatively independently of the basis of this contact, and their sum total constitutes concretely that entity which one designates by the abstraction, society.'[39] Society, then, consists of the sum of social interactions.

In any specific historical phenomenon, of course, content and social form are fused since there can be no social development that is merely social and one that is pure content. This content can be both objective (e.g. 'technological progress', 'the domination of an idea'), or subjective and refer to 'the countless sides of the personality'. This fusion of form and content does not, however, prevent the scientific study of either aspect. All sciences proceed by abstraction. The political historian, for example, might extract the political significance of events or the economic historian might extract all that is associated with human material needs and their satisfaction from the totality of events. Sociology too proceeds in the same manner since

> in fact it extracts the purely social element from the totality of human history, i.e. what occurs *in* society, for special attention; or, expressed somewhat succinctly and paradoxically, it studies that which is 'society', in society [*was an der Gesellschaft 'Gesellschaft' ist*].[40]

Simmel takes 'the sole object of a sociology as a specific science' to be 'the investigation of the forces, forms and development of sociation, individuals being together, their co-operation and their co-existence.'[41] He provides brief instances of what he intends such as the study of sociation in the aristocracy or a secret society — both of which are elaborated later in his *Soziologie* — but is at pains to point out that under 'the forms of human relationships' he includes not merely 'associations and combinations in the strict sense' but also 'opposition and competition'.[42] This would distinguish Simmel's understanding of 'sociation' from that version of 'socialisation' studies which were incapable of conceiving of any purpose of sociation other than integration in its naivest sense.

What methods should be pursued in the investigation of these forms of sociation? Simmel argues that they are 'the same as in all comparative psychological sciences'. What this implies is not merely the fact that sociology conceived in this way is quite similar to Dilthey's programme for a comparative psychology (in 1895 Dilthey prepared a paper 'On comparative psychology' which he withdrew from publication[43]) but also that Simmel conceives of 'certain psychological presuppositions' and 'primary psychological processes' that lie at the foundation of both history and sociology. These processes (such as love and hate, individual self-preservation, etc.) must be presupposed in order to conceive of 'sociations, group formations, relationships of individuals to a totality'. Not surprisingly, therefore, Simmel subsequently examines many of these processes from a philosophical or sociological perspective.

More specifically, in one of Simmel's many arguments by analogy, he argues that just as economic history applies economic abstractions to historical material, so sociology applies psychological abstractions to society. This is done in two ways: either it cuts a cross section through a historical development, for instance, in order to examine its social formation and specifically abstracts from it the process of domination and subordination, 'the modification of the social form through the quantitative changes in the group', etc.; or it cuts a cross section through 'individual developments' in order to see what relationships or forms of sociation they have in common.

Whereas sociology might presuppose certain psychological processes, it must be strictly demarcated from the philosophy of history which seeks 'to subsume historical facts in their totality, both external and psychological, under "general concepts"'. Instead, 'In complete contrast to this, sociology as a specific science . . . confines itself completely within the course of events and their immediate psychological significance.'[44] It cannot rely upon historical laws. None are to be found in view of the great complexity of history, and because any selection from cosmic events would be 'uncertain and subjectively limited'. For similar reasons sociology, too, is unlikely to discover laws of society.

It is interesting to note in passing that Simmel's essay was published in the same year as Windelband's key address on 'History and natural science' in which he argued that psychology had no part to play in history and should be relegated to the natural sciences.[45] Simmel's 1894 essay clearly argues the contrary insofar as psychological presuppositions are seen as a prior requirement for the study of history. Simmel's essay also unwittingly opposes Windelband's views insofar as Simmel's early conception of sociology is not totally dissimilar to Dilthey's notion of a comparative and descriptive psychology. As has been pointed out already, Dilthey strongly opposed Windelband's views on the nature and role of psychology. Whilst this may seem to link Simmel's work to the neo-Kantian debate on the natural and cultural or historical sciences, the suggestion of a direct connection would be misleading. There is little evidence to support the view that Simmel was directly engaged in the neo-Kantian debate or tradition. Indirectly, of course, it is clear that in an unacknowledged manner, Simmel took up much from Dilthey's earlier works.

In 1896, Simmel published an article entitled 'On the methodology of social science'[46] which was, in fact, a review of Stammler's *Wirtschaft und Recht nach der materialistischen Geschichtsauffassung*[47] – over a decade before Max Weber's more famous review of the revised edition of Stammler's work.[48] Besides being a critique of Stammler's study, it was also a vehicle for Simmel to expand upon his own conception of society as well as containing perhaps the only reference to the *Methodenstreit* in Simmel's work.

Since Stammler's study concerns the materialist conception of history, it is not surprising that Simmel should also confront a theory of knowledge that is not merely 'theoretical' but also practical. Already in *Über soziale Differenzierung*, Simmel had argued that if one examines the emergence of knowledge rather than its 'pure ideal content' then one must conceive of 'cognition as a sphere of human practice'. In his discussion of Stammler, Simmel returns more pointedly to the aim of a critique of knowledge initiated by Kant for the natural sciences. Why do the social sciences also require a critique of knowledge? Simmel suggests that

> social scientific cognition seems today to require a fundamental self critique [*eine prinzipielle Kritik seiner selbst*] since out of the endless dispute concerning its content only one thing is clearly illuminated: its inadequacy when confronted with the urgent crisis of the times, which indeed had to appeal to this knowledge above all other.[49]

But neither here nor elsewhere in this period does Simmel clarify what he means by 'the urgent crisis of the times'. Instead, he moves on immediately to the methodological debate surrounding the social sciences which he conceives as a fundamental opposition between an empiricism that is preoccupied with facts and historical descriptions of social life on the one hand, and 'a constructive systematic', on the other, which starts out from general concepts. It is an opposition which permeates practical issues and has practical consequences. Simmel argues that not only has Kant already shown how these two positions rely upon one another and are not independent but also that he himself has shown this to be the case for the study of history. Stammler, he argues, attempts to do the same for the social sciences.

Simmel appears to concur largely with that part of Stammler's substantive critique of historical materialism which centres around the relationship between 'the social economy' and law. Stammler's view is that whereas historical materialism argues that 'valid law in a society is merely the expression and product of its economic relationships', he argues that the law is the basis for 'a social economy'. Further, changes in technical production must be accompanied by modifications in the legal order. Simmel states that Stammler's arguments – which are, of course, more complex than this simple formulation – 'decisively dethrone the view that production as such . . . is the sufficient cause of a legal order'. Simmel takes this argument to be a 'typical error' whose general form is that

> in the case of the transformation of an element within a complex system, the next stage of development of the whole is taken to be exclusively the result of this individual element, whereas in reality it arises out of those combinations which the relatively unchanged continued existence of the remaining elements enters into with the changes in each of them.[50]

Despite the obscurity of Simmel's formulation here, it represents a decisive argument for the complexity of reality and the impossibility of extracting a single cause. It is an argument that Simmel returns to more forcefully – and more cogently – in his attempt to build 'a new storey beneath historical materialism' in *The Philosophy of Money*. As with many of his other early essays, the argument is not developed any further.

Rather, Simmel turns to what he finds most questionable in Stammler's work, namely his conception of society:

> Stammler seeks an absolutely precise concept of 'society' – in contrast to the merely natural communality, the mere sum of individuals; and he finds it in the fact that social life is 'a communal life of human beings that is governed [*geregelt*] by externally binding norms'. In this way, social life becomes the unified object of a special science . . . External regulation – which may be not only a legal but also a conventional one – is the *a priori* under whose precondition the sphere of society appears as a scientific entity.[51]

Society therefore exists where human behaviour is governed not by natural but by binding norms. Simmel, however, maintains that 'a mere secondary phenomenon, a secondary *conditio sine qua non* is elevated to the positive life-principle of society'. In opposing Stammler's conception of society, Simmel offers three counter examples. The first is the religious community which is not held together by externally binding norms but 'the awareness of a communal relationship to a high principle', or shared beliefs. This consciousness, 'this psychological interaction in the "invisible church" *is* already society' even before its members decide upon external norms of behaviour which is itself 'merely a type of organisation of already existing sociation'. The second example is that of a savings bank which certainly does rely upon external rules. But 'the positive principle of sociation is the reciprocally secured assistance not the form of technical regularity in which it is enclosed'. Finally, the case of simple association is constituted by a variety of forms of behaviour and relationships that are not bounded by external norms.

Simmel draws several negative conclusions from Stammler's use of 'external regulation'. First, Simmel maintains that

> To derive the concept of society from 'external regulation' is the same as if one wished to make the concept of purposive action dependent upon that of the human hand. For it may, of course, be that every purposive action can only be successful in the form of movement which the mechanism of our hand makes possible – but this technical precondition is certainly not the essence of purposive action. Regulation is no more the creative precondition for society any more than is language. Of course, there is no sociation without language in words or gestures; equally, there exists, on the other hand, no language without sociation. Accordingly it is, like regulation, a precondition or a form, a production or a co-product of society – but not its core or essence itself.[52]

Here Simmel wishes to assert the priority of sociation over 'external regulation'. More significantly, if we translate 'regulation' (*Regelung*) broadly as 'rule-following', then we see that Simmel moves decisively away from those present-day theories of society, interaction and communication which see rule-following as a fundamental precondition.

Simmel is concerned to undermine further Stammler's unclarified use of the notion of regulation. Simmel argues that

> the conduct of a person or a member of a group is thus 'regulated' if in the same conditioned situation the same action always results. Indeed, there is no doubt that, regardless of all the content of action, such a regularity of its forms must be present in order for a society to exist at all . . . Thus, regulation is merely the precondition for an already existing group to continue, not the formative condition of its emergence.[53]

According to Simmel, the regularity of conduct may ensure the continued existence of particular groups but cannot account for their original emergence. Similarly, 'in order for a rule . . . to be an "external" one, it does indeed already require a society'. In other words, if it is external to individuals it must have some basis elsewhere.

Finally, in this context, Simmel reiterates his own conception of society as an object of study in the following way:

if society is to be an autonomous object of an independent science, then it can only be so through the fact that, out of the sum of individual elements that constitute it, a new entity emerges; otherwise all problems of social science would only be those of individual psychology. Unity of several elements, however, is nothing but their interaction. . . . The fact that these interactions . . . result in the form of regulation . . . does not signify the essence but merely an attribute of sociation.[54]

Simmel continues by raising the objection against his own conception of society that two warring armies might also constitute a 'society' on this definition. He concedes that, unlike competition, this is a boundary of sociation that is marked by the excess 'quantity' of negativity repelling forces which predominates over positively attracting forces.

In the final section of his review, Simmel takes up Stammler's argument against relativism which takes the form of a distinction between subjective and objective social ideals or goals. As a 'unifying point of all social judgment' and as the 'ultimate goal of all social life' Stammler takes 'the community of freely intending human beings'. In contrast, Simmel argues that there exists no single normative ideal in society, merely a diversity of 'social ideals each of which forms an ultimate instance'. Thus, in contrast to any absolute ideal, Simmel maintains that 'we gain a secure — as distinct from a rigid — position, insofar as we take what is objective, in both knowledge and action, to be a *relational concept*'[55] that expresses this diversity. This does not rule out the possibility that in concrete social situations we act in such a manner '*as if*' they represent objective truth. Simmel's standpoint here is significant for three reasons. First, it not merely lies at the heart of his preference for relational concepts but also forms the basis for a conception of society in which there can be no hierarchy of values or goals. Secondly, it constitutes a central theorem of the sociology of knowledge as it developed in Germany after Simmel's death. Finally, and of most relevance to the present context, Simmel takes it to be a solution to the *Methodenstreit* in economics between 'the historical and dogmatic school'.

The validity of any economic 'law' derives from its abstraction from specific historical preconditions. Similarly, the latter is only made intelligible 'on the presupposition and with the application of certain *objectively* valid statements and concepts'. Both methods can only be extended reciprocally. Simmel concludes that this

> *regressus in infinitum* is the completely legitimate expression for the . . . incompleteness of our knowledge. Expressed in Kantian terms:

instead of two constitutive and, as such, irreconcilable principles we obtain two regulative ones, each of which forms the basis of the other. Thus, what we are concerned with is not a mechanical mixture or an eclectic compromise of opposed methods but with applying both of them as alternating levels of a *single* comprehensive methodology.[56]

It has been argued elsewhere — and we shall return to this later — that Simmel can be said to have made the concept of society itself into the 'regulative idea' of sociology, knowledge of which is never fully determinate.[57]

Some of the formulations of the nature of society and the tasks of sociology so far alluded to were expressed much more briefly in newspaper articles. In this context, it is interesting to note that, whatever the social theme of these much shorter pieces, Simmel usually felt it necessary to reiterate his concern for a clarification of the task of sociology and the concept of society. Rather than summarising these other articles in detail, some instances extracted from them should suffice.

In his newspaper article 'On the sociology of the family' (1895),[58] for example, Simmel prefaces his substantive discussion with a call for the clarification and demarcation of sociology's tasks. The 'new science of sociology' has not yet found its precise boundaries since 'For a long time, sociology seemed to be the magic word that indicated the solution to all the riddles of history as well as practical life, of moral theory as well as aesthetics, of religion as well as politics.'[59] This view, Simmel maintains, was particularly entrenched in France (presumably a reference to Comtean positivism). In Germany and the United States the new science has been understood either as 'a branch of psychology' concerned with the social aspects of the 'individual's mental processes', as 'the science of the common presuppositions of all knowledge relevant to society', as 'the philosophy of social events' or as 'the investigation of the forms in which human beings are socialised'. The latter is, of course, the version of sociology advanced by Simmel.

In the same year, Simmel reviewed le Bon's *Psychology of Crowds* under the title 'Mass psychology' (1895).[60] The book, 'in itself not particularly significant', fails to ask 'the fundamental question' as to how 'the mere sum of individual entities' becomes a crowd or a society. Simmel raises this question, in part, as the relationship between the individual and society:

In a unification of the rarest fruitfulness, the historical method in the humanities and evolution theory in natural science have combined to place the individual in an all-powerful, social–historical development. The individual appears in it merely as a point of intersection of social fibres. . . . Thus, society is everything and . . . the individual . . . a *quantité negligeable.*[61]

Simmel sees this view as now being challenged within sociology itself, though not by le Bon.

Two years later, we find Simmel using another review entitled 'Mass criminality' (1897)[62] as a vehicle for stating his views on laws in sociology. Here, having rejected both the explanatory power of 'human nature' and, at the other extreme, that of the social or psychological 'milieu' in the social and historical sciences, Simmel is prompted to raise the question of laws of society. Many sociologists seem to assume that 'the axiom of natural law-like regularity of all events' also points to the existence of social laws. Simmel argues that if we examine the development of a tree, for example, it would be a mistake to argue that 'a specific natural law' had brought about its growth since there are so many complex combinations of material and energy responsible for it. 'If we apply these reflections to society, as an extremely complicated structure that has developed out of countless elements taken together, then it follows that a specific natural law cannot be provided for it any more than the case of this tree.'[63] Simmel once more advances the proposition as to the complexity of society as a decisive argument against social laws at the macro-level.

Many of the arguments concerning both sociology and society re-appear in a major article in the following year which is an early version of a chapter of the *Soziologie*, namely 'The self-preservation of the social group' (1898).[64] Its significance lies in the fact that it is probably the last essay which Simmel wrote before the publication of his *Soziologie* in 1908 in which he takes up the nature of sociology and society in a general manner. *The Philosophy of Money* (1900) does not take up the issue of the tasks of sociology, though it does contain a number of passages on the nature of society. It could plausibly be argued, therefore, that by 1898 Simmel had secured to his own satisfaction the 'new and sharply demarcated complex of specific tasks' for sociology that he had announced in his letter of 1895. Thereafter, Simmel turned to the explication and elucidation of the tasks through substantive studies on money, competition, space, religion, etc., which are to be found either in the articles subsequently published in his *Soziologie* or in separate studies.[65] Again this confirms Tenbruck's view that Simmel had already established the major directions of his sociology by 1900. The task of its foundation would seem to have preoccupied him for the decade 1890–1900.

'The self-preservation of the social group', like the other articles considered so far, commences with the problem of the object of sociology and the nature of society. The remainder deals with various aspects of group formation and maintenance and is not part of our present concern. Simmel starts out by reiterating his earlier argument concerning the error of assuming that the object of sociology is 'everything that occurs in society' since merely 'a new name but no new knowledge is gained'. Therefore, 'the contents of social life cannot constitute its problem but rather their form . . . On the basis of this abstraction of the forms of society rests the whole justification for the existence of sociology as a distinctive science.'[66] It is thus similar to mathematics or linguistics which respectively abstract the 'spatial form' and 'linguistic form' from their object of study. Simmel repeats his earlier assertion that sociology is concerned with the forms of sociation whereas the purposes or goals of this sociation 'are dealt with in other sciences'.

> Since, however, human sociation always only arises out of such goals, we will thus recognise *the forms and laws of sociation* in such a way that we combine social phenomena of the most diverse contents and, in fact, *explore inductively* what is nonetheless common to all of them.[67]

More clearly than in the earlier articles, Simmel here asserts the task of searching for 'laws' of sociation to be derived from the 'inductive' investigation of social reality.

He gives the example of the formation of parties in social spheres other than the political. By means of an examination of what is common to these social spheres

> one discovers the laws and types of party formation as such, as a form of human communal existence itself; in this way we discover with the same method, for instance, super- and subordination, the formation of hierarchies, competition, the division of labour, emulation, representation and countless other forms of human sociation.[68]

In this manner, the notion of society is demystified insofar as it is seen to emerge out of 'the sum of all these individual means and types of connection that exist between its elements'. Society therefore exists 'where a number of people enter into interaction and form a temporary or permanent unity'.

The self-preservation of a social group or a society is not, however, identical with the self-preservation of its individual elements. Individuals survive while groups disintegrate just as, conversely, groups can be maintained while individuals become weaker. The latter instance perhaps accounts for the fact that society, for example, 'is taken to be a structure of autonomous reality, that leads a life according to its own laws and energies independently of all its individual agents'.[69] When we examine the major social organisations of society 'such a conception seems unavoidable', especially

> since they all appear as products and functions of an impersonal structure, in which individuals of course have a part as in a public possession without one being able to mention an individual by name who was its sufficient cause or specific aim, or whose contribution to it one could extract with any certainty. Rather, they confront the individual as something objective, split off from the conditions of personal life.[70]

Although Simmel does not argue this position here, it is clearly a basis for his theory of reification that is given much fuller treatment in his *Philosophy of Money*. It is a reification process that has also permeated much subsequent sociology. Simmel, however, is insistent that

> ultimately, in fact, only individuals exist, that human products outwith human beings only exist insofar as they are material nature, that in contrast, intellectual structures such as those named above only exist in human minds. Any attempt to conceive of them otherwise is a mysticism comparable with conceptual realism that makes human concepts into autonomous and substantive essences.[71]

Hence it is only as a methodological aid that we speak of the essence and development of such entities as the state, law, and fashion '*as if* they were this unified essence'. Similarly, we may speak of life processes as if they were autonomous entities whereas they are 'merely the complex of infinite mechanical interactions of the smallest parts of organic bodies'. These two views of society are manifestations of 'the conflict between the individualistic and the . . . monistic observation of social structures: the one corresponds to fact, the other to the limited capacity of analysis; the one is the ideal of knowledge, the other the stage that it has temporarily reached'.[72] Rather than remain at the heights of abstraction, Simmel maintains that we must seek to grasp 'the real individual processes' that constitute social structures. Simmel goes on to apply this dictum to the analysis of the self-preservation of social groups and the plurality of forms of sociation that underlie them.

This can only be achieved by separating out the forms of sociation from their content. Only this 'abstraction of sociation as form and type' of communal existence can isolate what is genuinely social science. 'Neither hunger nor love, work nor religiosity, technology nor the contents of intelligence are in and for themselves already social in nature; but the community and interaction of human beings makes them real and effective.'[73] This remains true even though 'the content of sociation, its concrete aim and interest often or always decides upon its specific formation'. Perhaps this is the point which is so often forgotten in asserting that Simmel was merely concerned with a rigid formalism in sociology. Not only was he strongly opposed to a reified conceptualisation of social forms but in his analysis he was at least aware of the dialectical relationship between form and content.

III

The argument advanced so far has suggested that Simmel's attempt to ground sociology as an independent discipline with a clearly demarcated field of study can be largely confined to a single decade, namely between 1890 and 1900. This should not be taken to imply that Simmel did not produce other sociological work subsequently. The period up to the publication of his *Soziologie* in 1908 constitutes a phase of Simmel's work in which he applied his schematic procedures to a variety of social processes and contexts. Shortly afterwards, however, his work took a more philosophical turn. Further, the confinement of his preoccupation with the foundation of sociology to this single decade should not lead us to assume that he in no way changed his views in subsequent years. Even though the *Soziologie*, for example, comprises a series of essays almost all of which had been published earlier in some form or other, it is a collection that contains many pieces which exhibit considerable reworking. Since readers of Simmel's works in translation are now most familiar with the extracts from the *Soziologie*, it is important to highlight the earlier writings, which are less well-known. Nonetheless, in the assessment of Simmel's foundation for sociology that follows reference will also be made to his better known essays.

Since Simmel ceased to preface his articles after 1898 with remarks on the nature of sociology and its tasks, we may presume that he, at least, no longer felt the need to defend sociology as an independent discipline every time he wrote upon sociological themes. But, at the same time, we should guard against the assumption that the often confident pronouncements on sociology and its object of study in his early writings signify a dogmatic assertion of the sociological problematic. Such an interpretation ignores the fact that Simmel seldom saw either his concepts or social processes themselves as closed off or finished: they remain open. This tentative approach to sociological problems — as indeed to those in the other areas he discussed — is exemplified in the hesitant nature of his formulations: the frequent use of 'perhaps', the reliance upon 'nuances' of meaning even from around 1890 onwards.

Whilst the 'approach' to his object of study is discussed at greater length in the next chapter, an example of the provisional nature of his speculations may be seen from the foreword to the *Soziologie*. Introducing the reader to almost 800 pages (in the first edition) of sociological analyses and reflections, Simmel is at pains to point out that it does not constitute a systematic textbook. Rather, the reader must fasten onto its first chapter — a reworked version of the earlier essay 'The problem of sociology' (1894) — in order to follow the succeeding analyses comprising a further nine chapters and thirteen 'excursions'. Simmel speaks of

> the present attempt at *giving the fluctuating concept of sociology an unambiguous content, dominated by one, methodologically certain, problem-idea.* The request to the reader to hold on, uninterruptedly, to this one method of asking questions, as it is developed in the first chapter (since otherwise these pages might impress him as an accumulation of unrelated facts and reflections) — this request is the only matter which must be mentioned at the head of the book.[74]

Thus, when we turn to the table of contents, we find that here too Simmel feels it necessary in a footnote to qualify their apparent specificity since 'The ultimate intention and the methodological structure of these studies required their arrangement under few central concepts but, at the same time, required great latitude in regard to the particular questions treated under their headings.'[75] And even when we enter into the first crucial chapter on 'The problem of sociology', we find Simmel denying that the work is a systematic, completed treatise:

> If I myself stress *the wholly fragmentary, incomplete character of this book*, I do not do so in order to protect myself, in a cheap manner, against objections to this character. . . . Yet if this character should strike one as a defect, this would only go to prove that *I have not been able to clarify the fundamental idea of the present volume.* For according to this idea, nothing more can be attempted than to establish the beginning and the direction of an infinitely

long road — *the pretension of any systematic and definitive completeness would be an illusion.*[76]

Simmel's contemporaries, however, were often less than satisfied either with his foundation for sociology or with his insistence upon the provisional nature of his formulations and analyses.

Tönnies, reviewing *Über sociale Differenzierung*, was the first to challenge Simmel's foundation for sociology.[77] Almost two decades before the publication of the *Soziologie*, Tönnies detected in Simmel's earliest sociological work the 'unfinished' nature of his speculations and the absence of connections between the various chapters. Tönnies objected to what he saw as Simmel's equation of sociology's problems with those in psychology and metaphysics. Further, he maintains that the difficulty in making generalisable statements in sociology is hardly an argument against 'laws of social development', especially since the concept of a law is hardly elucidated by Simmel. Similarly, Simmel's hostility to the concept of society as a 'collective expression' is, according to Tönnies, based on a false nominalism. In short, Tönnies was convinced neither by what he took to be the weakest chapter of Simmel's book nor by the elaboration of many of his concepts in the work as a whole.

A decade later, Durkheim also challenged Simmel's foundation for sociology as represented by his essays 'The problem of sociology' and 'The self-presentation of the social group'. The latter was translated for the *Année Sociologique* by Durkheim himself. Writing to Bouglé about this article, Durkheim asserted that though Simmel had 'a sense of the specificity of social facts' he was reluctant to 'pursue his ideas to their conclusion'. Nonetheless, the article was 'lively, agreeable to read and certainly in the spirit of the *Année*'.[78]

In his limited review of Simmel's work in 1900, Durkheim refers to Simmel having provided 'a notable, an almost violent, effort to trace the limits of the subject matter of sociology'.[79] Nevertheless, he was doubtful as to whether he had succeeded in this task, though he was sympathetic to the notion of obtaining 'a clear idea of what constitutes the domain of sociology'. The confinement of sociology to the study of forms of sociation 'serves merely to keep it tied to metaphysical ideology when it actually shows an irresistible need to emancipate itself from this sphere'.[80] Furthermore, with regard to Simmel's separation of social form and content, Durkheim maintains that 'such an assertion . . . though far from being accepted as a self-evident axiom, may yet overwhelm a student'. The argument that the distinctly social lies in forms of sociation reduces the social group to a sort of empty form of trivial cast that can indifferently receive any kind of material whatever! The claim is that there are arrangements which are encountered everywhere, whatever the nature of the ends attained. But clearly, all these ends, despite their divergences, have characteristics in common. Why should only these common characteristics, and not the specific ones, have social value?[81]

The concrete specificity of the content cannot be divorced from its social form.

Not only is the notion of social forms too wide and vague for Durkheim but also 'The most general aspect of social life is not . . . either content or form. . . . There are not two different kinds of reality which, though intimately connected, are distinct and separable; what we have instead are facts of the same nature, examined at different levels of generality.'[82] Since the criteria for the degree of generality of analysis is missing in Simmel's work 'there is no rule for deciding in an impersonal manner where the circle of sociological facts begins and where it ends'. Durkheim is led to conclude that one can applaud Simmel's

subtlety and ingenuity, but we think it impossible to trace the main divisions of our science as he understands it in an objective manner. No connection can be discovered among the questions to which he draws the attention of sociologists; they are topics of mediation that have no relation to an integral scientific system. In addition, Simmel's proofs generally consist only of explanations by example; some facts, borrowed from the most disparate fields, are cited but they are not preceded by critical analysis, and they often offer us no idea of how to assess their value.[83]

Thus, Durkheim firmly rejected Simmel's foundations for sociology in favour of his own search for causal explanations based on social facts *sui generis*. Ironically, we find Simmel in *The Philosophy of Money* declaring that 'exchange is a sociological phenomenon *sui generis*, an original form and function of social life'.[84] But even this formulation suggests that what interests Simmel is the 'forms' of social life whereas, for Durkheim, 'the term "form" as used by Simmel, has only a metaphorical significance'.[85] Similarly, the whole dimension of social 'interaction', which, it is often argued, constitutes the key to Simmel's foundation of sociology rather than the concept of form, is totally ignored by Durkheim.

From a quite different direction, Simmel's foundation of sociology was sharply criticised by Othmar Spann, whose critique appears to have been accepted by Max Weber with some qualifications.[86] Simmel's 'psychologistic concept of society' is based on his 'definition of societal interaction as the interaction of *psychological* entities'. But a 'specifically *social* criterion for interaction' can, Spann argues, only be derived from an adequate conception of society itself that is not grounded in the interaction of psychological entities. Instead Simmel defines society 'more in the sense of a collective name' for a whole diversity of interactional forms and relationships. Spann concludes that Simmel neither positively nor negatively successfully demarcated sociology as an independent discipline.

In his incomplete assessment of Simmel 'as a sociologist and as a theorist of the money economy' (c. 1908/9), Max Weber speaks of Spann's 'perceptive criticism' of Simmel's conception of sociology and society before the appearance of his *Soziologie* and maintains that 'in relation to the earlier work which Spann criticised, Simmel's recently published *Soziologie* shows some notable, but not *fundamental*, modifications'.[87] From this incomplete assessment, it is possible to glean a limited number of criticisms of Simmel's work.

Weber intended to examine Simmel's 'sociological style of work . . . with respect to both method and function'. Weber wishes to avoid a major concern

> with Simmel's *own* explications of the nature of sociology and the meaning of his sociological method; rather, we prefer to grasp his method by examining the manner in which he deals with individual problems. In a period, however, when sociologists who are to be taken very seriously maintain the thesis that the *only* task of sociological theory is the definition of the concept of society, these questions must be taken up beforehand.[88]

With regard to Simmel's 'method', Weber regards Simmel's argument by analogy and the whole 'analogical procedure' as resting upon 'the dubiousness of its basic principles (particularly pronounced in Simmel's treatment of sociological problems)'. This leads specialists to regard the analogous element of Simmel's arguments 'as something "external"' and 'where the specialist is dealing with questions of "facticity", empirical questions, Simmel has turned to look at the "meaning" which we can obtain from the phenomenon (or can believe we can)'.

But in the only remaining opening passage to Weber's critique, he focuses upon Simmel's conception of sociology as

> a science concerned with 'interactions' among individuals. Now it is clear that the concept of 'interaction' has a good deal of ambiguity in it. In its widest sense as the *reciprocal* influencing of several (however delimited) 'units', 'interactions' appear . . . in the most manifold nuances.[89]

Interaction has even been taken as an axiom of several sciences. But it is too general to constitute a specific foundation for a science since 'within the realm of physical reality an influence that is not somehow "reciprocal" in the strictest sense of the word and as a *general* phenomenon is scarcely conceivable.'[90] Similarly, when Simmel introduces the concept into sociology, in relation to domination for instance,

> one finds this concept of 'interaction' extended so far that only with the greatest artificiality will one be able to conceptualise a pure 'one-way' influence, i.e. an instance of one person being influenced by another where there is *not* some element of 'interaction'.[91]

Though the manuscript breaks off at this point, we can already see that Weber was unconvinced by the concept of social interaction as a basis for sociology even though, unlike Durkheim, it is this aspect of Simmel's work which he sees as crucial to Simmel's attempt at a foundation for sociology.

In the light of Weber's other writings and his brief comments in this incomplete assessment, it is clear that he would probably concur with Spann regarding Simmel's psychologistic theory of society. Such a view was shared by other contemporary commentators. Koigen, for example, saw Simmel's notion of society as rooted in a form of sociological atomism; individuals are almost Kantian things-in-themselves.[92] Unlike Kant's *Ding-an-sich* 'Simmel recognised it as an ego, as a kind of atom. The atom retains a quality. It is to be found in a plurality of relations to other atoms.'[93] Whilst recognising Simmel as 'the sociologist of differentiation', Koigen maintains that the total conception of society remains fragmentary.

> The whole, to take a musical expression, is shaped through 'counterpoint'. 'Harmonic' composition is not to be employed. The forms of sociation run free and parallel to one another, both burdened and enriched by thousands of 'episodes'. Modernity has found here a dynamic expression: the totality of fragmentary, centrifugal directions of existence and the arbitrariness of the individual elements are discerned. In contrast, the concentric principle, the element of the monumental is not attained. The conscious tendency towards a lack of system . . . reacts back upon the conception.[94]

Less poetically, Koigen is asserting that Simmel's conception of society remains atomised and fragmented. The aesthetic analogy he employs relates to an aesthetication of reality that must be examined in the next chapter.

Whereas other commentators such as Masaryk[95] lamented the

totally inadequate nature of Simmel's foundation of sociology in his *Soziologie*, especially as an orientation for the diversity of studies within it ('we have several very good and valuable studies, but sociology as a whole and as a system is not contained in the book'),[96] one contemporary, Alfred Vierkandt, was more sympathetic to Simmel's enterprise.[97] Vierkandt suggests that Simmel's *Soziologie* with its initial chapter on the problem of sociology should not be seen as a textbook, a groundwork or a total presentation of sociology but concerned 'as it were, with a series of variations upon the theme: "What is the task of sociology?"'.[98] That is, unlike many other contemporaries, Vierkandt implies that in order to understand Simmel's foundation of sociology and its aims one must look not merely at his programmatic statements but at the concrete application of his social theory to specific areas of social life. This enables Vierkandt to see 'three groups of questions' to which Simmel addresses himself: the nature and diverse types of social forms and relations whose 'characteristic qualities' are described and analysed; 'the causes which bring about and maintain these phenomena'; and 'the effects that they produce'. Vierkandt sees Simmel's sociology as primarily concerned with the first of these tasks whereas 'the question of the causal connection, especially the effects of these relations, is to some extent secondary in significance'.[99]

Unlike some other contemporary commentators, Vierkandt does not see Simmel as open to the charge of psychological reductionism. Indeed, Vierkandt largely applauds Simmel's significant demarcation of sociology from psychology based on three distinctions: 'psychology is in fact solely concerned merely with the material world, sociology, in contrast predominantly with the éxternal world, and expressed more precisely, with the social and cultural external world'; secondly 'psychology is always merely concerned with the circumstances of a *single* person . . . sociology, however, with *several* entities'; thirdly, for the psychologist, 'the causal sequence that he investigates is limited to the sphere of inner life' whereas the sociologist 'investigates those causes which are contained in the social and cultural environment and the effects' upon social relations.[100] As Simmel puts it, sociology's concepts are 'absolutely nothing substantial or particular, rather a mere relational form'.[101]

The preceding selection of responses to Simmel's attempt at a foundation for sociology should prompt some examination of the framework within which he conceives of this project. Simmel's sociological programme has often been reduced to the simple label of 'formal' sociology. This 'highly independent, difficult to classify thinker'

(Troeltsch)[102] has become rigidly categorised as a 'formal' sociologist. Simmel's contemporaries, however, were more inclined to emphasise his concentration upon a ceaseless interaction of elements of society rather than the formalism of his analysis. Perhaps what they often had in mind is the nature of his substantive studies rather than his programmatic statements that are largely confined to either his early writings or their much more seldom subsequent elaboration — the opening chapter of the *Soziologie* and the much later *Grundfragen der Soziologie*. Those who attended his lectures never attached the label 'formal' to his mode of exposition. More often than not they would refer to a dialectical method. This would suggest the existence of a disjunction between Simmel's more programmatic statements and his substantive achievements.

IV

In his own incomplete account of his development (c. 1908/9), Simmel points to what he saw as significant in his own intellectual tasks.[103] Having argued that his early concern with the philosophy of history led him to conclude that 'history' signifies 'the formation of immediate . . . events', he goes on to assess its importance for the demarcation of sociology as an independent discipline in the following manner:

> This separation of the form and content of the historical image, that emerged for me purely epistemologically, was then pursued by me in a methodological principle within a particular discipline: *I secured a new concept of sociology in which I separated the forms of sociation from the contents*, i.e. the impulses, goals, material content *that only by being taken up by the interactions between individuals became societal*; in my book, therefore, *I have undertaken the investigation of these types of interactions as the object of a pure sociology.*[104]

Simmel here highlights the separation of form and content, the concern for 'forms of sociation' and types of social interaction. In turn, it is social interaction itself which constitutes the unifying principle of society.

Thus, in order to examine Simmel's foundation for sociology as an independent discipline, we need to examine his conception of social form, social interaction and society. At various times, each of these concepts had been taken as the central feature of Simmel's sociological project. In the 1920s, Maria Steinhoff examined Simmel's concept of form 'as a basic category of sociology'.[105] The significance of the concept of form and the defence of Simmel against the more naive charges of 'formalistic sociology' has been forcibly presented by Friedrich Tenbruck.[106] More recently, Becher has argued that the concept of interaction is central to an understanding of his sociology.[107] Finally, on the basis of Simmel's essay 'How is society possible?', as well as his earlier writings, Karin Schrader-Klebert has argued plausibly for 'the concept of society as a regulative idea' in Simmel's conception of sociology.[108] The succeeding brief analysis of the three concepts is therefore indebted to these earlier studies. However critical of aspects of Simmel's work, all suggest that his sociology cannot be reduced to the naive, negative labelling of formalism advanced by Sorokin, Abel, Aron and many others.

The irony of the reduction of Simmel's work to that of sociological formalism is that he regarded concepts as rigid formations, almost as violations of life. Nonetheless, Simmel is concerned to establish a formal as opposed to a material object for sociology. This he sees in the forms of sociation that must be abstracted from social reality though it is not, as Tenbruck rightly points out, a plea 'for the establishment of categories of a high degree of abstractedness'.[109] Similarly, the distinction between form and content upon which the abstraction of forms of sociation rests is not a 'pure abstraction, insofar as — just like his concept of society — it possesses a *fundamentum in re*'.[110] In both cases, the notions of forms of sociation and society are not grounded, as some commentators have argued (notably Lieber and Fürth), in a neo-Kantian formalism since Simmel's typological concepts are inseparable from the analysis in which they are located.

However, as Steinhoff pointed out, this is only the start of a series of problems with Simmel's concept of form. Rather than a single definition we find a variety of formulations in his work: in 1894 Simmel speaks of extracting 'the purely social element' from society whereas later he is concerned with 'pure form', with 'social configurations' etc. Whereas, as we have seen, Simmel in his early writings seems to take the process of sociation as psychologically given — and thus opens himself up to the charge of psychological reductionism — 'the "objectivity of sociation" is for him the ultimate goal, and this not merely in the theoretical foundation but also in his individual analyses'.[111]

Social interaction and forms of sociation can congeal, as it were, in 'objective structures' and, at times, social interactions appear to be located in two aggregates: as a fluid stream or flux and as rigid structures. Though Simmel recognises the latter in his early works, the emphasis is upon flux and the emergent rather than upon the existent. In the *Soziologie* and earlier in *The Philosophy of Money*, however, Simmel speaks of 'independent agents of the societal unity', 'the abstractions of group functions that have become concrete', 'the objectivation of group solidarity', etc. Social relations become crystallised in supra-individual forms. Such 'objective structures present themselves in the most diverse types of phenomena: as specific organs of the division of labour, as cohesive symbols, as timelessly valid norms'.[112]

The actual analyses of forms of sociation suggest such a rich diversity that it is the grossest misunderstanding of Simmel's work to suggest that he sought to develop an abstract classification of social forms in a systematic manner. Even though Simmel does sometimes distinguish the social forms that he studies, for instance, between formal modes of behaviour (subordination, the division of labour, etc.) and the embodiment of social interactions in specific forms (hierarchy, co-operation, competition etc.), this in itself never constitutes a system. Even though Simmel may use 'forms as ideal-types', as Tenbruck argues, this does not lead to an endless typification and taxonomy of social relations that is so often seen as the end result of 'formal' sociology.

Social forms, however, are not the only feature of social reality highlighted by Simmel. As Tenbruck points out, 'Forms represent a specific "layer" of reality. Although they cannot — and are not meant to — account for interaction itself, they are operative in it; they account for its patterns.'[113] Interaction cannot, therefore, be explained by its forms. Hence, it has been possible to argue, along with Becher, that the concept of interaction [*Wechselwirkung*] is crucial to an understanding of Simmel's sociology.[114] When Simmel described the object of 'a pure sociology' as the investigation of types of interaction, he went on to say that 'Starting out from this sociological significance of the concept of interaction, however, it gradually grew for me into a comprehensive metaphysical principle as such.'[115] Even as early as *The Philosophy of Money*, the principle of the interaction of everything with everything else is clearly formulated. The importance of the concept therefore extends far beyond Simmel's strictly 'sociological' writings.

Becher has shown that Simmel's early study of Kant is important for his development of interaction in two ways. First, Simmel argues that the concept of interaction cannot be derived from the reciprocal relation between monads since 'interaction requires two spatial, materially existent, active entities'. Already, Becher suggests, Simmel is advancing the important distinction that is crucial for his concept of social interaction: 'Simmel does not develop his concept of interaction and, as a result, that of society like Kant from the ego but, going beyond Kant, from the dual category of the self and you. At the same time, this allows him to demarcate sociology from psychology.'[116] Secondly, 'Simmel criticises Kant from hypostatising functions and relations as material realities' thereby 'anticipating on the one hand, the dynamics of his later concept of interaction and, on the other, preventing the hypostatisation of his concept of society'.[117] More specifically, and moving further away from the Kantian problematic, Simmel asks how society itself is possible and not how knowledge of society is possible: the transcendental subject is replaced by the commitment of empirical subjects to interaction.

Becher is also inclined to see the dynamic of the concept of inter-action as rooted in Simmel's *Lebensphilosophie*. The problem here, however, is that, in the period of Simmel's foundation of sociology, it hardly holds the prominent position that it does in his later phil-osophy. Nonetheless, in his *Philosophy of Money* the opposition between life and form and life as form, on the one hand, and life as process on the other is already pronounced. The concept of inter-action, in view of its dynamic, belongs to life as process. Insofar as the notion of ceaseless interaction implies the openness of social reality it reinforces Simmel's opposition to systems and calls into question, once more, the concept of a 'formal' sociology. The notion of the ceaseless flux of development, already prominent in his *Moralphilosophie* (1892), is also one significant basis for the relationism that not merely exists as a category in his thought but as a feature of modern society itself.

But what of the specific sociological relevance of the concept of interaction? Becher rightly insists that 'Simmel does *not* start out from the isolated individual, *not* from society and also not from the oppo-sition between individual and society although this opposition greatly concerned him.'[118] The notions of 'interaction' and 'social interaction' are clearly related but the concept of social interaction has a specific location in Simmel's sociology. The contents of interaction do not provide the basis for social interaction since Simmel deliberately removes the contents of interaction from his formal sociology. Rather, Simmel is forced 'to locate the sociality of interaction in the *con-sciousness* of those interacting'[119] without at the same time hypo-statising or psychologising the concept of social interaction. Social interaction does not take place without the consciousness of individual participants but neither is it merely *in* consciousness. Further, social interaction can take place 'between social poles on one and the same level' and also between different levels (e.g. between the individual and supra-personal social forms such as the state). Interactions can also be institutionalised in rules, as Simmel recognised in his critique of Stammler, but this is merely an 'attribute' of sociation and not its essence. At its most abstract level, we have seen that in his first attempt to ground sociology Simmel also elevated interaction to a 'regulative world principle'. Finally, as an element of Simmel's methodology, interaction becomes a concept of causality not as a single chain of cause and effect but as 'a comprehensive interdependence', thereby removing any possible basis for a monocausal theory of history.

However, to return to the concept of social interaction, it is plausible to argue that Simmel's conception of society as an object of sociology is to be derived from the interaction of socialised individuals. Hence there exists

> no interaction in itself, in its abstract conception . . . rather always a whole wealth of diverse types and forms of interactions. This is what Simmel implies by the concept of form. Sociation is interaction. Interaction always presents itself in a particular form. Hence, society too is always a formed society or it does not exist. Form and sociation are identical.[120]

Interaction is differentiated for Simmel according to content and form. The inner motivations of individuals constitute an inner side to interaction and its content. Individual interests and motivations take on a particular form and are realised in forms of interaction.

Does this mean that society, for Simmel, is merely a sum of social interactions? Certainly Simmel was opposed to society as an unspecific general concept since it so readily becomes 'the name for the pseudo concrete totality of all human determinations'. In her persuasive article on Simmel's 'phenomenology of society',[121] Karin Schrader-Kelbert seeks to show how the concept of society constitutes a 'regulative idea' in his sociology in order to avoid

> the naive epistemological alternative of other theories of society that from the outset either destroy society as something subjective or hypostatise it as something objective. Simmel realises that the concept of society can never be the fully determined result of cognition because it is not the sum total of mediated phenomena but rather its transcendental possibility. The ontological presupposition of the idea of society is itself an implication of historical experience and therefore only an element in the totality of its knowledge that cannot be absolutised into the ontological substratum of the totality.[122]

In his essay 'How is society possible?' (1908), Simmel does in fact inquire in a seemingly Kantian manner into 'the a prioristic conditions under which society is possible'.[123] But whereas the unity of nature requires the knowing subject, 'the unity of society needs no observer. It is directly realised by its own elements because these elements are themselves conscious and synthesizing units'.[124] The notion of society is mediated through the experience of individuals' sociation, whose forms are not 'antecedent causes' of society but 'part of the synthesis to which we give the inclusive name of "society".' By means of the concept of form as a mediation of the transcendental and real synthesis, Simmel seeks to establish a notion of society that is neither a 'real product' to us nor a 'purely transcendental presupposition of sociological experience'.

Hence, in 'How is society possible?', Simmel moves far away from his own earlier epistemological naiveté towards a consideration of the '*a priori* effective conditions or forms of sociation' that make society possible — even though the three *a prioris* are given merely as examples. The first *a priori* is the social mediation of action: action is always 'social' action. The relations between actors is always the product of social abstractions since it is not possible either to completely know the other person as an individual or to know the other as an object with fixed, thing-like qualities. Hence, actors have recourse to thought-experiments. Other actors are reduced to types:

> We are all fragments, not only of the general human being, but also of ourselves . . . The practice of life urges us to make the picture of a person only from the real pieces that we empirically know of them, but it is precisely the practice of life which is based on those modifications and supplementating on the transformation of the given fragments into the generality of a type and into the completeness of the ideal personality.[125]

Typification thus mediates between knowledge and action.

The second *a priori* hinges on the concept of the social role as the 'mediation of sociability and sociality' insofar as 'every element of a group is not only a societal part but, in addition, something else'.[126] Simmel also presupposes that 'life is not completely social', that there exists non-sociated being as identity itself and therefore that the individual is not merely a bundle of roles. The third *a priori* is that of 'the phenomenological structure of society':

> the life of society takes its course — not psychologically but phenomenologically, viewed purely in regard to its social contents as such — as if each of its elements were predestined for its particular

place in it. In spite of all discrepancies between it and ideal standards, social life exists as if all of its elements found themselves interrelated with one another in such a manner that each of them, because of its very individuality, depends on all other and all others depend on it.[127]

Simmel is convinced that the presupposition of the synthesis of individual possibility and the general determination necessary for sociation takes place through the vocation (*Beruf*).

Schrader-Klebert draws out the critical implications of this third *a priori* that are not necessarily followed up by Simmel himself. She suggests that

> the self-foundation of sociology by means of the idea of society requires a concept of abstract utopia, a philosophical–historical premise. Then and only then can the idea of society fulfil its function as a critical concept, if its transcendentally grounded meaning is ultimately to be transformed into a postulate of practical reason; if its . . . presupposition of a mediation of theory and practice is also still to be reflected in the results of knowledge; if its claim to know reality also entails seeing through this reality; if its task is to be more than a description of what already exists then the object as the standard of critique must itself also imply a postulate for practice.[128]

Simmel's critique of society only partly fulfils this *a priori*. Some of his best work, such as *The Philosophy of Money*, does contain a remarkable critique of the capitalist division of labour, the commodity structure and the attendant reification. Similarly, Simmel is aware of the relationship between theory and practice but he does not work out the full implications of Schrader-Klebert's assessment of his third *a priori*. In terms of contemporary critical theory, Simmel does not provide what Habermas terms 'a philosophy of history with a practical intention'. Indeed, Simmel hardly followed through the implications that this third *a priori* has for a philosophy of history. Ultimately, it cannot counter the criticism which Schrader-Klebert makes at the end of her analysis when she states that 'Any self-foundation of sociology remains *aesthetic* if it does not extract the consequences from its relationship to the practice it presupposes.'[129]

3 A Sociological *Flâneur*?

An observer is a *prince* who is everywhere in possession of his incognito.

Charles Baudelaire

Simmel has not made it easy for people to understand him and has preferred to dazzle them with semi-journalistic fireworks. *Épater le bourgeois* was also for him an all too easy maxim to follow.

Ernst Troeltsch

I

There may, at first sight, appear to be a vain hope of ever discussing Simmel's methodology and still less his 'method'. Of all his contemporaries who have attained 'classic' status, Simmel stands alone in his contempt for methodology. He viewed an excessive concern with it as a kind of fetishism. Hence, it is not surprising that we do not find discussions of methodology as a discrete and separate body of argument in his works. Even in his major sociological works, actual discussion of methodology plays a very subordinate role. The first few pages of his earliest sociological work, *Über soziale Differenzierung* (1890), are devoted to a very brief argument concerning 'the impossibility of sociological laws'.[1] In the preface to *The Philosophy of Money* (1900) less than a page is devoted to the methodological intentions of this study, namely 'to construct a new storey beneath historical materialism'.[2] Similarly, contemporary reviewers of his *Soziologie* (1908) were annoyed at the absence of the elaboration of its methodological premises, particularly in view of the fact that there appeared to be so little to hold the whole volume together.[3] Later, the *Grundfragen der Soziologie* (1917) omitted as one of its basic questions (*Grundfragen*) that of methodology.[4] Even in his fleeting, tangential and neglected contribution to the *Methodenstreit* in political economy, 'Zur Methodik der Socialwissenschaft' (1896) — actually a review of Stammler's critique of historical materialism — Simmel concerns himself only briefly with 'the conflict between the historical and dogmatic schools of economics'.[5] All this might suggest that we can applaud Simmel's healthy disrespect for an overelaborate discourse or, more often, monologue upon methods and methodology that for several decades now has been commonplace in sociology, but it does not make the search for Simmel's own methodology any the easier.

Within his work as a whole, Simmel is remarkably unreflexive with regard to his methodology. His apparently intuitive approach to the object of study might lead us to see him as possessing no method at all. We have already seen that many of his contemporaries were uncomfortable when confronted with his unsystematic or, more accurately, his anti-systematic approach. But this lack of reflection upon his own procedure, should not obscure from us what is distinctive about Simmel's approach to his subject matter. Rather, the key to this 'approach' must be sought in other features of his work.

We have already pointed to the unsystematic and fragmentary nature of Simmel's work. His contemporaries certainly applauded him more for his flashes of insight into discrete social phenomena than for any of his systematic treatises. Simmel himself never permitted the republication of a new edition of his largest work, the two volume *Einleitung in die Moralwissenschaft* (1892–3), partly on the grounds that he saw it as his 'philosophical sins of youth'.[6] And yet it is one of the few of his major works whose origin cannot be traced back to countless shorter essays. In terms of his sociological writings, the most famous, his *Soziologie*, is, without doubt, the most fragmentary and readily confirms what one can only describe as Simmel's conscious essayism.[7] Where he does attempt to develop a major structured piece of work on a single theme, such as *The Philosophy of Money*, we find not only that it has its origins in earlier sketches that were published as essays — this, in itself, is not uncommon in other authors — but that the whole architecture of the work is not held together by a central argument but by myriad analogies and meandering enlightenments.[8] Extensive though Simmel's published work in book form may be, there can be little doubt that

> Simmel is the master of the philosophical essay. In the last instance, all his writings, even those of the early period, are either independent essays or collections of them ... his major *Soziologie* is constructed from a loose sequence of extremely diverse and nonetheless totally

enclosed essays and 'excursions' that are characterised by Simmel himself as fragments of that which he takes to be the science of society.[9]

Simmel is thus one of those writers who, according to Adorno, 'entrusted to the essay, speculation concerning specific objects that are culturally already preformed'.[10] The essay form in which Simmel was most at home possesses 'an aesthetic autonomy' that is both anti-positivist, anti-systematic and anti-academic. Hence, Simmel's favourite mode of presentation makes the search for an orthodox causal—analytical 'method' both mistaken and redundant.

Indeed, Simmel's conscious essayism points to an approach to his subject matter that moves in quite a different direction. Simmel does not set out to test hypotheses under experimental conditions, he consistently opposes the construction of a system in philosophy or sociology (and would on this basis have opposed von Wiese's taxonomy of social relations — his *Beziehungslehre*)[11] and only exceptionally does he write in an academic style with consistent definitions, footnotes and surveys of existing literature. The majority of his works do not follow any of these directions. From the outset, they can be readily distinguished from all of them. As Frischeisen-Köhler suggests with regard to most of Simmel's works,

> They are distinguished even in their external form from the scientific working community. They are free creations of a free mind that never require reference to the results of predecessors or verification by co-researchers . . . One cannot extract from the works themselves when they appeared, which impulses might have had their effect upon them, where they might have engaged in the course of scientific development and which standpoints and theories they might be opposing. They are, as it were, autonomous, timeless forms [*Gebilde*] that, as if enclosed within an invisible frame, preserve the 'pathos of distance' in all directions in a proud and exclusive reserve.[12]

This passage points to a number of features of Simmel's work that are essential to an understanding of his approach to his object of study. In his *Philosophy of Money*, for instance, Simmel provides few clues as to the contemporary reference point of his work. It does not even appear to be concerned with the consequences of a money economy within any specific mode of production even though many of its consequences clearly relate to contemporary capitalism. No reference is made to any earlier studies of the money economy except that of Marx and even then only tangentially. It is true that, for once in Simmel's

work, one can clearly detect a theoretical standpoint that he is opposing, namely historical materialism, but even here its tenets are seldom
explicitly stated. Finally, the absence of a historical dimension to the
study of money enables Simmel to introduce a bewildering array of
historical instances and analogies that are never related to one another
and which never appear in any historical sequence. This detachment
from historical specificity, this 'pathos of distance' of which Köhler
speaks is even discussed on many occasions in *The Philosophy of
Money* but nowhere does Simmel himself make explicit the fact that he
is committed to this same pathos.

   If one turns to Simmel's fund of essays, then this view is confirmed
in a most illuminating manner. They not merely share many of the
features of the essay as a form that have been outlined by Lukács[13]
and Adorno[14] but also highlight Simmel's approach to his subject
matter in general, whether one examines his essays, his books or his
lectures. If the majority of Simmel's work consists of essays (or collections of them) and if a feature of the essay form is its fragmentary
nature, then it is not surprising that the overall impression of much of
Simmel's work should also be one of fragmentation. Further, it sheds
a new light upon Simmel's concern with social 'forms' in so far as he is
preoccupied not merely with the 'forms' of social interaction as subject
matter but also with the 'form' in which his insights are presented. It,
too, is a privileged form of interaction. And this is largely the essay
form. Simmel would probably have concurred with Lukács' judgment
that 'The essay can calmly and proudly set its fragmentariness against
the petty completeness of scientific exactitude or impressionistic
freshness.'[15] or with Adorno's view that 'The essay does not obey
organised science's and theory's rules of the game; in the words of
Spinoza, it makes the order of things identical to that of ideas.'[16] The implication of the essay form as outlined by Lukács and Adorno is that we
should not seek in it the kind of conceptual precision that we find in
'organised science'. As Adorno says of the essay,

> Just as it denies what is originally given [*Urgegebenheiten*], so it
> refuses the definition of its concepts. . . . The essay . . . takes up the
> anti-systematic impulse into its own procedure and introduces con-
> cepts unmodified, 'immanently' just as it received them. They are
> only made more precise through their relationship to one another.[17]

For this reason, Kracauer is correct when he argues that 'Simmel unceasingly changes perspectives and constant meaning attached to concepts is almost never to be found in his work.'[18] This perspectivism,
which we must examine in detail below, has other consequences. It

enables Simmel to remain, as it were, incognito. Just as the consistency of definition is absent so too is the author's identity. There is no identity of thought and object; rather, a distance between the two. As Adorno comments,

> The freedom from compulsion to identify gives to the essay at times what eludes official thought — the element of the inerasable, the indelible colour. Certain foreign words in Simmel's work — cachet, attitude — betray this intention without they themselves being treated theoretically.[19]

This often gives to his work an elusiveness which hides from the reader any commitment on the part of the author. Having interested us in a whole range of phenomena, Simmel is often strangely reluctant to commit himself to any judgment on them. Somewhat cryptically in this context, Kracauer remarks: 'Instead of pronouncing with infinite certainty upon good and evil, beauty and ugliness, the true and the false, he seeks instead in his work — and this is very typical — to preserve his incognito, often even nervously.'[20] This absence of the author from the text, reinforced by a shifting perspectivism, serves to produce the illusion that Simmel himself in his essays has no standpoint at all. It confirms what Adorno described as '*die Standpunktlosigkeit des Essays*' and leads to the essay form often being attacked as relativist.

Indeed, some of his contemporaries saw this lack of standpoint as a distinctive feature of Simmel's approach to his work. Kracauer, for instance, argued that even though his work was rooted in certain 'basic experiences and ideas',

> This basis, however, does not include within itself the personal value attitudes of the philosopher. Yet it does not follow from this that evaluative decisions are totally absent for Simmel; rather, it merely follows that all such decisions play no decisive organisational role within the work as a whole. They guide the work, as it were, without carrying it; they are an ornament but neither an element of construction nor even a basis.[21]

Others, like Koppel, saw this absence of standpoint as part of a wider contemporary tendency in German thought. Of Simmel's 'epistemological standpoint', Koppel remarked

> it is, at first glance, not a new standpoint, not to have one and to accept the rejection of the demand to have a fixed point. . . . Yet the theory itself, in its rejection of all norms and their trust against reality arises out of a unified conception . . . which, perceived with the highest intuition, elaborated with the strongest graphic

power has, at the same time, been actualised in two artists, in Hofmannsthal and Stefan George.[22]

It is to this aesthetic conception of reality that we must return later.

For the moment, this absence of a standpoint may seem all the more surprising for a writer who, in *The Philosophy of Money*, concerns himself with the consequences of a money economy and the division of labour, with reification and alienation. But we seldom get the impression that Simmel engaged himself fully with such issues. Simmel's accounts always appear strangely unlocated whilst Simmel himself remains uncommitted:

> In a chapter of his *Philosophy of Money*, he impressively describes
> . . . which relationships exist between the intellectualisation of human beings and their entrance into the capitalist economic form and shows how the perfection of external life, like that which he terms the 'culture of things' is purchased at the price of the impoverishment of inner culture and the totality of individuals. In all this, nothing lies further from the philosopher than the pathos of the revolutionary and the world-reformer. Hardly ever, and then only in an incidental comment does he reveal his own person and when he describes contradictory value-positions one can at most gain an inkling as to which party he himself subscribes.[23]

In his brief articles for newspapers and journals, Simmel sometimes lets slip his incognito but in his major works this is seldom the case. In this respect, and as an 'observer' of social life who successfully preserves his incognito, Simmel has much in common with the *flâneur*.[24]

A closely related feature of Simmel's writing is the consistency with which his essays and often sections of his major works turn upon or at least commence from unresolved paradoxes and antinomies. A large number of Simmel's essays start out from a duality of concepts, an antinomy or a paradox either in the very first sentence or at least in the first paragraph. In the essay collection, *Philosophische Kultur* (1911),[25] for instance, nine of the thirteen essays commence from some form of duality or paradox being posed in the very first paragraph. 'The adventure' commences with the dual significance of action or experience, 'Fashion' with the dualism of the whole of life, 'The ruin' with the struggle between intellectual will and natural necessity, 'Michaelangelo' with the dualism that exists in the basis of our spiritual existence, and so on. In Landmann's collection of Simmel's essays, *Brücke und Tür*,[26] six of them start out from an antinomy, paradox or polarity. This mode of commencing an essay is not confined to a particular period in Simmel's work. It extends from his early essays — such as 'Dante's psychology'

(1884)[27] or 'On the psychology of money' (1889)[28] – down to his wartime writings. The mere numerical consistency of this manner of approaching the subject matter of many of his essays need not, of itself, clarify Simmel's style of work. But it is reinforced by the nature of the antinomies themselves, some of which recur throughout his work. Most predictably, perhaps, the dualism of form and content and subject and object are very common. But the dualism of the individual and society, subjective and objective culture, and thought and life, not merely figure prominently as the opening problematic to Simmel's essays but like the other antinomies actually permeate his work in a more fundamental sense.

Although Simmel was never formally a member of the neo-Hegelian revival in Germany, some of his contemporaries such as Frischeisen-Köhler or Max Adler were able to point to what Adler termed a 'great affinity' between the work of Simmel and Hegel.[29] The often latent and largely incomplete dialectical turn in Simmel's thought may provide the key to the manner in which he so often commenced his essays. In particular, the subject–object dialectic of Hegel's *Phenomenology* is a constant theme of Simmel's cultural criticism in the form of a fundamental tension between subjectivity and objectivity, between subjective and objective culture. But Simmel's dialectical turn is not merely incomplete but also radicalises the subject–object dualism of his later work as a life-form duality and renders it unbridgable. That is, a historical and social opposition becomes an 'exemplary instance of a comprehensive fundamental tension between subjectivity and objectivity, and this means ultimately between the individual and society, a tension that is interpreted as being basically tragic'.[30] It is possible to view these starting points of Simmel's essays over a long period of time as expressions of some of the central themes of Simmel's social theory.[31] The radicalised dualities of neo-Hegelianism, together with a conception of society as a whole as composed of fragments of interaction, provide Simmel with a central problem of his analysis of forms of interaction – that of seeking the connections between the most disparate forms of interaction.

A further consequence of operating within these polarities and antinomies is that the contradictions which they express are never resolved. The reader is always left with the ambiguities, the paradoxes of social life. In so far as the text retains the residues of Hegelian dialectics, it is always a dialectic that remains incomplete and unfinished. Dialectics is dissolved into ambiguity and paradox. In the first paragraph of one of Simmel's most archetypical essays – and

Landmann rightly chose it as the title of his collection of Simmel's essays, 'Brücke und Tür' ('Bridge and door') — Simmel commences his reflections upon what unites and divides social relationships with a passage that highlights not merely this pervasive ambiguity but also his notion of social reality itself:

> For us, the image of external objects possesses the ambiguity that in external nature everything can be taken to be connected but also everything can be taken to be divided. The unbroken transformation of matter as well as energies brings everything in relation to everything else and makes a *single* cosmos out of all individual elements. On the other hand, however, objects remain spellbound in the unmerciful separation of space, no material part can commonly share its space with another, a real unity of diverse elements does not exist in space. . . . In contrast to nature, it is only given to human beings to create bonds and to resolve things and to do this, in fact, in the distinctive manner that the one is always the presupposition of the other.[32]

With this as his starting point, Simmel goes on to analyse the reality and the symbolism of the bridge that connects and the door that separates. Though he starts out by discussing this ambiguity in nature, it is clear from Simmel's views elsewhere that he conceives of society in a similar manner.

There is another dimension of both the extensive use of unresolved paradoxes and ambiguities and the absence of a standpoint in Simmel's essayism. Simmel has the capacity for setting up the most stimulating ambiguities in social life without resolving them. As Karl Scheffler said of him, Simmel possesses 'an astonishing talent for narrowly missing the mark at the decisive point by a hair's breadth'.[33] It would be tempting here to relate this to the aesthetic distance which Simmel establishes between himself and his object of study. For the moment, however, we must remain with some of the other features of his approach before we turn to the issue of the aestheticisation of reality in some detail.

Not unrelated to the aesthetic stance in Simmel's work, is the uniqueness of his approach. Nothing annoys the positivist tradition more than the non-reproducibility of a particular methodology. The further we move away from Simmel's earliest works, which are indeed influenced by positivism and Spencerian evolutionism, and the more we examine the conscious essayism that he develops in the 1890s, the more Simmel adopts not merely an aesthetic model for his work but also one that is bound up with a belief in the uniqueness of the work of art. That is, his essays conform more to what Schlegel referred to as 'intellectual poems' — and we must remember that Simmel in fact published several poems in *Jugend* — and take on that 'aesthetic autonomy' referred to by Adorno. Again, his contemporaries were quite aware of the distinctiveness of Simmel's mode of presentation. In his review of *The Philosophy of Money*, Vierkandt pointed to this artistic uniqueness when he suggested that

> in its form and content, Simmel's book must be characterised as masterly, one might say written as a virtuoso. The psychological analysis of semi- or completely unconscious processes . . . is as brilliantly carried out as it is presented. Mastery of the linguistic and stylistic difficulties which confront the discussion of such subtle psychological processes and Simmel's capacity for subsuming immense series of processes and situations under a single concept and characterising them with the fewest apt words deserves the highest astonishment. In that the author has disclaimed the historical analysis of the theme, he is successful, within the atmosphere so artificially produced, in creating a prize exhibit that is not merely a master work of psychological analysis and presentation, but also forms the expression of a rich personality.[34]

Vierkandt's assessment of Simmel's analysis in *The Philosophy of Money* implies not merely the aesthetic attraction of the mode of presentation but also its uniqueness. The fact that his approach cannot be reproduced not merely associates it most firmly with the concept of style in the work of art — which is how Simmel was fond of viewing his 'method' — but also implies that reducing it to social scientific propositions destroys it. This point was made explicit by Frischeisen-Köhler when he maintained that,

> Just as the best of a work of art is lost when one attempts to reproduce its content in a language other than that of the artist, so too the content of many of Simmel's cultural–philosophical works appears to be so bound up with the inimitable personal art of their creator that it disappears in its translation into the impersonal form of a scientific report.[35]

Köhler goes on to suggest that Simmel's essays are 'intellectual expressionistic works of art'. Whether the judgment upon these essays as being 'expressionistic' is accurate or not will be dealt with below. What is important to stress here, however, is that this uniqueness and inimitability of style of presentation is decidedly bound up with a mode of theoretical production that takes the non-reproducible work of art as its model. Within the division of labour, too, Simmel seeks to preserve intellectual labour as a unique, non-reducible form. This is one of the central thrusts of his arguments against Marx's labour theory of value in *The Philosophy of Money*.

Taken together, the non-reproducibility of Simmel's work and his own defence of the uniqueness of not merely the work of art but also of intellectual labour suggest that he was seeking to defend a form of intellectual production that was being challenged. Simmel, like Benjamin, was aware of the threat to the 'aura' of the work of art brought about by its reproducibility. What Benjamin described as the 'aura' rests upon 'the unique phenomenon of a distance' and this is an aesthetic stance that is central to Simmel's approach. This threat to the uniqueness of the work of art emerges out of its mechanical reproducibility. As Benjamin argues, 'Around 1900 technical reproduction had reached a standard that not only permitted it to reproduce all transmitted works of art and thus to cause the most profound change in their impact upon the public; it also had captured a place of its own among the artistic processes.'[36] This period broadly coincides with Simmel's highest point of awareness of the reduction of use-values to commodities in so far as this is the critical impulse behind his analysis of the consequences of the money economy in *The Philosophy of Money* (1900). It also coincides with his espousal of a notion of the autonomy of the work of art, his association with the circle around Stefan George and hence with some commitment, at least, to one response to the challenge of artistic reproduction, 'with the doctrine of l'art pour l'art, that is, with a theology of art'.[37]

In order to substantiate these claims, it is necessary to investigate further the mode of theoretical production employed by Simmel. A closer examination of Simmel's manner of working and his relation to his subject matter might prompt comparison with Benjamin's analysis of the *flâneur*. It might raise the question of how far Simmel himself is a 'sociological *flâneur*'. The particular aesthetic stance employed by Simmel with its distance from reality might, at least around the turn of the century, be related to a movement with which his work was most often identified by his contemporaries, namely, impressionism. Whereas the aestheticisation of reality is common within that sociological tradition which, in part, has its origins in Simmel's work, an understanding of Simmel's particular version of aestheticism must, at least, be attempted.

II

Among the features of Simmel's approach to his object of study that have already been outlined are his conscious essayism, his preoccupation with the fragmentary, his tendency not to reveal himself in his writings, his aestheticisation of reality and distance from it and the centrality of the work of art as a model for his own essays. In various ways, all these aspects prompt a comparison with Benjamin's analysis of the *flâneur*. An examination of the extent to which Simmel is a sociological *flâneur* might therefore serve to clarify his mode of intellectual production.

In his analysis of 'the *flâneur* who goes botanising on the asphalt', Benjamin commences with the significance of the popular physiologies – scenes from everyday life etc. that have their counterpart in Britain in Dickens' *Sketches by Boz* – within which is presented 'the colossal parade of bourgeois life . . . Everything passed in review . . . Days of celebration and days of mourning, work and play, conjugal customs and bachelor's practices, the family, the home, children, school, society, the theatre, types, professions.'[38] It is the literature of the stroller through the city, the literature of the person who wanders through a variety of social situations and contexts and remains detached from them because he or she is merely an observer. The literary product of such wanderings is the social *vignette* that is both 'harmless and of perfect bonhomie'.[39] At this point, Benjamin locates these writings within the context of an adaptation to life in big cities and cites Simmel on the nature of interpersonal relations in big cities that forces individuals to confront many different social groups without positive interaction.

Later, Benjamin argues that the *flâneur* can be 'turned into an unwilling detective' who 'only seems to be indolent, for behind this indolence there is the watchfulness of an observer'. Acute observation of the myriad of social interactions and social types suggests an intense interest in unlocking the key to hidden relationships. We might say that whereas 'in the *flâneur* the joy of watching is triumphant', the results of this observation must be systematised in some way to be of interest to the sociologist. But the formalisation and typification of what is observed with extreme sensitivity is the task of someone even further removed from what is observed than the *flâneur*. The sensitivity of Simmel's social *vignettes* is much more striking than his attempts to formalise social interactions and social situations. It suggests its social location – that of the *intérieur* and the *salon*. Here, of course, it is not so much the *intérieur* that separates Simmel from the *flâneur* – since

Benjamin rightly observes that 'the arcade is the classical form of the *intérieur*, which is how the *flâneur* sees the street'[40] – but the *salon*.

Just as the early physiologies could present a 'parade of bourgeois life', so too Simmel's essays offer us an array of forms of interaction, social processes and social types that even in his most critical works such as *The Philosophy of Money* are 'harmless'. Simmel's distance, and an attendant pathos, is ultimately one that is not disturbing. This feature of his work was highlighted by Kracauer when he suggested that

> Simmel is full of interest in the world but he holds all that he has interpreted at that distance which is expressed in the concept of interest understood in its widest sense; i.e., he never engages his soul and he forgoes ultimate decisions. There is nothing more character-istic of his works in fact than that they so strongly arouse interest. It is for this reason that in them distinct phenomena are investigated that have immediate relevance to the life of civilised man. Yet the reverse side of this is, in fact, that they *only* arouse interest. One does not feel pressured by them in a specific direction, they indicate no course in which our life should flow.[41]

Simmel arouses our interest in phenomena whilst at the same time maintaining a distance from them. He might '*épater le bourgeois*', as Troeltsch puts it, but does not fundamentally disturb him.

The interest that Simmel's work arouses in us is, in most of his essays at least, confined to the fragments of social interaction from which we should derive aesthetic satisfaction. As Freund remarks

> aestheticism pervades his sociological studies, for he was one of the rare sociologists of his time, as well as ours, to call attention to the subtle, so to speak fleeting and impalpable, aspects of social rela-tions, such as courtesy, coyness, attire, faithfulness, or gratitude. One can regret that he has hardly been followed in this orientation since sociologists . . . neglect those expressions, filled with subtlety, which make meetings between human beings so charming.[42]

That 'charm' of which Freund speaks is, of course, predicated upon a mode of experiencing human relationships that presupposes an aesthetic distance. Benjamin says of Baudelaire, with reference to a similar sensi-tivity, that 'to it he owed his enjoyment of this society as someone who had already half withdrawn from it'.[43] Such a judgment could equally apply to many of Simmel's essays. Simmel, too, could extract from the seemingly most insignificant details of social life the most interesting connections. In this respect, we might see Simmel as a *flâneur* for the intelligentsia, providing them with the most subtle analyses of all manner of social phenomena without disturbing any of them.

The charm that Simmel extracts from social phenomena, however, is not derived from the same social detachment that is necessary for the *flâneur* to engage in his speculations. We do not associate Simmel's social *vignettes* with tramping the streets of Berlin like Baudelaire's ragpicker even though he too seems to collect fragments of social settings and experiences. But this is despite the fact that there is a remarkable affinity between Benjamin's analysis of Baudelaire's work and Simmel's sociological essays. On Baudelaire's poetry, Benjamin argues that of 'The social experiences which are reflected in his work . . . The most important among them are the experiences of the neurasthenic, of the big city dweller, and of the customer.'[44] The consumer appears extensively in Simmel's analysis of the consequences of a money economy in *The Philosophy of Money*, as well as in his essays on 'Fashion', 'The problem of style', 'The Berlin Trade Exhibition' and elsewhere. The role of city life in transforming social relationships is also central to *The Philosophy of Money* which contains the outline for the famous 'Metropolis and mental life' essay of 1903. More fundamentally, we may recall Simmel's identification with 'the Berlin milieu' of the turn of the century. Like Dickens away from London, Simmel appeared totally lost in Strasbourg. Most remarkable of all, however, is the location of the first of the social experiences mentioned by Benjamin, that of the neurasthenic. Only in the late nineteenth century were persons suffering from an atonic condition of the nervous system referred to as 'neurasthenics', though the condition itself had been classified in the 1850s. This condition was not unknown to Simmel himself. In a passage towards the end of *The Philosophy of Money*, for instance, Simmel speaks of 'the delicacy, spirituality and differentiated sensitivity of so many modern people' in the context of hyperaesthesia and agoraphobia and reflects upon such people's experience for whom 'reality is not touched with direct confidence but with fingertips that are immediately withdrawn'.[45] Simmel's own deep aestheticism might also be seen in this context. But most remarkable of all, one of Simmel's contemporaries described him as 'the intellectual neurasthenic' (Koppel).[46]

Prior to examining the difference between the social location of Simmel's reflections and that of the *flâneur*, it is possible to pursue further the affinities which exist at the level of Simmel's methodological intentions. Simmel possessed the remarkable capacity for illuminating the details of social life. Like the image of the ragpicker in Baudelaire, Simmel collected fragments of social life; for Simmel, however, they were often the fragments of sociability. This theme, as we shall see, is also central to impressionism in art. For the moment, however, it is the fragmentary that is of significance. Simmel gives preference, as Kracauer remarked, to 'the small detailed work', to 'psychological microscopy'.[47] Related to this, one of Simmel's rare and explicit methodological intentions is his assertion of 'the possibility — which must be demonstrated — of finding in each of life's details the totality of its meaning'.[48] Starting out from the 'detail', Simmel hopes to extend his analysis to 'the totality and the highest level of generality'.[49] But if we examine his essays and, for instance, if we examine every section of his *Philosophy of Money* (which contains six chapters each of which is split into three sections), then we find that Simmel starts out with a series of generalisations and often, as we have seen, with a paradox or antinomy before moving onto the particular and then finally returning to the level of generality again. But what is always striking in Simmel's essays is not this level of generality which today might often seem trite but the brilliant illumination of the particular and its interconnections. Kracauer is thus justified in suggesting that

> Simmel very early on proved himself to be a master in the — for his purposes often necessary — elaboration of fragmentary images of the world; out of the minute piece of a curve he hit upon its course in its complete scope, and even though he might have only a scant knowledge of a chain of thought, he nonetheless soon sensed in which intellectual organism it emerged, developed the whole mode of presentation of this individual element and showed how the phenomenon that interested him must be conceived from this element.[50]

Later, when he was much less interested in sociology, Simmel was to elevate this preoccupation with the fragmentary into a metaphysics of life.

It is through the examination of the particular and the fragmentary that Simmel hopes to grasp what is universal. Through sensitive reflection upon each of life's fragments one can arrive at an understanding of some aspect of society as a totality. But society conceived as a totality is an absent concept in Simmel's social theory. Though the striving towards totality may be present in his work, it is a goal that is never realised. Simmel, as the astute wanderer, can connect seemingly isolated fragments of social life with other apparently unrelated fragments. But the universal generalisation that so often opens and concludes his written work always stands in an uneasy relationship to these connections. The principles of the fundamental interrelatedness of phenomena and of interaction might well lie at the heart of

Simmel's theory of sociation but they do not and cannot of themselves lead to a conception of society as a totality. Hence, it is appropriate to argue that 'In Simmel's view, society, compared with the real inter-action of its parts, is always merely secondary, only the result.'[51] Sociology's task is to extract from the complex phenomena of social and historical concretions what is 'really only society, i.e., sociation [*Vergesellschaftung*]'.[52]

Simmel's justification for emphasis upon the fragmentary, upon the particular in its individuality is an aesthetic one. In an essay on 'Socio-logical aesthetics' (1896), Simmel writes, 'The essence of aesthetic ob-servation and interpretation lies for us in the fact that what is typical is emphasised in the particular, what is normal is emphasised in the accidental and the essential and significant in things is emphasised in what is superficial and fleeting.'[53] The fleeting glimpse of the frag-mentary is summed up in the title of some of Simmel's contributions to the *Jugendstil* journal, *Jugend* — 'Snapshots *sub specie aeternitatis*'. The snapshot (*Momentbild*) is literally a momentary image of a scene that we choose to retain. The photographer can wander through the most varied situations. His snapshots retain the fleeting images he has captured in the camera. What he records is both fleeting and repro-ducible. In a not dissimilar manner, Simmel seeks to preserve what is unique and transitory whilst at the same time extracting from it its essential form, its typicality. But Simmel is not the photographer who is the documentary reporter. Rather, his interest lies in awaken-ing and retaining an aesthetic enjoyment of social phenomena. What Baudelaire said of his friend Constantin Guys could also be applied to Simmel: 'Everywhere he sought the transitory, fleeting beauty of our present life, the character of what the reader has permitted us to call *modernism*.'[54] Less flatteringly, Troeltsch was to describe Simmel as 'a child and favourite of modernity with all its terrible sicknesses and weaknesses'.[55]

But what is the social location of this collector of fleeting images? Is Simmel a *flâneur* in the sense of a stroller through the streets of Berlin? In a somewhat different context, Coser has spoken of Simmel as 'a stranger in the academy' whose marginal position perhaps enabled him to achieve such insight into social life.[56] But, of itself, this would not distinguish him from the *flâneur* who 'still stood at the margin, of the great city as of the bourgeois class. Neither of them had yet over-whelmed him. In neither of them was he at home.'[57] Clearly the notion of marginality would require further elaboration in Simmel's case. The notion of the stranger is certainly a powerful image in his work which exemplifies the centrality of detachment (and presumably marginality) and aesthetic distance. Simmel insists that the stranger is not to be seen 'as the wanderer who comes today and goes tomorrow, but rather as the man who comes today and stays tomorrow — the potential wanderer, so to speak, who, although he has gone no further, has not quite got over the freedom of coming and going'.[58] Simmel goes on to suggest that the stranger is able to adopt 'a distinctly "objective" attitude, an attitude that does not signify merely detachment and non-participation, but is a distinct structure composed of remoteness and nearness, indifference and involvement'.[59] Whilst it is always the over-whelming detachment that strikes us in Simmel's response to the social world compared to his engagement in it — and this is testified by his contemporaries — there is a sense in which Simmel is part of the bour-geois class and yet marginal to it, in the Berlin metropolis but yet detached from it.

A recent commentator upon Simmel's aestheticism suggests his social location: 'a typical member of the German cosmopolitan educated bourgeoisie in the period of the "fin de siècle".'[60] But in the context of Simmel's marginal position within Berlin University and the relative ineffectiveness of the educated bourgeoisie within the dominant power structures of Wilhelmian Germany one must surely question the notion of 'typicality'. Nor was Simmel such a confident member of the edu-cated bourgeoisie as, say, Max Weber. Similarly, whilst Simmel himself, as well as his contemporaries, recognised the extent to which his creativity was tied to a particular location, namely Berlin, it must again be emphasised that Simmel is not the naturalistic commentator and documenter of its social life. Rather, his reflections are those derived more from detachment than engagement. The aestheticisation of reality that so often permeates them suggests a retreat to the interior. This retreat is reinforced by the intellectual salon society maintained by Simmel at the turn of the century in Berlin. An examination of the precise location of many of Simmel's social *vignettes* would suggest a close affinity with the images of sociability that are typical of im-pressionism. They are the images of a section of the bourgeoisie that is no longer confident, that feels the need to distance itself from a reality it no longer controls. Even when confronted with aspects of the feudal—capitalist class structure in Simmel's work, a distance is always pre-served which gives the impression that only an 'observer' could extract the distinctive aesthetic charm from them that Simmel does. And the notion of *distance* is itself so central to his work and life that it cannot be analysed merely as the illumination of the social dimension of physical distance. Levine, for instance, points to the crucial role of the concept in Simmel's sociology but not in his whole perspective on the world when he writes

> Simmel wrote a pioneering and penetrating account of the influence of physical distance on human relations. Furthermore, nearly all of the social processes and social types treated by Simmel may readily be understood in terms of social distance. Domination and subordination, the aristocrat and the bourgeois, have to do with relations defined in terms of 'above' and 'below'. Secrecy, arbitration, the poor man, and the stranger are some of the topics related to the inside—outside dimension.[61]

Social distance does lie at the heart of Simmel's sociological concerns. But this is because it is part of a much deeper distance that Simmel himself maintains with his subject matter. It is the stance of the aestheticisation of reality.

III

Simmel's aestheticism was often remarked upon by his contemporaries but has subsequently seldom been examined in any detail. This is all the more surprising since it is both a central feature of his approach and one which he makes quite explicit in his writings. Only one recent article in English takes up the centrality of Simmel's aestheticism. Murray Davis examines whether 'Society is a work of art? . . . it constitutes Simmel's central vision and . . . around this aesthetic model the overwhelming profusion of Simmel's sociological insights — that on first reading appear in such chaotic dissociation from one another — actually cohere.'[62] Though Davis goes on to show the close connections between Simmel's aesthetics and his sociology, he fails to come to grips with the deeper significance of his aestheticisation of reality since he does not consider the social and ideological location of Simmel's approach.

In contrast, a recent article by Sibylle Hübner Funk is not merely one of the few recent German commentaries on this feature of Simmel's work but also contains the only discussion of the pervasive aestheticism within it. The debate surrounding Simmel's aestheticism rests upon the distinction between the proposition that he often studied and used aesthetic insights in his work and the proposition that

Simmel's works, *Kant und Goethe, Rembrandt*, and *Philosophie des Geldes* demonstrate in numerous places that Simmel not merely *consciously* concerned himself with art but also *transposed* its specific structural features onto social phenomena. On his own admission, for instance, he owed knowledge of the significance of the principle of interaction [*Wechselwirkung*] for the constitution of society to *art* and *metaphysics*![63]

Thus it is not merely a question of the use of aesthetic insights for the study of society but of the aestheticisation of social reality itself.

This means that we should be concerned with the ideological dimension of aestheticism and aesthetic experience. 'An experience is characterised as aesthetic when it is understood as an end in itself, closed off and autonomous and not as a means to an end. The best example of this is supplied by the "sociability" practised in bourgeois circles at the turn of the century.'[64] One need only recall here Simmel's analyses of forms of sociability which include not merely his essay on sociability but also many of his shorter pieces on the same theme. More importantly, however, the author seeks to highlight the key elements of Simmel's 'aesthetic world view' which she characterises as

> Subjectivism, aristocratism and romanticism — three labels for one and the same attempt to escape from the social tendencies of the present, which were manifested typically in a permanent, self-differentiating division of labour, in a growing intellectualisation of human relationships to their world and in a radicalisation of the subordinated masses.[65]

These dimensions of aestheticism, which are all related to 'the flight from reality'[66] substitute an aesthetic for an ethical stance vis-à-vis reality. Henceforth, the ethical dimension of life remains problematical. On the one hand, it has been suggested that where the 'structures of human action and their real results are viewed from aesthetic standpoints, then in fact, the moral content of social reality does not completely disappear. Rather, the result is a new kind of ethics. Karl Lamprecht characterised it as "aesthetic ethics".'[67] In contrast, some of Simmel's contemporaries saw the moral dimension disappear from his social theory, despite the fact that he was the author of a weighty tome on moral philosophy. In his perceptive review of *The Philsophy of Money*, Rudolf Goldscheid argues that

> behind Simmel's whole work there stands not the ethical but the aesthetic ideal. And it is this aesthetic ideal which determines his whole interpretation of life and thus his whole scientific life activity.

What holds him back from all democracy is this feeling . . . that he
denotes with the category of distinction [*Vornehmheit*] . . . for him
this distinction is always only expressed as aesthetic and not as
ethical distinction. Out of this pure aestheticising element of his
nature there emerges that excessive cobweb-like feature of his
presentation of real circumstances. It is also this intentional pure
aesthetic ideal . . . that leads him to a false pathos of distance in
relation to all practical life. I might almost say that he is too refined
[*vornehm*] to commit himself to the correctness of his own views;
he is a sceptic, to whom scepticism itself is still much too little
differentiated, and thus ultimately, at least in relation to himself,
he adheres to the pathos of distance. Out of all this there emerges
a powerless hyper-objectivity that often introduces something
artificial into Simmel's exposition such that he seldom draws the
consequences of his own views with complete realism.[68]

The category of distinction or excellence forms part of Simmel's defence
of individual creativity and what has been termed his 'aristocratism'.
Though it is possible to suggest that 'as a scientist he felt himself to be a
member of an "unassailable aristocracy", of the so-called "aristocracy
of education",'[69] one must nonetheless also recognise that Simmel was,
at the same time, not completely at home or welcome within that group.

Goldscheid was not alone in recognising this pervasive aestheticism
in Simmel's work, though he was probably the only contemporary
reviewer to relate it to 'the pathos of distance' and to draw out the
political implications of this stance. Von Wiese, reviewing Simmel's
Soziologie, saw that

his observations run the danger of ending in scattered fragments.
Surely they contain not only a great many fine observations, but
also peaks of the most valuable insights; but they lose themselves
in playing with the fullness of forms with the subtlest and nicest
of nuances. At times the interweaving of his thoughts resembles
a spider's web studded with glittering drops of dew; but a substantial breeze can destroy it.[70]

The 'fragmentary and incomplete character' of Simmel's sociology
would, von Wiese argues, be incapable of being synthesised in a system.
As we have already seen, this was a common charge made against his
sociology. But von Wiese is more explicit with regard to the origins of
this fragmentation. In Simmel's *Soziologie*, the

accumulation of thought-fragments is readable as a sequence only
because of the fact that, with all his tendency towards abstraction,
Simmel is by no means clumsy in dealing with concepts . . . his
presentation has great aesthetic attractiveness. From a certain

aspect, I would even call his sociology the sociology of an aesthete, a sociology for the literary salon. Simmel is a cultural psychologist with a cosmopolitan cast of mind. In his work we never encounter mere book-wisdom or dry, pedantic erudition; rather, one feels the rich internal agitation of the explorer, his examples are vivid, interesting, psychologically well-selected, and presented with individual originality . . . But in its mosaic form and its aestheticism, this sociology has a distinctly personal, Simmelean character.[71]

What von Wiese's insight into 'sociology for the literary salon' suggests is not merely that Simmel in fact ran a salon but that he conceived of sociology itself, in part, as a form of sociability. Sociability in general may well be a play-form of sociation but in Simmel's work it has a more specific social location. The illumination of human interactions, gestures and situations has always been a feature of salon society. Could it be that Simmel elevated it to a form of sociological discourse? There is certainly a whole tradition surrounding symbolic interactionism and other associated tendencies in modern sociology that feeds upon this kind of discourse and whose practitioners illuminate the *nuances* of social interaction whilst, at the same time, maintaining this 'pathos of distance' in relation to social reality itself.

Few of the more recent practitioners of these traditions, however, have been aware of the social foundations of their own reflections upon social reality. Simmel himself, and his contemporaries, provided many clues as to the roots of his own reflections. In his essay on 'Sociological aesthetics' (1896) and in *The Philosophy of Money* (1900) — which takes up most of the notions surrounding an aesthetic stance from this earlier essay — Simmel relates contemporary aestheticism to the tendency to distance oneself from reality. Simmel suggests that the distinctive 'interest in items from a distance seems to be a distinctive sign of modern times'.[72] Simmel is inclined to relate this distance to the modern money economy and urban life which, on the one hand, objectifies all social relationships whilst, at the same time, creating a need to preserve an aesthetic distance. Hence

> an inner barrier develops between people, a barrier, however, that is indispensable for the modern form of life. For the jostling crowdedness and the motley disorder of metropolitan communication would simply be unbearable without such psychological distance. Since contemporary urban culture, with its commercial, professional and social intercourse, forces us to be physically close to an enormous number of people, sensitive and nervous modern people would sink completely into despair if the objectification of social relationships did not bring with it an inner boundary and reserve.[73]

This means that we now enjoy objects aesthetically through maintaining a distance from them. The object of our observation 'has now become an object of contemplation from which we derive pleasure by confronting it with reserve and remoteness, without touching it. It seems to me that the essential features of aesthetic enjoyment are foreshadowed here.'[74] It creates an 'aesthetic indifference' to 'the real existence of an object', to its utility. Our appreciation of the object 'becomes aesthetic only as a result of increasing distance, abstraction and sublimation'.[75] Where attempts were made to overcome this distance, as in a naturalistic stance vis-à-vis reality, it broke down.

Such an aesthetic distance is not merely a feature of Simmel's approach to his object of study but also constitutes his own response to the reification of objective culture. The radical opposition between subjective and objective culture, between individual creativity and reified social forms is first developed most fully in his *Philosophy of Money* where Simmel argues that human interaction leads to 'the creation of higher supra-individual formations' that are 'ideal products of human conceptions and valuation, which in our mind now stands beyond the will and action of the individual as "pure forms" '.[76] Despite the fact that Simmel subsequently recognises the historical form of human objectification in the division of labour and commodity production, his analysis of some of the features of reification is undertaken totally within the context of the inevitable tragic dualism of subjective and objective culture. The critique of reification becomes the critique of culture without any historical dimension or concretion.

The response to this tragic contradiction is the inward retreat to subjectivism, the retreat to the *intérieur*. Such a stance is crucial to an understanding of Simmel's social and political world view.[77] In terms of his 'methodology', it is fully in keeping with the aestheticisation of reality. The observer who Baudelaire describes as a prince can continue to observe undisturbed provided he can also retreat. Aesthetic retreatism was much more advanced by the end of the nineteenth century and especially amongst a powerless intelligentsia in Wilhelmian Germany. This more recent form of aestheticism pervaded the academy just as much as the arts. Hamann and Hermand express it as follows:

> What must be described with the adjective 'feuilletonistic' in the realm of impressionist science, may best be characterised in art with the concept of 'aestheticism'. In both cases, one is as equally opposed to attachment to a world view as to any form of objective search for truth in order not to capitulate before the danger of a supra-individual commitment.[78]

The particular form which this aestheticism takes in Simmel's work must be examined in greater detail.

IV

If we have established that the sociological work of Simmel's middle period at least is permeated by a fundamental aestheticism and if we take seriously his comment that method for him is akin to the notion of style in art, then we should expect that a writer as sensitive as Simmel would take up in his approach to his subject matter elements of all the current artistic styles. In other words, given the period within which he was active, we would expect naturalism, impressionism, *Jugendstil* and expressionism to be reflected in the work of a writer so committed to the aesthetic stance. Indeed, it should be the case that Simmel not merely applies analogies from cultural movements to aspects of social reality or illuminates social phenomena through aesthetic insights but that Simmel's approach — in other words, his 'method' — is in fact constituted by one or several aesthetic movements. This thesis should be investigated despite the fact that Simmel himself developed an increasing interest in aesthetic questions and a decreasing interest in sociology, especially after 1908. This was not merely the year of publication of his *Soziologie* but also of his membership of the 'Association for Aesthetic Research', which included Wölfflin amongst its members.

If we merely examine the artists upon whom Simmel wrote, then a preliminary glance at his studies in aesthetics might reveal an initial difficulty in substantiating this claim. The artistic and literary figures upon whom Simmel devoted most of his attention are seldom his contemporaries. Only studies of Goethe (first in *Kant und Goethe* [1906], then more substantially in *Goethe* [1913]), and *Rembrandt* (1916) appeared in book form. Amongst the other artistic figures to whom Simmel devoted his attention are, chronologically the following essays or reviews: 'Dante's psychology' (1884), 'Michaelangelo as poet' (1889), 'Rembrandt as pedagogue' (1890), 'Leonardo da Vinci's Last Supper' (1905), 'Michaelangelo' (1910), 'Rembrandt's religious art' (1914), 'Rembrandt and beauty' (1914), 'A study of Rembrandt' (1914), and 'On death in art' — on Rembrandt — (1915).[79] Amongst Simmel's contemporaries upon whom he wrote are the following reviews or essays: 'Gerhart Hauptmann's "Weber"' (1892), 'Böcklin's landscapes' (1895), 'Stefan George' (1898), 'Polymeter' (1898 — on

Paul Ernst), 'Stefan George' (1901), 'Rodin's sculpture' (1902), 'Rodin's art' (1909), 'The seventh ring' (1909 — on George), and 'Rodin in Remembrance' (1917).[80] Of these contemporaries, Simmel had a close relationship with Paul Ernst and, to a lesser extent Stefan George, as well as corresponding with Rilke and Rodin, whom he visited in Paris.

In itself, this catalogue of his published essays and reviews of artists and writers explains very little of Simmel's aesthetic commitments. The content of some of these essays and studies might provide further evidence of Simmel's approach. Lukács, for instance, argued that Simmel's studies of Goethe, Michaelangelo, Rodin and Rembrandt 'displayed the pathbreaking element of his way of looking at things' more than any of his other works.[81] For Lukács, this was characterised, as we shall see, by impressionism. To take another example, the essays on Stefan George coincide with the publication of *The Philosophy of Money* and the height of Simmel's affinity with the George circle, of which he was never formally a member. Possibly what appealed to Simmel in George's poetry was what Lukács called 'the impressionism of the typical. All his poems are symbolic snapshots'.[82] Again we are confronted with Simmel's affinities to impressionism. But this is not the only aesthetic movement that concerned Simmel during his lifetime.

If we turn to Simmel's own writings and those of his contemporaries and students, then we find evidence not merely for the view that Simmel was deeply committed to an aesthetic stance but that, at varying stages of his life, the major artistic movements of his day permeate his 'method' and world view to a greater or lesser extent. Is it possible, for instance, to view Simmel's work as moving chronologically through the phases of German art and culture that he would have experienced, namely, naturalism, impressionism, *Jugendstil* and expressionism?

In Simmel's earliest phase of commitment to some form of positivism and Spencerian evolutionism, it is possible to detect a naturalistic stance in his atomistic psychology. In his substantial work on moral philosophy, Simmel argues with considerable naivety that 'ethics will advance to the description of the *real* processes of moral life just like history, statistics, etc.'. Earlier, in his *Über sociale Differenzierung*, Simmel 'seeks to grasp reality directly as an uninterrupted continuum'.[83] This study, his first 'sociological' work, is certainly not free from epistemological naivety. Though it contains some central themes of his later work — on conflict, for instance — the treatment of social differentiation and the principle of energy saving (*Kraftersparnis*) as well as what Böhringer describes as his 'speculative atomism' (derived from Fechner's work) does not betray the subtlety of his later works.[84]

In general, Simmel's early works remained neglected by his con-temporaries. Certainly they do not contain the same degree of insight into social processes and relationships as is to be found from the mid 1890s onwards. By then, Simmel was establishing his essay style that became so distinctive as to gain him recognition as 'the master of the philosophical essay'. He was also developing the aesthetic stance that remained a consistent feature of his work in its several phases up to his death in 1918. In 1896, in his essay on 'Sociological aesthetics', Simmel was already analysing the importance of distance between subject and object in art. The human subject must, Simmel argues, be brought closer to reality through art and

> This reduction is short and easy in naturalistic art forms. For this reason naturalistic art does not require determined and far-reaching intellectual activities for its enjoyment; its approaches are quite direct . . . Man can be most quickly and most directly excited by naturalistic art, because the object and the subjective reactions to it are here in closest proximity.[85]

However, it is clear both from Simmel's own views expressed in this article and from his later essays that he does not favour naturalism which was 'a desperate attempt to overcome distance, to catch the closeness and immediacy of things. But no sooner had one got very close, than sensitive nerves could already no longer bear the contact and shied away, as if they had taken hold of red hot coals.'[86] This increasing distance is seen here and especially in his *Philosophy of Money* as having its origin in the deeper penetration of the money economy which weakens the 'immediacy of impression and active interests in things'. In the modern world, 'a deep psychological trait' is expressed in this expanding distance between ourselves and our objects. The oscillation between remoteness and closeness is a mani-festation of 'the same neurasthenia':

> A period which simultaneously idolises Böcklin and impressionism, naturalism and symbolism, socialism and Nietzsche seems to find its highest pleasures in life in the form of oscillation between the ex-treme poles of all that is human: exhausted nerves, oscillating be-tween hypersensitivity and indifference can be excited anew only by the most obfuscated form and the most earthy proximity, by the tenderest and crudest stimulations.[87]

Here Simmel is suggesting that this contemporary oscillation prevents a commitment to any one style or aesthetic movement. The pervasive 'neurasthenia' certainly prevents attachment to naturalism for any length of time. Not surprisingly, none of his contemporaries saw Simmel's work as expressing a commitment to naturalism.

In contrast, many of his contemporaries and students did view his approach as firmly rooted in impressionism. Assessing his contribution to the philosophy of art, Emil Utitz argues that

> Simmel, without any academic restriction whatsoever, could also philosophise upon anything because the emphasis lay precisely upon philosophising itself. The impressionist painter, too, painted everything . . . Thus, Simmel philosophised upon God and upon fashion, on a Japanese vase and on money, on history and on the future, on ruins and the Alps, on Michaelangelo and on Goethe.[88]

Like impressionism in art, it was not so much the content that was significant — though, as we shall see, neither Simmel nor impressionist painters took 'everything' as their subject matter — but the manner in which it was presented.

It is, however, Lukács who makes out the strongest case for Simmel as an impressionist. In his article on Simmel published in 1918, Lukács says of him that

> he is the true philosopher of impressionism. This does not imply that he had merely made manifest what the impressionistic development of music, the visual arts and poetry had expressed: rather, his work is to be seen much more as a conceptual formulation of the impressionist world view; it is the philosophical structuring of this sense of the world out of which the greatest works in this tradition have emerged, an equally problematic formation of the essence of the epoch that lies immediately behind us as is presented in the works of a Monet or Rodin, a Richard Strauss or a Rilke.[89]

Simmel was indeed impressed by the work of Rodin and Rilke and corresponded with both. But what is significant in Lukács' assessment is the features of impressionism that he highlights since they do open up the possibility of an analysis of Simmel's 'method'.

Lukács sees impressionism as a transitional form which 'rejects completion of the fateful and fate-creating ultimate formation in principle and not out of an incapacity to achieve it', though for some of its adherents this hides 'a cleverly masked impotence'. The fundamental problem facing impressionism is that of form since 'Impressionism experiences and evaluates the major, rigid and eternal forms as the violation of life, its wealth and its multi-colouredness, its richness and its polyphony; it is always a glorifier of life and places every form in its service.'[90] But when it seeks 'the eternal forms in their perfection' that are enclosed and cut off from life, it must connect them once more with that life in order that the particular work may be 'a true work, a self-sufficient world, a microcosm'. Hence,

> Every major impressionist movement is nothing other than the pro-test of life against the forms which solidify too much in it and which become too weak in this paralysis to be able to incorporate its rich-ness in forms. However, because they remain contained in this ele-vation of the apperception of life they are, in their very nature, transitional phenomena; preparation for a new classical period that makes eternal the richness of life, that is revealed through its sensi-tivity in new, rigid and strict but all-encompassing forms. Seen from this standpoint, Simmel's historical situation can be formulated in the following manner: he was a Monet of philosophy that has still not yet been succeeded by a Cézanne.[91]

Impressionism rejects rigid forms and systems. It is loath to complete a whole system of thought or to close off those fragments and elements that might express 'the richness of life'. Whereas Cézanne is bolder and more secure in the structures of what he paints, Monet perhaps remains unsure and at a greater distance from the reality he paints.

However, the negative dimension of impressionism is its perspectiv-ism. Simmel, according to Lukács, 'was the most productive adherent of methodological pluralism; the pathos of his philosophising arose out of the astonishing knowledge of the infinite diversity of philosophical possibilities of foundation and objectification'.[92] It was this 'method-ological pluralism' or what Landmann has termed Simmel's 'impres-sionistic pluralism' that led many to conclude that he was a relativist, particularly in view of 'this pluralistic-unsystematic tendency in his thought'. Lukács, however, argues that this is unjustified since he

> adhered to the absoluteness of each individual foundation [*Setzung*] , he looked upon each as necessary and unconditional, yet he did not believe that there could be any kind of *a priori* attitude towards the world that would really encompass the totality of life. Each offered only a single aspect and not the totality itself. What separates Simmel here from the pluralistic and yet unified system of philosophy that is sought after today is precisely his remaining with the assess-ment of the individual aspects.[93]

Simmel remained attached to 'a genuine impressionistic pleasure in the characteristic sensitivity' towards what is qualitatively unique.

Conversely, this meant that Simmel adhered to a conception of social reality that was constituted by a myriad of interrelationships. What interests him is the particular aspects of the totality of society and never that totality itself. Hence,

Simmel's importance for sociology — I am thinking here primarily of his *Philosophy of Money* — lies in the fact that he drives the analysis of determinations so far and crowns it with such sensitivity as has never been carried out before him and yet, at the same time, he makes evident with inimitable precision the sudden changes in the determinations, their autonomous limitations, their halting before that which they cannot determine.[94]

Lukács here grasps what it is that we remember from reading Simmel's best works: the 'sensitivity' of his analyses and the 'inimitable precision' or, as Gadamer puts it, the 'seismographic accuracy' with which he pinpoints the most unlikely chain of connections between the seemingly most insignificant social interactions.

Yet completely in keeping with impressionism, Lukács recognises that 'Simmel's sociology is only an "experiment" and not a conclusion; his *Soziologie* bears the stamp of his impressionism much more strongly than the great treatise on money; and his incursions into the philosophy of history are . . . conceived as fragments.'[95] But it was the studies of Goethe, Kant, Rembrandt, Michaelangelo and Rodin which, Lukács argued, 'displayed the pathbreaking element of his way of looking at things'. They also demarcated the impressionistic stance that was neither historical nor systematic:

> Simmel's impressionism sees in each of these geniuses a unique, specific but at the same time eternal and *a priori* possibility of attitudes towards the totality of life: his pluralism not merely refers to the individual forms of existence [*Setzungsarten*] but also to the individual realisations within each form of existence . . . But because Simmel's impressionism is a genuine and philosophical one, each of the world views becomes something absolute.[96]

Thus, Simmel's impressionism extends not merely through the description and analysis of a whole variety of social processes and forms of social interaction but also to individual, unique forms of existence.

Lukács' interpretation of Simmel's work as firmly located within impressionism highlights a number of features of that movement within his work. Simmel certainly takes the problem of form as central to his social analysis though his later writings suggest that the concept of form lapses into formalism. At their best, Simmel's analyses of social relations and processes seek to capture 'the richness of life' with considerable sensitivity. This richness is, of course, unstructured in that it can derive from a whole variety of aspects none of which is given any particular preference. Everything is provisional or, as Lukács puts it, 'an experiment'; nothing is finished, completed or incorporated within a single system. We are dazzled by the illumination of the parts whilst the whole remains obscure. As one contemporary observed, Simmel's mode of presentation can be compared 'with a firework, that is certainly brilliant to look at but leaves behind it no tangible product'.[97]

Other students of Simmel have also been aware of his impressionism. Karl Mannheim, who attended his lectures in Berlin in 1912, argued much later that Simmel possessed a capacity

> for describing the simplest everyday experiences with the same precision as is characteristic of a contemporary impressionistic painting which has learned to reflect the previously unobserved shades and values of the atmosphere. He might well be called the 'impressionist' in sociology, because his was not an ability to take a constructive view of the whole of society but to analyse the significance of minor social forces that were previously unobserved.[98]

Once more, it is the 'view of the whole of society' that is seen to be absent in Simmel's work. Perhaps the fragments of human interaction are to represent the lost totality, the vision of society as a whole.

But what is the relationship between these fragments? Simmel merely offers us aspects and snatches of social relationships from the absent totality. But, Lukács argues, 'These individual aspects stand in the most diverse and intricate relationship to one another . . . this network of interrelationships must remain a labyrinth and cannot be a system.'[99] Although we do perceive a totality in an impressionist image when we stand at a distance from it, viewed from close by it too reveals its composition out of a 'labyrinth' of colour in a manner not found in earlier art forms. Kracauer went so far as to suggest that 'Simmel's work resembles a single labyrinth of ways many of which suddenly terminate as dead ends and cut through one another obliquely.'[100] And here we are once more confronted with the *flâneur* who creates 'the mythical aspect of the big city as a labyrinth' and who is at home in 'the labyrinthine character of the city itself, the labyrinth, whose image is embedded in the flesh and blood of the *flâneur*'.[101]

Not just the big city but also society itself is, for Simmel, a giant labyrinth. His method too allows him to conceive of society as a labyrinth since he is 'an eternal wanderer between things; an unlimited capacity for combination allows him to step out from any point in any direction'.[102] Not surprisingly, therefore, Simmel conceives of society as a network of human relationships. Often the actual relationships between diverse aspects of social interaction remain hidden. It is one of the tasks of Simmel's sociological perspective to reveal these hidden connections, to reveal 'the intersection of social circles' (*Die Kreuzung sozialer Kreise*).[103] Indeed, Kracauer outlines the 'core principle of Simmel's thought' as follows:

> *All expressions of cultural life . . . stand in an inexpressible plurality of relationships to one another, none is capable of being extracted from the contexts in which they find themselves associated with others.* This standpoint is one of Simmel's fundamental experiences upon which his understanding of the world rests.[104]

It is an 'intellectual labyrinth with its many-stranded branches through it, individual side paths and branch lines'.[105]

Simmel finds his way within the social labyrinth by postulating 'two types of relationships between things'. The first is 'the relationships of *fundamental interrelatedness* [*Wesenszusammengehörigkeit*] of the most diverse phenomena'. The implication of this principle is that no individual element can be fully understood in isolation and cannot be abstracted from the 'context of diversity in which it is enmeshed'. Hence one of Simmel's basic intentions is 'to release each cultural phenomenon from its falsified autonomy and to show how it is embedded in the major constellations of life'.[106]

To the sociologist, it is the interrelatedness of forms of individual interaction that is important since 'the interaction between individuals is the starting point of all social formations'.[107] In fact, it is social interaction itself which constitutes society:

> Society is not an absolute entity which must first exist so that all the individual relations of its members . . . can develop within its framework or be represented by it: it is only the synthesis or the general term for the totality of these specific interactions. Any one of these interactions may, of course, be eliminated and 'society' still exist, but only if a sufficiently large number of others remain intact. If all interaction ceases there is no longer any society.[108]

It is the task of sociology to comprehend these interactions and to demonstrate their fundamental interrelatedness. The web or network of social relationships that goes to make up society is itself located within a social process that, as we saw in an earlier chapter, has been dehistoricised. Impressionism, too, rejected a historical dimension and was faced with a composition crisis. In Simmel's case, this prevents him, as Mannheim argues, from taking 'a constructive view of the whole of society'.

This is reinforced by the alternative method employed by Simmel to illustrate the interrelatedness of social phenomena, namely that of *analogy*. Here, too, Simmel searches for 'the liberation of things from their individual isolation'. But the excessive use of argument by analogy is itself rooted in aestheticism. If we think of the analogies Simmel draws, then we find that they conform to the range suggested by Kracauer:

> He emphasises, for example, the affinity between the structural relationships of the work of art with those of some social organisations, or considers how chosen processes of social and inner psychic life operate according to one and the same schema. The economic order is compared with the legal order, analogies between art and play, with adventure and love are rendered visible.[109]

Here, of course, the analogies often remain little more than a heuristic device that may produce suggestive affinities but do not lead to the examination of real connections.

In both instances highlighted by Kracauer — the interrelatedness of phenomena and the employment of analogies — we are confronted with real or suggestive interrelationships that are located within an absent totality. Therefore, we might expect that the interrelationships and the fragments of social processes dealt with by Simmel would themselves be clear and focused. But in keeping with an impressionist stance, there is almost always an indefinite atmosphere surrounding Simmel's social forms. As Kracauer argues, 'None of Simmel's forms live in historical time. A thin air swirls around them; they do not appear in sequence; we know nothing of their historical milieu.'[110] This vagueness and imprecision of location and definition extends to Simmel's work as a whole.

In his perceptive account of Simmel's relationship to impressionism, Richard Hamann aptly describes the nature of Simmel's texts and teaching as follows:

> Time and time again one finds expressions in which he characterises graphic clarity and logical determination of form as an intellectual forgery. As a life creating energy, he only trusts those of a personal origin since the clear perfection of concepts has led to a linguistic slipperiness within which one comes into contact with the wealth of the actual and the particular merely from outside. Therefore, he demands a prose style that does not limit itself to the results of thought but also seeks to reflect the movement of thought. . . . Thus, in his lectures, Simmel supported particular thought processes, in fact, through swirling hand movements that were often the sole binding element in his chain of thought. Hence philosophising as the manifestation of a pre-established idea gradually steps into the background. Instead of being concerned with a logical connection, one gives way completely to momentary inspiration.[111]

This mode of philosophising is confirmed, for instance, in the introduction to *Philosophische Kultur* (1911) where Simmel quite explicitly states that the fundamental aspect of philosophy lies not merely or not even in its content but in 'a definite intellectual attitude to the world and to life, a functional form and mode of looking upon things and dealing with them internally'.[112] What this mode of philosophising rests upon is a sophisticated concern for the activity of philosophising itself conceived as the preoccupation with strands of meaning. Thus, in the place of detailed explanations there stand 'brilliant, suggestive symbols, unusual words or philosophical ciphers that have nothing to do with the content itself but rather merely with supporting the elegance of the formulation . . . the refined brokenness that expresses itself in the shift in certain nuances of meaning'.[113] The preoccupation with 'impressionistic mental vibration' (Hamann) in Simmel's work results in the indeterminate nature of even the details of social life that he so brilliantly illuminates.

The impressionist stance has three other consequences that can be dealt with more briefly. The first — already alluded to — is the imprecision of even the details of social life, quite apart from the absence of a conception of society as a totality. Adorno refers to the frequent use of such terms as 'attitude' and 'cachet' in Simmel's work as an indication of this imprecision. We have already seen that Simmel conceived of philosophy as an 'attitude'. Kracauer, too, detected the indeterminate nature of Simmel's stance:

> Where previously hard boundaries were drawn, there now emerge crossings, here one thing flows into another. Not for nothing is 'nuance' a catchword of the times. Everything shimmers, everything flows, everything is ambiguous, everything converges in a shifting form. It is the realm of chaos in which we live.[114]

This capacity to conjure up 'particular psychic intricacies, moods of the most fleeting kind' is evident in Simmel 'just as in Schnitzler, Hofmannsthal, George, Rilke, etc.'.[115]

The indeterminacy is reinforced by a second feature of Simmel's texts that was commented upon by his contemporaries and which has also already been referred to briefly. Margarete Susman suggests that 'time and time again, two words confront us in his writings: the words "perhaps" and "so to speak" that otherwise do not occur in any significant philosophy'.[116] Similarly Kurt Gassen relates that 'Everyone who reads Simmel or has even heard him themselves will remember that characteristic subtle, hesitant, to some extent hypothetical manner of expression, in which the word "perhaps" . . . played such a prominent role.'[117] Ernst Bloch concludes that 'Simmel was a philosopher of the "perhaps" [*ein Vielleichtdenker*] like few others before him' and that 'Simmel's "perhaps" belongs solely to that general, constant, indecisive pathos of life' to which he was prone.[118] In the context of impressionism, Hamann points to the frequency with which 'Simmel uses the phrases "perhaps", "one might say" or "it may well be" instead of describing dogmatically the true state of affairs'.[119] As we shall see, this indecisiveness has important implications for Simmel's social and political stance and world view.

Finally, the implication of the fact that there is, in his work, no constructive view of the whole of society or a conception of society as a totality but instead a wealth of memorable *vignettes* and social fragments, suggests that this uncertainty means that we cannot generalise from individual instances with any degree of certainty. The 'flight into the unbounded' (Hamann) can easily be associated with the fleeting impression instead of the systematic analysis with the review or essay rather than the scientific treatise. When Coser comments on the increasing frequency with which Simmel published in non-academic journals, the conclusion to be drawn from this is not that Simmel remains an outsider in the academy but that this expresses his preference for the 'feuilletonistic' mode of addressing his public which is, of course, not unconnected with the refined discourse of the salon. Similarly, Bloch associates this extensive use of 'perhaps' with a form of intellectual coquetry whose social location Simmel himself so well described. The fleeting impressions that Simmel leaves behind are indeed the momentary images or snapshots (*Momentbilder*) that he refers to in a collection of pieces for the Munich *Jugendstil* journal *Jugend*. Whilst the significance of the notion of snapshots is discussed in the next chapter, the fact that he published in a *Jugendstil* journal around the turn of the century should prompt us to question Simmel's relationship with this aesthetic movement.

Within Simmel's own work and commentaries by his contemporaries there are no direct references to the *Jugendstil* movement. Subsequent commentators, too, have seldom made a connection between his work and the *Jugendstil* movement. Ernst Bloch, referring eliptically to Simmel's development, speaks of 'Simmel's early neo-Kantianism (most recognisable in his *Problems of the Philosophy of History*, 1892) also blended later with its "constituents of form" in the almost mother-of-pearl, almost sparkling flow of life that came from diverse kinds of *Jugendstil*, then predominantly from Bergson.'[120] More specifically, one recent commentator suggests that his *Philosophy of Money* is 'a delicate philosophical total design in *Jugendstil* in which things flow away ethereally above all distances and oppositions and in this manner are once more connected with one another "organically".'[121] There might well be a case for suggesting that Simmel's preoccupation with form in such a work can be compared with the intervening of brilliant colours in *Jugendstil* design that gives an artificial structure to the whole artistic work. The content recedes into the background and is submerged in the formal designs. However, this would have to be a tentative judgment in the absence of a detailed study of his works.

However, some of Simmel's contemporaries did detect a move towards expressionism in his later work. Utitz detects his dependency upon expressionism in his wartime writings. Certainly the existential element and the existential decisionism of the wartime essays *Der Krieg und die geistigen Entscheidungen* (1917) do have strong affinities with expressionism. Frischeisen Köhler, commenting upon the later period of Simmel's work suggests that 'If it is permitted to characterise Simmel as an expressionistic thinker, then his philosophy of culture is the attempt to conceive of culture itself as the expressionistic creation of life.'[122] Both the philosophy of culture and Simmel's version of a *Lebensphilosophie* belong to the later period of his work. But this is the period in which Simmel increasingly lost interest in sociology and turned more explicitly towards the philosophy of culture and metaphysics. Expressionism may surely have influenced the mature Simmel but it is not the key to his sociological writings. Besides, even in his later writings such as 'Die Krise der Kultur' (1917), Simmel argues that expressionism also failed to capture life 'by the direct expression of psychological processes', assuming that

> by externalising inner dynamics in a work of art without regard to either the form appropriate to that work or to objectively valid norms, life could at last be given the form of expression genuinely appropriate to it without any falsification by external form. But it seems to be in the nature of inner life that it can only ever be expressed in forms which have their own laws, purpose and stability arising from a degree of autonomy independent of the spiritual dynamics which created them.[123]

Hence, expressionism could not overcome 'the real, ubiquitous tragedy of culture'. Nor indeed could futurism in whose manifestations we see that 'once again the forms that life created as dwelling places have become its prisons'.

This tragedy of culture and the separation of objective and subjective culture was not first outlined in Simmel's last writings but in his earlier sociological works, most notably in *The Philosophy of Money*. As we have seen, however, there is general agreement upon the impressionist stance in his sociological work to say that of the four aesthetic movements outlined here it is impressionism itself which most fundamentally permeates Simmel's sociological writings. It is to some of these impressionistic fragments and snapshots as well as his more substantial sociological analyses that we must now turn in the next chapter.

V

The search for a method in Simmel's work has led us to conclude that no systematic method exists. Rather, the notion of approach or stance vis-à-vis social reality — perhaps, even, Simmel's 'attitude' — is more appropriate. In turn, this can only be elucidated by reference to his consistent aestheticism and its various dimensions. Of the various possible aesthetic traditions with which Simmel was acquainted, it has been suggested that only impressionism holds the key to his sociological work.

On the question of method and approach, it is one of the ironies that many writers have seen this as his specific contribution to sociology. Rudolf Heberle writes:

> It is Simmel's method and procedure of analysis rather than the content of his findings which constitutes his unique and lasting contribution to the advancement of sociology. Thus we are confronted with the paradox that the philosopher who started out to redefine the subject matter of sociology gained his place among sociologists rather because of his methodological ideas.[124]

This is perhaps overstating the case for Simmel's approach being his major contribution to sociology, especially since Heberle does not examine it in detail. More appropriately, Kracauer, who was much closer to Simmel, concludes that 'Simmel has exercised a broad and deep influence upon the intellectual life of his period that does not so much derive from the results as from the distinctive style of his thought.'[125] The distinction between 'his *methodological* ideas' (Heberle) and 'the distinctive *style* of his thought' (Kracauer) does, of course, reflect a distinction between science and aesthetics.

4 'Snapshots *sub specie aeternitatis*'?

Simmel est toujours très intéressant dans les *détails*.
Henri Bergson (1912)

Simmel dealt with problems *sub specie aeternitatis* while feigning to deal with them *sub specie momenti*.
Arthur Salz

I

Between 1897 and 1907, Simmel frequently contributed to the Munich *Jugendstil* journal *Jugend*. His contributions varied from poems of diverse length, aphorisms, fables and short articles with such titles as 'Theistic phantasies of a fin-de-sièclist' (1898), 'Justice' (1898), and 'The metaphysics of laziness' (1900). None of them was ever reprinted. They all appeared anonymously under the signature 'S.', 'G. S.' or 'Fridolin'. Between 1900 and 1903, seven contributions consisting largely of parables appeared under the title 'Momentbilder *sub specie aeternitatis*' — literally, snapshots viewed from the aspect of eternity. At that time, *Momentbild* was the word in use to describe snapshots. It still retained the literal meaning of a fleeting or momentary image or picture. But, interestingly enough, the literary 'snapshots' are not accompanied by actual snapshots since *Jugend* was firmly committed to *Jugendstil*. Simmel's contributions are surrounded by *Jugendstil* designs, and other graphics that belong to an aesthetic movement which sought to preserve individual creativity against the reproducibility of new art forms thrown up by capitalism, such as photography.

The content of Simmel's 'snapshots' in *Jugend* are not important in the present context. Rather, it is the title of these pieces itself which serves to illuminate his mode of approaching his subject matter during the major period of his sociological production, namely, around the turn of the century. Indeed, the title of these pieces 'Snapshots *sub specie aeternitatis*' serves to summarise many of the aspects of Simmel's approach that have been outlined in the previous chapter, as well as providing a way into the substantive content of his works in this period.

The paradox of the snapshot is that although it is literally a fleeting image, it is also one that can be made to endure. As Benjamin — who wrote on the social consequences of photography — puts it, 'A touch of the finger now sufficed to fix an event for an unlimited period of time. The camera gave the moment a posthumous shock, as it were.'[1] Simmel would want to say that what interests him is not merely the fleeting image that the snapshot provides but also what can be seen as enduring about that image. In Simmel's terminology, the snapshot of social reality may capture a transitory content but the sociologist should be concerned with the more enduring social forms within which that content is embodied. Another way of looking at Simmel's snapshots is to see them as the product of what Hamann terms 'impressionistic *feuilletonism*' of which Simmel was a master and within which he was perfectly at home.

But even a series of discrete snapshots or social *vignettes* does not constitute a sociology. Sociological snapshots, as fragments of social interaction and social processes, require something to bind them together. In this respect, Simmel's conscious essayism as the particular form in which he presents these fragments and his acute difficulty of holding together aspects of interaction under the principle of their fundamental interrelatedness or through analogies both point to the absence of a binding element. Connections are certainly made between the most disparate phenomena but they are more often than not aesthetic rather than real connections. As such, the connections are aesthetic rather than concrete historical ones. In other words, they can easily become eternal connections devoid of historical concretion.

What are we to make of these fleeting images viewed from the aspect of eternity? Kracauer suggests that none of the social phenomena examined by Simmel 'live in historical time'; 'Rather, everything that is interwoven in the past and future he transposes into eternity, that is, into the sole form of existence in which it can exist as pure essentiality and can also be contemporary with us at any time.'[2] The analysis of the money economy and its peculiar social formations in *The Philosophy of Money*, for instance, moves in the direction of dehistoricised social forms of interaction. Similarly, the essay on conflict leaves us with the eternal forms of the conflict relationship and its historical instances fade into insignificance. In other words, the reduction of social inter-action and social processes to their timeless forms is confirmation of their aestheticisation.

But it is not merely the content of Simmel's texts that are viewed from the aspect of eternity, that are viewed *sub specie aeternitatis*. The form itself in which his reflections are presented also takes on this aspect. Again, both Lukács and Adorno, in their different ways, seek to highlight what is distinctive about the essay form, of which Simmel was an acknowledged master. Lukács, for instance, sees the essay form as enabling one to discuss the eternal as if one is discussing the transitory. The critic is

> always speaking about the ultimate problems of life, but in a tone which implies that he is only discussing pictures and books, only the inessential and pretty ornaments of real life — and even then not their innermost substance but only their beautiful and useless sur-face. Thus, each essay appears to be removed as far as possible from life, and the distance between them seems the greater, the more burningly and painfully we sense the actual closeness of the true essence of both.[3]

More specifically in relation to Simmel's essays, we have Salz's comment that though Simmel ostensibly discussed topics *sub specie momenti* — i.e. snapshots — he was actually concerned with viewing them *sub specie aeternitatis*. Similarly, Adorno suggests that this is a feature of the essay form which 'does not search for the eternal in the transitory and distill it but rather seeks to eternalise the transitory.'[4] In so doing, the transitory, fleeting glimpses of the everyday world come to be seen as something alien. The danger of an obsession with the fleeting, the transitory and the paradoxical is that it has no limits, no boundaries. Either everything merges into everything else or the snapshots do not cohere. As Hamann argues, the extreme form of 'impressionistic *feuille-tonism*' lapses into trivialisation: 'The result of this wandering into the unbounded is an intellectual semi-obfuscation that almost borders on frivolity. Thus, one flirts with things that are really uninteresting only in order to create a charmed atmosphere or to awaken the impression of an eloquent futility.'[5] Though coquetry is a central theme of Sim-mel's writings on sociability and though the wide range of his essays itself suggests a form of intellectual flirtation on the author's part, this judgment of trivialisation is perhaps too harsh for his better works. Nonetheless, Simmel's 'psychological microscopy' and his tendency to be a collector of snapshots does tend to leave the question of the ranking or ordering of his subject matter in some doubt. What is not in doubt is the centrality of snapshots from which is extracted some external meaning structure. Lukács, probably correctly, associates this approach with impressionism. Simmel, Lukács argues, possesses 'the capacity for seeing the smallest and most inessential phenomena of everyday life so strongly *sub specie philosophiae* that it becomes transparent and behind its transparency reveals an eternal constellation [*Formzusammenhang*] of philosophical meaning.'[6] In the absence of historical specificity, these more enduring forms and connections that are often aesthetic rather than concrete give to his social theory a resignatory pathos, a 'false pathos of distance'.

There can be little doubt that Simmel's approach to social phen-omena has its roots in a distinctive aesthetic stance. Already in 1895 in an essay on 'Böcklin's landscapes',[7] Simmel was making explicit the meaning of the title of his later contributions to *Jugend*. There he expresses his response to Böcklin's landscapes precisely from the perspective of grasping the eternal in the momentary image when he states that,

> Spinoza demanded of the philosopher that he view things *sub specie aeternitatis*, that is, purely according to their inner necessity and sig-nificance, detached from the arbitrariness of their here and now. . . . Böcklin's paintings affect us as if we looked at their content trans-posed in the sphere of such timelessness; as if the pure, ideal content of things, set apart from any historical momentariness, from any relationship to the past and future, stood before us. Everything is just like the moments of a summer's day where nature holds our breath, where the passage of time is arrested. It is not eternity in the sense of an immeasurable passage of time, that is, not eternity in a religious sense, in whose sphere we feel ourselves to be. Rather, it is simply the suspension of temporal relationships, as when we term a natural law eternal, not because it has already existed for a long time but because its validity has nothing at all to do with the ques-tion of the past or the future.[8]

More specifically, Simmel takes the example of Böcklin's trees in his paintings. The artist captures something very specific, namely, 'the moment in which he presents them, whether it is their first buds, their midday maturity or their autumnal decline, is their eternity.'[9] Though Simmel is concerned here with an appreciation of Böcklin's landscapes, his other writings suggest that the preoccupation with 'the suspension of temporal relationships' and the attempt to grasp the meaning of the totality of life from its fleeting moments as an ex-pression of their eternal significance lies at the heart of his sociology too.

The more radically we advance the thesis that Simmel's sociology consists of snapshots viewed from the aspect of eternity the more we are inclined to emphasise the fragmentary conscious essayism of his approach. This would suggest that he presents us with a series of unrelated snapshots of social interaction. But is it possible to challenge this conception of his work? Certainly, the preponderance of the essay form in Simmel's work would confirm the judgment outlined so far, as would the seemingly fragmentary major work, the *Soziologie*, which comprises ten apparently separate chapters and thirteen 'excursions'. But there is one substantial study that might hold the key to Simmel's success in relating diverse aspects of social interaction and snapshots of social life, namely his *Philosophy of Money*. Tenbruck argues that Simmel's

> sociological period . . . reaches its real high point and completion in the *Philosophie des Geldes* (1900) . . . several shorter articles on sociology after 1900 are only the rounding off and development of positions already definitively reached earlier, additional studies that contribute nothing essential to the total work.[10]

If we accept this view of *The Philosophy of Money*, then it would be worthwhile concentrating our attention upon this major work, together with a number of related essays. However difficult Simmel found it to maintain the structure of this work — and despite its symmetry of three analytic chapters and three synthetic chapters each divided into three sections, there is little doubt that he found the architecture of the whole work a strain — it remains his most substantial, coherent and sustained work upon social theory. It is also the one major sociological work that Simmel completed during the period within which he contributed to *Jugend* (1897—1907). The first edition appeared in 1900 and the second revised version in 1907.

II

Despite the fact that Simmel's *Philosophy of Money* appears to possess a symmetrical structure seldom encountered in his other works, the actual coherent *form* of the work hides a disparate *content*. The 'analytical part' of the study — the first three chapters — 'relates money to the conditions that determine its essence and the meaning of its existence'.[11] The 'synthetic part' — the last three chapters — is where 'the historical phenomenon of money . . . is studied . . . in its effects upon the inner world – upon the vitality of individuals, upon the linking of their fates, upon culture in general'.[12] One might infer from this description that the analytical part of Simmel's study outlines the preconditions for the emergence and study of a money economy (e.g. a theory of value or 'its preconditions in non-economic concepts and facts'), whereas the synthetic part examines the actual historical nature of social relationships as they have been transformed by money (i.e. 'its consequences for non-economic values and relationships'). But money is taken by Simmel to be 'the symbol of the essential forms of movement within this world'. Hence, the work is not to be defined merely in terms of its content: 'The unity of these investigations does not lie, therefore, in an assertion about a particular content of knowledge and its gradually accumulating proofs but rather in the possibility – which must be demonstrated – of finding in each of life's details the totality of its meaning.'[13] In other words the details of social life, the 'snapshots' of social reality, hold the key to an understanding of the human social totality. This declared methodological aim is also the key to an understanding of Simmel's conception of society. Furthermore, it unwittingly renders the structure of *The Philosophy of Money* less significant.

There can be little doubt that Simmel had considerable difficulty in maintaining the architectonic structure of this major study of one of the most elusive social phenomena. It was not merely, as he explained to Rickert, that particular sections of the work, such as the exposition of his own theory of value, presented him with considerable problems. Even when he had revised the volume in 1907, he was still not satisfied with it. Indeed, he suggested to his friend Hermann Keyserling, that it might be better not to read *The Philosophy of Money* straight through:

> I would recommend that you omit the second chapter or at most leaf through it in order to see whether one or two places in it perhaps appeal to you (in any case, a very remarkable psychological fact). This chapter is the most technical in the book and will, as a whole, hardly interest you. Indeed, I would take it to be not unreasonable for you to start with the last chapter and only then read further from the first chapter onwards.[14]

Nonetheless, unlike the *Soziologie*, his *Philosophy of Money* is a structured work, however unhappy Simmel might have been about its final form.

Perhaps the advantage which Simmel possessed in this work was his concentration upon a particular object that so well suited his aesthetic approach as well as his whole notion of society. Money had come to preoccupy Simmel much earlier than the date of the first publication of his *Philosophy of Money*. Eleven years earlier in 1889 he had published an article entitled 'On the psychology of money'[15] which, in the space of fourteen pages, already contained many of the themes of his major work, albeit in an abbreviated form. What preoccupied Simmel in 1889 was the peculiar feature of money within the teleology of means and ends, namely that 'the in itself merely indifferent means' should become an end of human action, which stamped its own indifference and 'colourlessness' upon those who were caught within its machinations. Money is 'the common point of intersection of different series of ends'[16] and hence, in order to reflect their divergence, it must remain indifferent, 'colourless' and 'lacking in quality'. Simmel briefly illuminates some of the different contexts within which money functions to transform relationships, such as the sale of women and the blasé attitude, that are taken up in much greater detail in his *Philosophy of Money*.

But already it is clear that what really interests him is the symbolic significance of money rather than merely the historical development of a money economy. This is exemplified in the manner in which the article concludes with an analogy between the notion of God and that of money. The passage is significant enough to quote in some detail. Simmel suggests that

> If one were to express the fact – in both a melancholy and sarcastic tone – that money is the god of our time, then there are indeed significant psychological relationships to be found between the two apparently so opposed notions. The fundamental significance of the notion of god lies in the fact that all the diverse elements of the world succeed in unifying in him, that – in the beautiful words of Nicholas of Cusa – he is the *coincidentia oppositorium* . . . the psychological affinity with that of money is clear from what has been stated. The *tertium comparationis* is the feeling of peace and security that precisely the possession of money in contrast to all other possessions secures and refers to the same psychological feeling which the devout person finds in his god. In both instances, it is the transcendence of the particular that we find in the object observed, the trust in the omnipotence of the highest principle. . . . Just as God in the form of belief so money in the form of the concrete is the highest abstraction to which practical reason has ascended.[17]

What is interesting about this passage is not merely that it forms the basis for a fuller elaboration in *The Philosophy of Money*, but that money symbolises a particular form of abstraction that unifies the most diverse phenomena. More specifically, money transcends the particular interests to which it is put. As the most mysterious social abstraction, it can also serve to symbolise social relationships as a totality in such a way that any examination of one of its particular uses or contexts — however trivial — can lead us to its universal significance. In short, it is a perfect phenomenon to be studied by a methodology that takes as its starting point the relationship between the particular and the totality.

In other words, money as an object of study fully accords with an approach to social reality that seeks to demonstrate the 'fundamental interrelatedness' of all phenomena. Whereas the analogy drawn between God and money is an instance of Simmel's search for the unexpected strands that link disparate phenomena, the passage as a whole and, more especially, *The Philosophy of Money*, points to a second task that Kracauer characterises as being

> to grasp what is diverse as a totality and somehow to be master of this totality, to experience and express its essence. From the prin- ciple that everything stands in relationship to everything else there follows directly the unity of the world. Each individual constellation is present within it, it is only a fragment of the whole totality of the world, without whose previous grasp and comprehension one can only bring to light fragmentary, incomplete constellations.[18]

Does Simmel, however, commence his analysis of social phenomena from a conception of this totality or does he start out from the par- ticular individual phenomenon in order to show how it is enmeshed within the totality? It has already been suggested that in many of his analyses 'an abstract moment . . . of general concepts' becomes 'the starting point of his observations'. This would be true of those social analyses that encompass a whole range of objects such as 'The inter- section of social circles' or 'Super- and subordination' and which in his *Soziologie* are self-enclosed analyses. Yet in *The Philosophy of Money* both examples are treated within the unifying context of the transformations brought about by a money economy. But it is doubt- ful whether we can conceive of the generalities from which Simmel so often commences his analyses in the *Soziologie* as entailing a concept of the social totality.

Much more common, of course, is the search for the totality from the seemingly insignificant elements of social interaction. The danger here, however, is of never advancing beyond the individual element. As Kracauer comments, 'Always when Simmel observes individual forms, he sets them apart from the macrocosm and detaches them from their interwovenness with phenomena; he treats them as independent entities, he disdains the incorporation of the individual microcosm in the global totality.'[19] It is this concern with the social microcosm, combined with the seemingly insignificant social phenomena so treated, that led many contemporaries to assume that Simmel was *merely* concerned with fragments. Bloch, for instance, says, 'One thinks of Simmel: here too it is always merely the colourful, nervous, purely impressible margins of life that are painted.'[20] But in some of his works, Simmel does seek to grasp the totality of social relationships. Whether he is ever successful is an issue that must be investigated.

His contemporaries were agreed that he came closest to analysing the totality of social relations around a single theme in the study of money. Altmann, reviewing *The Philosophy of Money*, argued that 'only an economic phenomenon like money . . . could in its totality give an image of the world in which everything is part of the whole'. Similarly, Schmoller maintains that Simmel produces an analysis of 'money or, one could almost say, of modern economic forms as a whole; for he extends far beyond money, he assembles everything that he has to say about the modern economy around money as the centre of these phenomena.'[21] As is often the case, this positive assessment of Simmel's work is most fully elaborated in Kracauer's judgment that

> The most outstanding example of the . . . mastery of the totality is offered by the *Philosophy of Money* . . . all the spheres of material that are at all accessible to the author are here traversed and the countless relationships are indicated which establish connections between the equally innumerable phenomena within these spheres. Simmel placed one cross section after the other through the social and individual life of men in the age of the developed money economy. . . . In none of his other works does the author outline such a comprehensive picture of the interconnectedness and entanglement of phenomena. He clearly extracts their essence in order to melt it down once more into a multitude of connections . . . and reveals the many common meanings that reside within them.[22]

What this suggests is that, unlike many of his essays, his social analysis in *The Philosophy of Money* moves away from discrete snapshots towards a conception of society as a totality. The features of this social analysis must therefore be examined in some detail in order to confirm whether this judgment is an accurate one.

Again, this is not to argue that Simmel was successful in presenting society as a totality. Nor is it to suggest that he was unaware of the difficulties involved in relating fragments to a wider totality.

As Schrader-Klebert points out, 'it is one of Simmel's convictions that knowledge must necessarily be fragmentary'. In this way we can understand the fragmentary nature of his *Soziologie* as emerging 'out of the openness of the research situation'. But the problem is more complex than this:

> Since, however, not only the temporary but also the constitutive openness of empirical science determines that any total mediation remains a claim that cannot be fulfilled, so Simmel's theory of the 'example' must not only be taken to be the mastery of science's problem with regard to its starting point but also as the mastery of the contradiction between the claim to total mediation, i.e. to a system, and the fact that this claim cannot be fulfilled in an empirical science.[23]

Arguments by example and by analogy abound in all Simmel's works but they can be seen to possess this wider methodological significance.

From the very outset in *The Philosophy of Money* Simmel maintains that 'the ever-fragmentary contents of positive knowledge seek to be augmented by definitive concepts into a world picture and to be related to the totality of life'.[24] This is his real aim rather than presenting a 'philosophy' of money that might involve 'the abstract philosophical construction of a system' which maintains 'a distance from the individual phenomena'. Philosophy's problem 'is nothing less than the totality of being' and in setting itself such a wide task tends to minimise the fullness of the very totality it seeks to grasp. In contrast,

> The great advantage of art over philosophy is that it sets itself a single, narrowly defined problem every time: a person, a landscape, a mood. Every extension of one of these to the general, every addition of bold touches of feeling for the world is made to appear as an enrichment, a gift, an undeserved benefit.[25]

It is this advantage of an aesthetics of the particular that Simmel wishes to preserve in his *Philosophy of Money*.

Not surprisingly, therefore, Simmel claims that 'not a single line of these investigations is meant to be a statement about economics' since a philosophy of money 'can only lie on either side of the economic science of money'. Money is merely 'an example' for the presentation of relations in society as a whole. Hence, the aim of the book is 'simply to derive from the surface level of economic affairs a guideline that leads to the ultimate values and things of importance in all that is human'.[26] To take up merely the economic aspects of production and exchange is to view the problem 'from *one* standpoint' that is insufficient for Simmel's purpose.

This does not mean that Simmel wishes to ignore this 'standpoint'. Rather, it must be incorporated into a wider framework in order

> to construct a new story beneath historical materialism such that the explanatory value of the incorporation of economic life into the causes of intellectual culture is preserved, while these economic forms themselves are recognised to be the result of more profound valuations and currents of psychological or even metaphysical pre-conditions. For the practice of cognition, this must develop in in-finite reciprocity. Every interpretation of an ideal structure by means of an economic structure must lead to the demand that the latter in turn be understood from more ideal depths, while for these depths themselves the general economic base has to be sought, and so on indefinitely.[27]

A basic aim of *The Philosophy of Money* is, therefore, to discredit what Simmel took to be historical materialism's one-sided emphasis upon economic factors. The basic economic categories such as production and exchange are much more than merely 'economic' concepts. The objects they seek to apprehend can be viewed from other sides: political, aesthetic, etc. But Simmel is not merely saying that the economic is merely one aspect of phenomena amongst others. He is also saying that some economic phenomena such as money are symbols or indices of much more fundamental processes – the objectification of subjectivity, the quantification of qualities. Ultimately money and the money econ-omy are only 'examples' of the fate of all culture. Hence it is not diffi-cult to gain the impression when reading *The Philosophy of Money* that 'the attempt at a philosophy of money has no foundation in the object itself but is the result of an intellectual activity that results from the personal attitude',[28] of the author. The role of this 'philos-ophy' of money is both analytic and synthetic in the sense that the analytic part (the first three chapters) examines the presuppositions whilst the synthetic part (the last three chapters) organises the frag-ments of the science. It is possible, as Lieber has argued, to see the supra-historical or ahistorical analysis of the analytic part as correspond-ing in some sense to the analysis of the abstract form of money (via a theory of value) and the historical concretion of the consequences of a money economy as the concern with the 'content' of money.[29]

III

What are the presuppositions from which Simmel commences his analysis of money? Simmel operates with a subjectivist theory of value that has important relativist implications. It is a theory of value derived from marginal utility theorists such as Menger and Böhm-Bawerk. The problem of a subjective theory of value is that it views the economy completely from the perspective of the subject's demand for goods. As Simmel says, 'the world of value is my demand'. Value becomes totally relative in relation to consumer demand. The economy as a whole is viewed from the side of demand, from the standpoint of consumption and exchange. For its part, exchange is viewed exclusively from the standpoint of use values, of goods rather than, as in Marx, of commodities. Simmel himself was aware of the relativist implications of a totally subjective theory of value. In 1898, while working on his *Philosophy of Money*, Simmel complained to Rickert that

> the concept of value seems to me to not only contain the same kind of *regressus in infinitum* as does that of causality but also contains a *circulus vitiosus* because, if one follows through the connections far enough, one always finds that the value of A is based on that of B, or that of B is only based on that of A . . . I see no end to the difficulties since, in any case, I am convinced of the fact that I can only maintain my relativism if it is capable, as it were, of solving all the problems which are presented by theories of absolutism.[30]

Some of Simmel's contemporaries, such as Kracauer, recognised in the work as a whole 'a theoretically grounded relativism'. Clearly the theory of value espoused by Simmel was its fundamental presupposition.

Yet in examining the economic presuppositions advanced by Simmel, we need to examine the process of exchange since value and exchange 'are mutually conditioning' and are both equally 'the basis of practical life' and since the economy itself is 'a special case of the general form of exchange'.[31] Nor does the significance of exchange end there since, as we have seen, it is central to his notion of social interaction and society. In short, it is 'a sociological phenomenon *sui generis*'. Indeed, in the first half of *The Philosophy of Money*, money is taken to be a symbol for one form of social life, namely, exchange.

But what kind of an economy does Simmel postulate within which the exchange process takes place? As one recent commentator points out, 'Simmel still postulated the concept of exchange for a "solipsistic economy as it were", that is, one in which the isolated person does not confront other persons but directly confronts nature'.[32] Indeed it is

not merely exchange that is conceived in this way; Simmel also speaks
of 'the exchange with nature which we call production'.[33] Fully in
keeping with this limited conception of production, which totally
ignores the *social* nature of the production process, we find Simmel
arguing that 'exchange is just as productive and value-creating as is
production itself'.[34] Furthermore, the exchange process is seen as the
same in a subsistence and a market economy. All this is possible because Simmel operates with a totally subjective notion of exchange
and the economy. Hence, *'it is of great importance to reduce the economic process to what really happens in the mind of each economic
subject.'*[35] Having done this, there is no difference between the exchange of goods or land and the exchange of labour power for money
wages. All involve the same 'subjective process of sacrifice and gain in
the individual mind'.[36] It is not surprising, therefore, that at the close
of the analytical part of his study Simmel should concern himself with
the psychological consequences of money transactions. Nor is it surprising that economic objects are viewed entirely from a subjective
standpoint as when Simmel maintains that 'economic objects have no
significance except directly or indirectly in our consumption and in the
exchange that occurs between them'[37] and that 'the economic form of
value lies between two limits' — demand and consumption. In short,
'exchange, i.e. the economy, is the source of economic values'.[38] In
other words, exchange and not production is the central feature of
any economy.

Having briefly examined some of Simmel's presuppositions with
regard to the economy within which money transactions assume their
significance (i.e. exchange in the economy), it is fruitful to investigate
the relationship between exchange and society as a whole. We have
already seen that Simmel characterises exchange as 'a sociological
phenomenon *sui generis*'. It is also 'the purest and most developed
kind of interaction which shapes human life'.[39] Social interaction *is*,
in fact, exchange insofar as 'every interaction has to be regarded as an
exchange'. But both social interaction and exchange are also constitutive for Simmel's conception of society. In a crucial passage, Simmel
writes that

> society is a structure that transcends the individual, but that is not
> abstract. Historical life thus escapes the alternative of taking place
> either in individuals or in abstract generalities. Society is the uni-
> versal which, at the same time, is concretely alive. From this arises
> the unique significance that exchange, as the economic—historical
> realisation of the relativity of things, has for society; exchange raises

the specific object and its significance for the individual above its singularity, not into the sphere of abstraction, but into that of lively interaction which is the substance of economic value.[40]

The universality of exchange relationships or ceaseless reciprocal interaction avoids both the hypostatisation of society and a simple atomistic conception of society as a mere sum of individuals. Whereas for Marx, production relations might be seen as central, for Simmel it is exchange relations in the widest sense that are constitutive for society. But each relationship is relative to all the others and none has priority. This is ultimately what would distinguish Simmel's conception of society from that of Marx when he wrote: 'What is society, whatever its form may be? The product of people's reciprocal action'.[41] Taken out of context, it is a remarkable Simmelian formulation.

Where does money fit into Simmel's conception of exchange and society? Simmel argues that 'the interaction between individuals is the starting point of all social formations'.[42] Money is *the* symbolic object of this interaction, 'For money represents pure interaction in its purest form; it makes comprehensible the most abstract concept; it is an individual thing whose essential significance is to reach beyond individualities.'[43] Formulated differently, money 'is nothing but the pure form of exchangeability'. As such it is a 'supra-individual formation', one of the 'reified social functions'. What this implies is that

> The function of exchange, as a direct interaction between individuals, becomes crystallised in the form of money as an independent structure . . . exchange . . . is obviously one of the purest and most primitive forms of human socialisation . . . exchange is one of the functions that creates an inner bond between people – a society, in place of a mere collection of individuals . . . exchange is a form of socialisation. It is one of those relations through which a number of individuals become a social group, and 'society' is identical with the sum total of these relations.[44]

Within the context of the exchange relationship, 'money is the reified function of being exchanged' and as such achieves a quasi-autonomy from those performing the exchange. What this implies, in turn, for a theory of reification is that it is universal in money economies. There is no sense of the historical specificity of the reification process.

In summarising some of the essential features of Simmel's theory of exchange and the role of money, it is already possible to see the advantage of this particular object of study for someone who sees both individuals and history as composed of fragments. Given that Simmel argues that 'we are all fragments' and maintains that the past 'comes down to us only in fragments', he requires some mode of analysis that enables him to transcend 'the single elements'. Its basis is provided by a conception of society as rooted in exchange and ceaseless mutual interaction. It requires, as Simmel himself points out, a relativist theory of truth that 'makes possible a final uniformity of interpretation with reference to the variety of things, and which provides a general context for the interpretation of economic value'.[45] In other words, 'The finiteness of existence is only transcended through the conditioning of every content of being by another content, which in turn is equally conditioned — either by a third factor which undergoes the same process or by an interaction of the two'.[46] Again, Simmel himself later admitted taking up this mutual interaction and 'comprehensive metaphysical principle'.

The advantage of taking money as the object of study might be substantiated within this context. Money symbolises interaction in abstraction and 'represents pure interaction in its pure form'. Every interaction is an exchange which is itself 'the purest sociological occurrence, the most complete form of interaction'.[47] Social interaction is also the basis of society and exchange is a form of socialisation into society. Simmel's most successful analyses in *The Philosophy of Money* are of the psychological consequences of money transactions and the effects of money — the quantification of the qualitative, the reduction of qualities to indifference — upon human relationships. The exchange process is at the very heart of both his concept of the economy and, more widely, social interaction and society itself. Money symbolises this exchange process as infinite interaction only if we remain within the exchange process. Simmel, unlike Marx, is not concerned with money as capital and is not particularly preoccupied with the exchange that takes place between capital and labour. Indeed, faced with Marx's labour theory of value — which Simmel argues, 'is, at least philosophically, the most interesting theory' of value — he felt compelled to devote some considerable space for an attack upon it. Marx, however, is not merely concerned with the exchange process under capitalism but with its production process. This cannot be a central feature of Simmel's analysis since he sees value as created in exchange and not in production. Hence, in what seems to be the most 'Marxist' of Simmel's analyses, namely the consequences of the division of labour and the attendant alienation and fragmentation of its human agents, the whole discussion is placed within the context of a theory of cultural alienation of which the production process is merely an 'example'. Indeed, in keeping with our earlier interpretation of Simmel's work, it is at least plausible to argue that the very act of viewing economy and society as based on exchange itself involves an aestheticisation of reality and a distance from it since if we merely concentrate our attention upon this aspect we can never discover how value, commodities, etc. are produced.

There are, in fact, other important implications of Simmel's theory of money and exchange that clearly differentiate it from Marx's account. The absence of a historically specific account of the development of particular forms of exchange-economy, especially the capitalist form, gives a natural character to the economy and society which effectively destroys any basis for a critique of society. Human agents confront nature as an objective process. Even where he describes the alienating effects of a specific form of the division of labour — which he does not recognise as historically specific — 'Simmel makes the development of alienation independent of social relations: the victims of alienation confront only an objective process'.[48] Within the labour process, the workforce does not confront a social class that stands in opposition to them. The relationship between the capitalist division of labour and social class formation is not an object of Simmel's analysis, as it is, for instance, in Schmoller's account.

The ahistorical nature of Simmel's analysis of the money economy was noted by Mannheim when he wrote that

> Simmel in particular has characterised in many ways the empirically changing objects of the world that are associated with money forms . . . yet in so doing he has abstracted, in a completely unhistorical manner, the capitalistic money form from its capitalistic background and imputed the characteristic structural change to 'money as such'.[49]

Similarly, like Weber and Sombart, Simmel also spoke of the progressive rationalisation of the world yet overlooked 'that money calculation also existed earlier but that it is precisely in modern capitalism and only here that the category of the commodity becomes a universal category which structures the whole world view'.[50]

Instead, society as such is seen to rest upon exchange relations, regardless of their historical specificity. Hence, the preconditions for the exchange relationship itself also become the preconditions for the continuation of society, whatever its distinctive historical form. For instance, Simmel maintains that

> Without the general trust that people have in each other, society itself would disintegrate, for very few relationships are based entirely upon what is known with certainty about another person, and very few relationships would endure if trust were not as strong as, or stronger than, rational proof or personal observation.[51]

Yet it would be difficult, for example, to conceive of the wage labour—
capital relationship as based upon 'trust'. But in Simmel's account this
is merely one of many exchange relations that are, ultimately, accorded
equal status within the totality of the exchange process.

Again, it is important for Simmel to confront Marx's labour theory
of value in order to maintain his own theory of the centrality of exchange and a subjective theory of value. Yet if we turn to Simmel's
critique — which is located somewhat uneasily at the end of the fifth
chapter of *The Philosophy of Money* instead of within the second
where Simmel expounds his own theory of value[52] — we find that, in
many respects, it fails to come to terms with Marx's theory. Simmel
wrongly describes Marx's theory of money as a theory of labour money,
which Marx specifically rejects both in *Capital* and, more fully, in
A Contribution to the Critique of Political Economy. His own argument on value obfuscates the distinction between use and exchange
value with respect to labour power and, by implication, removes any
possibility of discussing commodity exchange rather than the exchange
of goods in a historically concrete manner. As Brinkmann argues,

> Simmel uses two concepts of value in an undifferentiated manner:
> on the one hand, his concept of value which . . . is orientated towards
> that of each individual valuation of an object . . . on the other,
> however, Marx's concept of value which commences from abstract
> labour.[53]

Hence, Simmel's critique centres around a number of examples of
concrete labour without again confronting Marx's distinction between
labour and labour power, between concrete and abstract labour.

Perhaps most significant of all, Simmel emphasises the genuine
problems of the distinction between mental and manual labour, between complex and simple labour, within a labour theory of value.
This was already the subject of some discussion at the time of writing.
But what is interesting in this context is that the major purpose of
highlighting this distinction is to preserve the freedom of the intellect
by asserting that mental labour is free. The socialist ideal would, Simmel argues, 'declare economic interests to be the source and common
denominator of all others'.[54] That common denominator involves the
reduction of complex to simple labour, the quantification of the
qualitative and reveals 'its crude and plebeian character'. The hierarchy
of value that lies behind Simmel's argument is expressed more poetically
in one of his 'Snapshots *sub specie aeternitatis*' entitled 'Money alone
does not make one happy' (1901). There he maintains that

Whatever we need to own, in order to enjoy, sooner or later we destroy through ownership: roast meat and wine, a garment and everything that we sensuously enjoy. But intellectual things and what possesses its value in this form — these stand over and above the question of possession and non-possession . . . The irremovable dividing line between plebeian and aristocratic values is that we can in fact possess the one without it making us happy and that the other makes us happy without us possessing it.[55]

The instance which Simmel provides in this context is one of Böcklin's landscapes. It points once more to the preservation of an autonomous aesthetic realm.

Yet despite the obvious wide differences between Simmel's and Marx's accounts of both economy and society, this did not prevent some Marxist writers coming to Marx through Simmel (Lukács) or being impressed by many of his analyses (Benjamin). The paradox of *The Philosophy of Money* is that *if*, especially in its later chapters, it is read as a phenomenology of commodity exchange in a capitalist society then it is possible to see it as a contemporary reviewer (Gold-scheid) viewed it: 'like a translation of Marx's economic discussion into the language of psychology'. Some of the fragments and 'snap-shots' within it and those written around the turn of the century then seem to prefigure subsequent Marxist analyses such as those of Benjamin. It is to Simmel's analyses and 'snapshots' of commodity exchange, money transactions and their consequences that we now turn.

IV

It has already been remarked that Simmel's work very seldom contains reference to or, still less, analysis of contemporary social events. This is also true of *The Philosophy of Money*. Yet in 1896 Simmel wrote a brief article on 'The Berlin Trade Exhibition'[56] of that year which provides a 'snapshot', as it were, of his response to one contemporary event, one that bears directly on the themes taken up subsequently in his *Philosophy of Money*. Masur argues that 'these who visited the *Gewerbeaustellung* of 1896 were overwhelmed by this demonstration of Germany's industrial potential, and the beginnings of Berlin's exist-ence as a world city date from this event'.[57] What was Simmel's response?

Simmel views the world exhibition as an instance of the duality of society in the following manner:

The dual meaning of 'society' expresses symbolically how much the enjoyment of socialising at least accompanies this sociation as a by-product, how it forms the resting point of the most heterogeneous interest groups and thus remains a binding force when the actual grounds and appeal of unification have lost their effectiveness. In the history of world exhibitions . . . the unavoidability of this fundamental type of all human sociation emerges most clearly.[58]

Instead of divergent interests, diverse products are exhibited in the social context of a form of amusement, almost as a form of sociability. But it is a distinctive form of amusement insofar as

The close proximity within which the most heterogeneous industrial products are confined produces a paralysis of the capacity for perception, a true hypnosis . . . in its fragmentation of weak impressions there remains in the memory the notion that one should be amused here.[59]

This is reinforced by a seemingly minor social arrangement in which at each stage of passing through the exhibition a small entrance fee is charged. In this way

curiosity is always aroused anew, each individual enjoyment appears more momentous and more accentuated as a result of the expenditure paid out for it; the many things that one must pass by arouses the impression that here still many more surprises and pleasures remain stored up. In short, the shading off of the guiding motif — amusement — is basically reached through these small restrictions that can only be overcome by means of a small sacrifice.[60]

It is, Simmel continues, as if paying a higher, once-only entrance fee would make everything appear the same, whereas our sense of enjoyment is heightened by each smaller payment.

Simmel points to the powerful effect upon the senses that this bewildering array of commodities had — what Benjamin later described as 'the enthronement of the commodity and the glitter of distraction around it'.[61] Our senses feel 'overpowered' and 'deranged'. On the other hand, 'precisely this wealth and colourfulness of over-hastened impressions is appropriate to over-excited and exhausted nerves' need for stimulation'. This wealth of products is derived from 'constantly increasing specialisation and ever greater one-sidedness of activities'. Yet

it seems as if the modern person wishes to compensate for the one-sidedness and uniformity of their product within the division of labour by the growing crowding together of heterogeneous impressions, by the increasingly hasty and colourful change in emotions.

The differentiation of the active spheres of life evidently comple-
ment one another through the comprehensive diversity of their
passive and receptive spheres.[62]

This need to compensate for uniformity and one-sidedness in production by diversity in consumption finds its high point in major exhibitions
that, despite the apparent 'average superficiality' of diverse impressions,
do perform this function.

Simmel is in no doubt that the 1896 exhibition of Berlin products
makes clear 'what a "world city" signifies and that, despite everything,
Berlin is one'. But what really interests him is the aesthetic dimension
of such an exhibition. The architecture of these exhibitions is 'a creation
for transitoriness', a 'conscious negation of the monumental style'. Thus,

> With regard to the architectural dimension, this exhibition perhaps
> signifies the focal point of that which the principle of exhibiting
> has so far achieved in aesthetic productivity. With regard to the
> other dimension of its fruitfulness, it stands, at least, relatively high:
> I mean the increase in what one might term the shop-window
> quality of things that is evoked by exhibitions. Commodity pro-
> duction dominated by free competition, together with the average
> preponderance of supply over demand must lead to a situation of
> giving things an enticing external appearance over and above their
> usefulness . . . one must attempt to excite the interest of the buyer
> by means of the external attraction of the object, even indeed by
> means of the form of its arrangement.[63]

In other words, it is necessary to extract 'the most charm from what
has least charm'. This Simmel conceives as an 'aesthetic superadditum'
which, with regard to commodities, seeks 'to give new aesthetic significance through the arrangement of their coming together – just as
the common advertisement has advanced to the art of posters'. Simmel
hopes that this 'aesthetic impulse will be developed further'.

Finally, Simmel sees the world of commodities in the exhibition as
mirroring the relation of the individual to society insofar as

> the individual object within an exhibition displays the same relation-
> ships and modifications as exist, characteristically, for the individual
> within society: on the one hand, subjugation by one's neighbour with
> different qualifications, on the other, differentiation at the latter's
> expense; on the one hand, levelling and rendering indifferent
> through identical environment, on the other, the elevation which it
> and the individual experience precisely through the totality of im-
> pressions; on the one hand, the individual is merely the element of
> a whole, merely the member of a higher unity, on the other, it none-
> theless advances the claim to be itself a whole and a unity.[64]

These interactions which take place in society, exist in the exhibition of commodities as aesthetic dimensions.

Simmel's analysis of the Berlin trade exhibition is significant for a number of reasons. It anticipates some of his central concerns in *The Philosophy of Money*, especially when dealing with the consequences of money transactions. It can be read as an analysis of 'the fetish commodity' in that it anticipates some of Benjamin's comments on world exhibitions which he saw as glorifying

> the exchange value of commodities. They created a framework in which their use-value receded into the background. They opened up a phantasmagoria into which people entered in order to be distracted. The entertainment industry made that easier for them by lifting them to the level of the commodity. They yielded to its manipulations while enjoying their alienation from themselves and from others.[65]

But the article also illustrates the extent to which Simmel's concern was largely with exchange and circulation of commodities within the context of which money can be seen as its most significant symbol. Similarly, if we look for economic analyses around the period of the first and second editions of *The Philosophy of Money* we find that they are confined to exchange and consumption. As well as the article on the Berlin trade exhibition, there is 'On the psychology of fashion' (1895), 'The sociology of competition' (1903), *The Philosophy of Fashion* (1905) and 'The problem of style' (1908).[66] Most of them are anticipations and developments of the central themes of the synthetic part of *The Philosophy of Money*.

What are its central themes? Lieber has argued that the first part of the book is devoted 'to the aim of demonstrating money to be symbol for *one* form of social life, *one* social life form: exchange', whereas the second part is concerned with how

> money transactions and exchange as such determines, in the sense of both a presupposition and as a consequence, the social unity of the opposites of buyer and seller; thus, money is the symbol for the social identity of diversity and contradiction.[67]

But since, as we have seen, society is unified through exchange and continuous interaction, 'the antagonisms of the modern capitalist money economy can also, for him, exist as the mere phenomenon of deeper forms of identity or even the unity of society without him having to deny this contradiction'.[68]

Even where Simmel comes closest to a critique of this economy in his examination of the consequences of the division of labour, the whole thrust of his argument is located within the 'deeper forms' of antagonism between subjective and objective culture. Nonetheless, it is worth looking at in some detail since it has prompted some commentators to maintain that

> in *The Philosophy of Money* at least, the power of the analysis lies precisely in the constant return of the argument to the process of industrial production. In this context, Simmel rediscovered major moments of Marx's theory of alienation that most interpreters (except Lukács in 1923) associated with Marx only after the discovery of the 1844 *Paris Manuscripts.*[69]

Yet any affinity between Simmel's analysis here and that of Marx need not rest upon his reading of Marx. Without in any way detracting from Simmel's originality, many strands of his analysis elsewhere can be traced back to some of his contemporaries such as Tönnies on rationality or Knapp on agricultural workers.

On the other hand, in the last chapter of *The Philosophy of Money* Simmel does draw a remarkable picture of alienation within the division of labour 'in terms of its importance within production as well as consumption'. The processes of fragmentation, atomisation, objectification, reification and standardisation are all dealt with as consequences of the division of labour that produces such consequences. It is 'modern' but not always explicitly capitalist. Elsewhere, for instance, the development of free wage labour is seen to be a consequence of the money economy as such. Whereas Marx speaks of the sale of labour power to capital, Simmel refers to a situation where 'the labour contract emerges as the purchase of labour as a commodity — and *this is the final result of the money economy'.*[70] Similarly, he points to the irrelevance of the individual personality in money transactions which we enter into in order to buy or sell particular one-sided qualities and activities. We become more dependent upon people's achievements and less upon their personalities. Both derive from

> one and the same process: the modern division of labour permits the number of dependencies to increase just as it causes personalities to disappear behind their functions. . . . The form of social life that would evolve were this tendency to be completely realised would exhibit a profound affinity to socialism, at least to an extreme state socialism. For socialism is concerned primarily with transforming to an extreme degree every action of social importance into an objective function.[71]

Stated in this manner, this particular result of the division of labour can occur in capitalist or socialist economies — the latter merely extending tendencies already in existence in the former. Both have their origin in 'the conditions of a money economy'. The aim of socialism becomes merely a technical one, an extension of processes already inherent in the reduction of qualities to quantities in the money economy. It aims at 'the elimination of all that is fortuitous and at an organisation . . . that makes all elements of life calculable.'[72] As such it is merely an extension of 'the calculating character of modern times', of 'the calculating intellectuality' that is embodied in more and more forms of life.

This 'calculating intellectuality', as an objectification of the mind and objective culture in general, expands in modern society at the expense of individual subjective culture. Its cause is the division of labour. Simmel analyses several of its dimensions. First, the specialised division of labour ensures that a 'product is completed at the expense of the development of the producer. The increase in psycho-physical energies and skills, which is the result of specialised activity, is of little value for the total personality, which often even becomes stunted.'[73] Secondly, the product becomes divorced from its producer insofar as

> the inadequacy that develops between the worker's existential form and that of his product because of greater specialisation easily serves to completely divorce the product from the labourer. Its meaning is not derived from the mind of the producer but from its relationship with products of a different origin. Because of its fragmentary character, the product lacks the spiritual determinacy that can be easily perceived in a product of labour that is wholly the work of a *single* person.[74]

Fully in keeping with Simmel's strong aesthetic sense, he contrasts this situation with the work of art which is 'the most perfectly autonomous unity, a self-sufficient totality' that 'requires only one *single* person, but it requires him totally'. In the case of the product of an advanced division of labour, however, which only serves a greater whole, 'the more objective is that whole and the more is its life independent of the subjects who produced it'.

This is reinforced by 'the separation of the worker from the means of production' since

> In that it is the function of the capitalist to acquire, organise and allocate the means of production, these means acquire a very different objectivity for the worker than for those who work with their own material and their own tools. . . . In so far as work itself and its direct object belong to *different* persons, the objective character of

these objects must loom extremely large in the worker's conscious-ness. . . . This process is continued and reflected in the fact that, in addition to the means of production, work itself is separated from the worker. This is the significance of the phenomenon indicated in the statement that labour power has become a commodity.[75]

Yet when Simmel goes on to point out the significance of this state-ment, he reduces it to an instance of a more universal process. Hence, Simmel maintains that

The fact that labour now shares the same character, mode of evalu-ation and fate with all other commodities signifies that work has become something objectively separate from the worker, something that he not only no longer *is*, but also no longer *has*. . . . The process by which labour becomes a commodity is . . . only one side of the far-reaching process of differentiation by which specific contents of the personality are detached in order for them to confront the personality as objects with an independent character and dynamics.[76]

Hence, the reduction of labour power to a commodity does not have any special significance for Simmel. It is part of the wider 'process of differentiation' brought about by the money economy and an instance of the separation of objective from subjective culture.

This process is also manifested in the product itself since 'the product of labour in the capitalist era is an object with a decidedly autonomous character, with its own laws of motion and a character alien to the producing subject'. The division of labour 'endows the product with objective independence' and has consequences for both producers and consumers. The independence of the product 'is most forcefully illu-strated where the worker is compelled to *buy* his own product'. For the consumer, the disappearance of personal custom work means that 'the subjective aura of the product also disappears in relation to the con-sumer because the commodity is now produced independently of him'.[77] It is, incidentally, one of the central aspects of Benjamin's analysis of both the work of art and the commodity that is hinted at here without being developed.

Simmel also maintains that the 'autonomy of production with reference to the consumer' is associated with another consequence of the division of labour, namely, the inversion of the social structure within production. Simmel argues that

the techniques of production are so specialised that the handling of its different parts is transferred . . . to increasingly more diverse people until the point is reached at which one part of the work on the humblest necessities is performed by individuals of the highest rank. Conversely, the subdivision of work by machine technology brings about a situation in which the roughest hands collaborate in the production of the most sophisticated products.[78]

From this tendency within modern production, Simmel draws the remarkable conclusion that

> This inversion of the typical relationship between the upper and lower strata of society indicates most clearly that *the division of labour causes the upper strata to work for the lower strata*. The only form, however, in which this may occur is through the complete objectification of the productive process itself in relation to both groups. This inversion is nothing other than a final consequence of the relationship that exists between the division of labour and the objectification of culture.[79]

The fact that both the upper and lower strata to which Simmel refers stand in the same relationship to the means of production does not appear significant. Rather, what interests Simmel is, once more, the extent to which a particular aspect of the division of labour is a manifestation of 'the objectification of culture'.

Yet it is not merely the specialisation of individuals with the division of labour that is of concern to Simmel. Rather,

> the specialisation of objects themselves contributes no less to the process of their alienation from human subjects, which appears as an independence of the object, as the individual's inability to assimilate it and subject the object to his or her rhythm. In the first place, this is true of the means of production. The more differentiated these means are, the more they are composed of a multitude of specialised parts, the less is the worker able to express his personality through them, and the less visible is his personal contribution to the product.[80]

This reaches its extreme in 'the automatic character of modern machinery' where the specialisation is 'akin to the character of a highly developed state administration which can evolve only on the basis of an elaborate division of labour among its functionaries'. Similarly, the machine too 'confronts the worker as an autonomous power'. In earlier processes of production, 'the undifferentiated tool is merely a prolongation of the arm', whereas 'the specialised tool is elevated to the pure category of an object'.

In many respects, this remarkable analysis of the consequences of the modern division of labour, more detailed and accurate in many respects than Durkheim's, seems to echo much of Marx's discussion in the central chapters of *Capital*, volume one. It appears all the more remarkable in view of the fact that in the previous chapter, Simmel had devoted a whole section to the critique of the labour theory of value. But what is significant is not merely the extent to which Simmel's analysis diverges from that of Marx but the context within which this whole discussion is set. The discussion both prior and subsequent to the analysis of the consequences of the division of labour explicitly concerns 'the process of objectification of culture'. Taken out of context, it is easy to see how it is possible to draw affinities between Simmel's and Marx's accounts. But it would lose sight of the fact that Simmel's study is of the transformation of social relationships and sentiments brought about by a money economy and not by a capitalist system of commodity production.

Indeed, in this last chapter of *The Philosophy of Money* within which the analysis of the consequences of the division of labour is presented, Simmel's concern, as its title suggests, is with 'the style of life'. Simmel sees the process of alienation from our environment as encroaching upon our everyday life. Even the objects that surround us in our homes – furniture, utensils etc. – have become specialised objects to which we have no genuine attachment as in earlier decades. This 'sense of being oppressed by the externalities of modern life is not only the consequence but also the cause of the fact that they confront us as autonomous objects', as a result of 'their impersonal origin and easy replaceability'. This separation of objects from people brought about by the impersonal commodity exchange of the money economy reaches its peak in the slot machine 'since by means of the vending machine the human relationship is completely eliminated even in the retail trade . . . The money equivalent is now exchanged against the commodity by a mechanical device'. This is also true of 'the five cent store . . . where the psycho-economic process runs not from the commodity to the price, but from the price to the commodity.'[81]

Even in those situations where the individual attempts to stamp the commodity with his or her individual personality, the consequences are quite ambiguous. As instances we may cite Simmel's discussions of fashion and style. In the case of fashion, it is

> one of those social forms which combines, to a particular degree, the attraction of differentiation and change with that of similarity and conformity . . . the spreading of fashion, both in breadth as well as speed, appears to be an independent movement, an objective and autonomous force which follows its own course independently of the individual.[82]

Fashion expresses both differentiation and communality. Earlier, in his 'On the psychology of fashion' (1895), Simmel saw fashion as a phenomenon that in terms of this opposition 'embodies that of socialism and individualism', 'a compromise between the tendency towards social equalisation and the impulse towards individual destruction'. But today the speed of change in fashion has meant that 'it becomes less dependent upon fashion. Both develop like separate evolutionary worlds'.

The speed of change in fashions is paralleled by 'the bewildering plurality of styles that are absorbed, presented and appreciated by our culture'. Again, Simmel argues that where the individual was surrounded by a single style over a period of time, this style was seen 'as being identical with its *contents*'.[83] It was, in other words, a part of the individual self. But where there are a plurality of styles, they suffer the same fate as products themselves since

> Through the differentiation of styles each individual style, and thus style in general, becomes something objective whose validity is independent of human subjects . . . the entire visible environment of our cultural life has disintegrated into a plurality of styles.[84]

Style and fashion are merely instances of 'all these phenomena, in which the cultural content becomes an increasingly conscious *objective mind* in relation not only to recipients but also to producers'.

In a later article on 'The problem of style' (1908),[85] Simmel examines the extent to which an attempt is made to preserve individuality within the bourgeois *intérieur*. These individuals seek to impress their own personality upon their home surroundings whose distinctive style 'is based upon one and only one especially distinctive personality'. Rooms are filled with objects through which individuals seek to express their personality. At the same time, however, these objects also belong to a particular style: they are already formed in a specific manner. In this way

> a supra-individual form and law is produced between the subjective personality and their human and objective environment; the stylised manifestation, form of life, taste — all these are limits, forms of distance in which the exaggerated subjectivism of the times finds a counterbalance and a cloak.[86]

Within their individual homes 'the person is the main object, the point as it were' around which objects are arranged and 'of all the objects we use it is in fact furniture that most thoroughly bears the cachet of some kind of "style" '.[87]

Elsewhere in *The Philosophy of Money*, Simmel maintains that 'the material contents of life become increasingly objective and impersonal, so that the remainder that cannot be reified becomes all the more personal, all the more the indisputable property of the self'. Within the *intérieur* there is a 'flight from the present'[88] a withdrawal of contact from the world which seeks refuge in the 'vividly felt charm of the fragment' away from 'the bustle and excitement of modern life'. This is in conscious opposition to our having become

> entangled in the instability and helplessness that manifests itself as the tumult of the metropolis, as the mania for travelling, as the wild pursuit of competition and as the typically modern disloyalty with regard to taste, style, opinions and personal relationships.[89]

All these dimensions of modern life are seen by Simmel as having either originated in or having been accentuated by the universalisation of money relationships.

But the pathos and sometimes melancholy that is expressed in Simmel's account of the retreat from objective culture would suggest that he was aware that it was not a satisfactory solution. He might have agreed with Benjamin's comments on the interior to the effect that the private citizen created in his living space an area separate from work in order

> that it should support him in his illusions. This necessity was all the more pressing since he had no intention of adding social preoccupations to his business ones. In the creation of his private environment he suppressed them both . . . This represented the universe for the private citizen. In it he assembled the distant in space and in time. His drawing room was a box in the world-theatre.[90]

Indeed, Simmel's notion of the inevitable tragedy of culture which is the context within which this whole discussion is set, would lend support to the view that he was aware of the seemingly paradoxical connection between interiority and society. As Adorno states it,

> The notion of intérieur is only apparently paradoxical. Inwardness exists as the confinement of human existence in a private sphere, which should be able to transcend the power of reification. However, as a private sphere it does itself belong, even though polemically, to the social structure.[91]

The retreat to an individual moral law and, later, to an early form of existentialism does not resolve this contradiction. Having established a tragedy of human culture, Simmel is left trapped within it.

V

It would be impossible to do justice to the wealth of insights that Simmel provides on the consequences of the extension of money relationships to all spheres of life. The preceding extraction of one of his central themes hardly begins to grasp the myriad connections that Simmel establishes between money payments and individual freedom, money's reduction of a whole range of social relationships to a near total indifference, money's transformation of female roles and its role in human alienation. At almost every level, Simmel is preoccupied by the paradoxical nature of money's functions; levelling differences or accentuating them; creating greater individual freedom or reducing it, and so on. He is also concerned to rescue fragments of interaction and social relationships from the flux of ceaseless interaction. This is especially important in an analysis of money relationships since there exists

> no more striking symbols of the completely dynamic character of the world than that of money. . . . Money is . . . an *actus purus*; it lives in continuous self-alienation from any given point and thus forms the counterpart and direct negation of all being in itself.[92]

Simmel's examples, his 'snapshots' are taken out of this dynamic process. They do not, as Kracauer pointed out 'live in historical time'. Rather they are rendered eternal as instances of forms of interaction.

Yet this ceaseless network of interactions, especially within the context of money relationships, did secure for Simmel an instance of the fundamental interrelatedness of phenomena without having to resort to a reified concept of a system of totality. Simmel could start out from any example, any fragment in order to establish its connection with a wider totality. In the case of money, it symbolises 'the relativistic character of existence' in which everything is related to everything else. The totality of relations is not constituted by a real historical totality but by aesthetic connections. Towards the end of *The Philosophy of Money*, Simmel reasserts the aesthetic ideal that justifies his preoccupation with fragments, with snapshots *sub specie aeternitatis*:

> The totality of the whole . . . stands in eternal conflict with the totality of the individual. The aesthetic expression of this struggle is particularly impressive because the charm of beauty is always embedded in a whole, no matter whether it has immediate distinctiveness or a distinctiveness that is supplemented by fantasy as in the case of a fragment. The essential meaning of art lies in its being able

to form an autonomous totality, a self-sufficient microcosm out of a fortuitous fragment of reality that is tied with a thousand threads to this reality. The typical conflict between the individual and supra-individual existence can be interpreted as the irreconcilable striving of both elements to attain an aesthetically satisfying expression.[93]

5 'A Philosophy of the Times'?

Around the turn of the century, we all certainly experienced the way in which the socio-economic interest of the period was elevated into the aesthetic interest.

Karl Joël

Simmel's philosophy of life (like that of Bergson too) is a philosophy from the perspective of a frog, a world view from below instead of from above. If all objective forms do emerge out of the mere movement of life, what then decides upon the value of these forms?

Siegfried Kracauer

I

Many of his contemporaries testified to the fact that Simmel, like few other writers of his period, captured 'the spirit of the times' and possessed a profound understanding of the nature of the society in which he lived. In his review of Simmel's *Philosophy of Money* entitled 'A philosophy of the times',[1] his friend and colleague Karl Joël maintained that the book was 'bound to a single place and a single period' and yet, at the same time, 'projected the soul of modern Berlin onto a universal level'. He characterised the period as one dominated by money which

> dumbfounds everything into mere nuances of its own impure colour, and we live without doubt in the age of giving nuances to everything, of transitions and relativities, of the transcendence of all contradictions under the domination of money that is without determination and yet determines everything. It is the age of percentages and units, of degrees and numbers, of majorities, of paragraphs, of minutes, of scales and measures . . . it is the age in which qualities die out in quantities.[2]

Another friend of Simmel's, the dramatist Paul Ernst, in a review of the same book, asserts that it is concerned with the basic question of the times: 'as to how far today, when we genuinely struggle with ultimate questions, we must always come up against the relativist answer. In other words, Simmel allows sociology to investigate the ultimate motive of the thought of our times.'[3] Similarly, Simmel's student Siegfried Kracauer maintained that 'the essence of the epoch announced itself in his philosophy' and that Simmel was 'the philosopher of West European civilisation in the period of its highest maturity'.[4] Another suggests that, at the turn of the century, Berlin University students 'went above all to Georg Simmel. They scented the instinct for the times which he brought with him; and because they needed an interpretation of the times from the modern perspective [*Zeitdeutung vom Modernen aus*] they went to him.'[5] Yet another contemporary suggested that Simmel was 'the only genuine philosopher of his time, the true expression of its fragmented spirit'.[6]

If there is little doubt that Simmel responded with 'seismographic accuracy' (Gadamer) to some of the key intellectual movements of his time – and Gadamer had in mind his reciprocal relationship to the George circle and the revolt against industrialisation[7] – and if he provides us with a bewildering array of analyses of contemporary social situations and contexts, then we need to ask what form his 'instinct for the times' took. Even on the basis of the preceding discussion of his work, it cannot mean that Simmel provides us with a wealth of concrete, empirical analyses of Wilhelman Germany. Simmel did not stand in the same relationship to his society as, say, Max Weber who not only presents us with contemporary analyses of aspects of German society but also pronounces with some confidence upon the issues of the day.[8] Simmel did write upon a number of contemporary social issues but what contribution he did make is seldom explicitly incorporated into his major works.

From the manner in which his contemporaries expressed the understanding Simmel had for his times it seems clear that what they have in mind is the fact that he captured a particular way of looking at the world, a mode of experiencing the world which they either shared or were sympathetic towards. Insofar as Simmel was attempting a phenomenology of social life, its historical dimension is that of the here and now. It is a version of applied phenomenology that is concerned with the description of modes of experiencing the world without recourse to their historical foundations. It becomes a philosophical 'attitude' towards the world that is shared by a specific strata of German society. It is not a concrete historical analysis of that society.

More specifically, if we look in Simmel's work for a critique of modern social and economic formations then what is striking is the extent to which this is transposed into a critique of culture. Writing in 1914, shortly after the outbreak of the First World War, Simmel looks back over the changes that had taken place in Germany since the *Gründerjahre* around 1870. He detects the emergence of a new intellectual movement, even a new strata from around 1880 onwards — presumably the generation that flocked to his lectures at the turn of the century. This was the generation

> upon whom Nietzsche and socialism had their effect, naturalism and the new appreciation of romanticism, Richard Wagner and the technology of modern work, the resurgence of metaphysics and religiosity and the specifically modern aesthetics of the style of life drawn together out of objectification and intellectualisation.[9]

In other words, it was a generation responding to the fundamental contradictions, as Simmel saw them, in German society, contradictions that were transposed onto a cultural plane. With the unleashing of Germany's 'immeasurable economic potentialities' after 1870

> our life suffered — to emphasise one point as being symbolic for many others — under the contradictions of a materialistic and an aestheticising direction. Perhaps materialism was at first the unavoidable shadow over this economic upswing — which then, as its no less extreme counterblow, called forth the pale, overrefinement of the aesthetes.[10]

Though Simmel might retrospectively see his own work as responding to this contradiction, it is evident that his own position was strongly opposed to materialism — even though he could discuss the material consequences of the division of labour in his *Philosophy of Money* — and in favour of an aestheticisation of reality.

Simmel's aesthetic stance has already been examined in relation to his approach to sociology. It had its roots, as we have seen, in a specific social setting. As Becher maintains,

> Simmel often characterised himself as a 'fin-de-sièclist'. He belonged to the Berlin upper bourgeoisie, whose 'customs' he knew and made his own. Typical of this highly civilised life . . . are the aesthetic circles in the 'salon' of the drawing room. . . . At the same time . . . Simmel's alert, critical mind not only allowed the contemporary cultural currents to pass through it but also, simultaneously, as a sociologist and philosopher of culture, to question their content. In so doing, he 'elevated the social reality of the *present* into scientific consciousness'.[11]

But this is the paradox of Simmel's social thought. On the one hand, he could reflect the latest modes of experiencing social reality and he could also be highly critical of them. On the other hand, however, the aestheticisation of reality led him to distance himself from the practical consequences of this critique. Simmel could startle or astound the bourgeoisie with his insights and critique, as Troeltsch recognised. Ultimately, however, they could remain undisturbed. How was this possible?

As Becher points out, Simmel himself saw one reason as lying in an intellectual tendency of the period: the reduction of the substantive to the relational, and cites a passage in his early *Einleitung in die Moralphilosophie* (1893) where Simmel detects a

> general tendency of modern thought, with its dissolving of substances into functions, the rigid and permanent in the flux of restless development — an intellectual tendency that certainly stands in interaction with the practical movements of a period which is directed against all rudiments of surviving, presumptive instances of a claim to eternity and finds in the liveliness of development, in the dynamic energy . . . the substitute for the peace and security with which the earlier modes of experience that strove for the substantive and unchanged were happy.[12]

By 1900 Simmel was even more convinced of the dissolution of forms into relations and our distance from anything enduring and permanent since we 'feel as if the whole meaning of our existence were so remote that we are unable to locate it and are constantly in danger of moving away from rather than closer to it'.[13] Looking back on his earlier work around 1908, Simmel is even more explicit about the consequences of this destruction of what is substantial. He is left arguing that

> the contemporary historical dissolution of all that is substantial, absolute and eternal in the flux of things, in historical mutability, in a merely psychological reality seems to me to be then only preserved against an unceasing subjectionism and scepticism if *one substitutes for every substantial, secure value the living interaction of elements which ultimately underlies, in turn, the same dissolution into infinity.* The central concepts of truth, value, objectivity, etc., revealed themselves to me as changing effective phenomena [*Wechselwirksamkeiten*], as the contents of a relativism which no longer implies the sceptical loosening of all determinations but rather means securing against this by means of a new concept of determination.[14]

And we are left with a thorough-going relationism that relies for its perspective upon a distance from reality that cannot, ultimately, be bridged.

All this suggests that what is required in examining how Simmel could, on the one hand, have such a sensitive ear for some aspects of cultural life and, on the other, view everything from such a distance is an investigation of the practical consequences of his aestheticisation of reality. This would lead in the direction of a study of the sources and consequences of his relativism and perspectivism, his refusal to commit himself on most social issues and the relation of all these factors to a philosophy of history that virtually reduced 'historical diversity' to 'a chaos'.

As a preliminary step, it might be useful to investigate some of Simmel's stances towards social and political issues since it would be mistaken to believe that he was totally unconcerned with social, political and economic life in Wilhelmian Germany. Though such an analysis must remain selective, it will give some indication of the features of his political 'perspective'. Thereafter it will be possible to relate this 'perspective' to Simmel's wider world-view, strands of which have permeated the whole of his work. We can then return to the question posed at the start of this study: namely, in what sense is Simmel 'a man without qualities'.

II

The mundane aspects of Simmel's political perspective are not well known and, in some respects, are not particularly helpful. His son Hans relates:

> I do not know whether my father belonged to a party. He voted 'liberal', i.e. Independent People's Party or, if the candidate seemed to have no chance at all, even for the social democrats too. In general, he was completely sceptical of all parties. He was filled with the deepest mistrust towards Wilhelm II's politics.[15]

In the 1890s, Simmel was not averse to occasionally publishing articles in socialist journals and newspapers and this is perhaps the decade in which he seems to have stood closest to the social democrats on some issues. As instances of this, we may cite a brief article on trades unions in 1892, and a review of a book on social medicine in 1897. Also discussed below is his article on the women's movement in 1896. Much later, and in a very different vein, Simmel's political views resurface in his wartime writings. Further, there is a persistent interest in socialism at least until 1900, as well as a critique of Marx's labour theory of value in his *Philosophy of Money*. Indeed it is socialism rather than any other political movement which engaged Simmel's attention. Finally, whilst much is often made of the marginality of his position in German society as a result of his Jewish origins, a specifically Jewish dimension of his thought is difficult to discover. Hence, the few surviving letters from the 1890s also suggest no great interest in Zionism as a political movement.[16]

Simmel's political stance on a limited number of issues is significant since, as Kracauer pointed out, in his major writings he always sought 'to preserve his incognito'. Furthermore, he seldom appears to commit himself to any position so that one hardly ever knows where his sympathies lie. The three articles discussed briefly below are therefore interesting exceptions.

In an article entitled 'A word on social freedom' (1892),[17] Simmel provides 'a theoretical discussion of the principles' upon which personal freedom is based in relation to the employment contract. The context was a report on a draft French law permitting an employer to dismiss an employee on the grounds of their membership of a trade union (no doubt raised in connection with the protracted French miners' strike of 1892).[18] Simmel's 'theoretical discussion' hinges on the distinction between a right and a duty. The crucial passage in his argument concerning such a law as was proposed as follows:

> If the state thus prevents the worker from exercising his right to join a trade union . . . then it can do this only from the standpoint that any such membership is no mere right in the usual sense but rather is a duty.
> At this point there is opened up a perspective in which the whole of social politics seems to be based primarily upon a unified fundamental principle. The raising of the standard of living is not only the worker's individual right but also his social duty; he *may* not only struggle for it, he *should* struggle for it.[19]

The weapons with which this struggle is fought are a logical consequence of the fact that 'whenever the communality imposes an obligation upon someone it must also secure for them the means for its fulfilment'. This implies that individual duties can only be understood within the context of the whole society since,

> The more the erroneous nature of the individualistic world-view is recognised, the more deeply one examines the close interaction of all social elements which connects each individual's action with some kind of consequence for the totality, so all the more lively is the interest of the whole in the free actions of individuals too and

every permissible act falls all the more under the perspective of an obligation.[20]

Yet the state, according to Simmel, preserves the freedom of each individual even though it might have its limits. In the case of the employment contract, the duty of the worker to raise his or her living standards finds its limit in the freedom of the employer.

Finally, Simmel raises a more general issue concerning individual freedom. We must always recognise that 'personal freedom is an ideal that emerges out of specific historical grounds', 'that it is merely a means to specific social and personal ends'. The recognition of the causes of this idealisation — which Simmel was to so thoroughly investigate in *The Philosophy of Money* — is itself 'a liberation from dogma'. It is then possible to conceive of another ideal that can also be historically determined, though Simmel is not too clear as to its specific nature. He stops short of professing a commitment to an alternative ideal.

That Simmel conceived of social goals as worth striving for may be seen in his review entitled 'Social medicine' (1897)[21] in which he argues strongly for state intervention in preventive medicine and health care. Again, he is at pains to counter individualistic solutions. Any preventive measure must be social in nature 'rather than individual therapy or case work', since 'an individual's problem and its solution rest in society and with the kinds of social action taken'. More generally, 'the growth of culture expresses itself in purposeful social action not directed toward unique and individual cases but toward causes and still more general causes. . . . We have to influence general conditions if we are to provide for the common good of all individuals.'[22] The specific application of this principle means that it is 'desirable to fight theft not through punishment and poverty, not by giving alms, but by establishing a social system wherein theft and poverty cannot appear'. Similarly, in the field of health, we should 'fight an illness not by curing it but by preventing; further, to maintain health rather than to prevent disease'. In short, it is 'high time that we became aware of the power of conscious intervention'.

Simmel also raises some general implications for social reform that are probably more explicit than in any of his other writings. He points to the apparent limitation of social reform within a single area by asking 'Of what use is the enforcement of housing regulations if the worker does not earn enough to rent a better apartment? . . . What is the point of emphasising the health benefits of leisure or sport when the great mass of people has neither time nor money for these?'[23] If one argues that health is a right then it would 'presuppose an even more basic reform of the social structure than does the idea of the worker's right to work'.

Ultimately, then, individual reforms cannot be restricted since 'individual reform presupposes social reorganisation, and social reorganisation, in its turn, presumes the reform of individual units'. Does this mean that the total transformation of society is the only solution? Simmel replies that

> To those favouring revolutionary means, we concede the interdependence of the parts of society. . . . Such interdependence seems logically to exclude the perfection of society by means of reforming its units. This difficulty can be resolved by acknowledging that while it is not possible to achieve ideal conditions for an individual without also achieving them for all individuals, one can work toward such an ideal in stages. . . . And this is a safer and more achievable path than that advocated by the revolutionaries who share our ends but not our means.[24]

Perhaps nowhere else did Simmel so explicitly favour social reformism as a political programme.

In the previous year, Simmel had reported briefly on 'The Women's Congress and Social Democracy' (1896).[25] Here Simmel argued that the significance of the Berlin congress lay in two directions: 'in the opposition between the bourgeois and social democratic women's movement' and in the fact that it 'has once more shown how much today the question of socialism is the "secret king" of all specific social questions'. The leaders of the workers' women's movement emphasised 'the uselessness of the bourgeois women's movement for the interests of working wome' since it remained embedded in the existing social order. Hence, the proletarian women's movement confronted the "ladies' movement" partly with indifference, partly with hostility'.

Simmel viewed the alternatives between the two positions in terms of the question of revolution or reform. The revolutionary perspective he states as follows:

> If the social democrats persist in their official standpoint that, by means of an internal revolution, they thus bring about the socialisation of the means of production and by this one and only possible means can remove all social abuses, all injustice, all present day repression, then it is a completely correct consequence that they reject all attempts to heal a fraction of these misfortunes in other ways. . . . Hence, on this basis . . . it would be an erroneous attempt on the part of the present day women's movement to seek any kind of connection with the social democratic movement.[26]

The alternative is not necessarily to abandon a belief in 'the complete transcendence of class distinctions and the private ownership of property'. Rather, Simmel argues that one can maintain this position and still press for reforms from below. The abolition of the poverty of the proletariat can remain 'the first and most urgent task of the times' whilst 'one can still just as little believe in the radical means of a revolutionary transformation of the total social system as, for instance, in a sudden miracle from heaven'.

Simmel's preference is again for social reformism. After listing a series of measures such as workers' insurance, free education and minimum wages, etc., he asks

> is all this not a 'socialisation of the means of production', a gradual levelling of social distinctions? . . . If I am not mistaken, then this more sober tendency towards — relatively — slowly advancing evolution that, rather than the improvement of individual elements out of a radically transformed total situation, allows the radical transformation of the total situation to develop as the sum of improved individual elements, has already taken root in further socialist circles.[27]

What is the relevance of these alternatives for the women's movement? Simmel does not deny that the bourgeois and socialist women's movements are moving in different directions as a result of the very different economic and social situation of the two groups of women. He views this as a contrast between the apparent 'freedom' of working class women to take up work — albeit factory work — and create a degree of economic independence unknown in bourgeois circles. There, Simmel sees women as being increasingly 'liberated' from household tasks without any alternative taking their place so that 'the home is experienced as an unbearable barrier' to social and economic freedom.

Within a class society, Simmel sees the apparent opposition between the two sets of circumstances as deriving from 'the same socio-economic order' in which diverse circumstances call forth diverse reactions. Hence, 'The contemporary mode of industrial production has, on the one hand, torn the proletarian woman from household activities and, on the other, curtailed the sphere of activity of the bourgeois women to within this remaining area.'[28] Simmel fails to examine the material circumstances of the two classes of women any further and merely goes on to see this as an instance of the general phenomenon that 'the development of objective circumstance progresses more quickly than the development and adaptation of individuals. The culture and technology of things makes demands and develops consequences that no longer accord with the historically developed personal conditions of life.'[29] Within the context of this universal predicament, Simmel concludes that despite the apparent discrepancies between the two wings of the women's movement they nonetheless constitute 'the sides of the same social total phenomenon'.

Despite Simmel's awareness of some of the issues involved here, it is an interesting instance of his failure to follow through the consequences of what he takes to be a specific problem in a concrete manner. Instead, the particular problem ultimately becomes universalised in the sense that it is seen as resulting from a general tendency in industrial society. Three years later, in his *Philosophy of Money*, he elaborates this discrepancy between objective and subjective culture, between the culture of things and the individual personality into a tragic ahistorical tendency.

As Simmel made clear in the 1890s, there was no political position that he saw more significant than socialism in all its facets. If he sometimes seemed to come close to avowing a socialist standpoint in this decade, then this can only be understood in the light of his concern for specific social reforms. It is a very pragmatic response to a limited range of socialist measures. This did not prevent him from being fascinated by a political position that was often reduced to a world view, to another interpretation of reality. In many respects, however, his *Philosophy of Money* marked the high point of his interest in socialism and Marxism — though the latter figured less in his writings, however much the two were often fused. In that work, the critique of the labour theory of value and the reduction of socialism to another instance of the rationalisation and even aestheticisation of the world — through its presumed preference for symmetry — was combined with an assertion of the importance of the individual. Later, this was to take on an almost existential significance with his formulation of the 'individual law' and his attempt to establish an autonomous ethics grounded in individuality.[30] This 'existential' current became even more marked in his early response to the First World War.

In the light of this it seems legitimate to inquire into the features of socialism that Simmel highlighted. Since, in his study of social differentiation, Simmel explains 'the struggle between capital and labour as a necessary process in which sometimes property and at other times labour predominate',[31] it is not surprising that he remained sceptical of its virtues, however critical he might be of capitalism. Indeed, his analysis and critique of socialism is confined to a limited number of themes.

As a world view, Simmel sees socialism as the end result of utilitarianism in the sense of the maximisation of the happiness of the greatest number. In his *Einleitung in die Moralphilosophie* its ideal is taken to involve a circularity in that it emphasises the expansion of the very economic culture it seeks to remove. Later, in an article on 'Socialism and pessimism' (1900),[32] Simmel argues that its ostensibly optimistic ideal readily produces its pessimistic opposite in the levelling process he attributes to socialism. The pessimism of the existing individualistic society has its counterpart in socialism:

> the dragging back of the individual into solitude, into the womb of things, in which all the differentiation of phenomena is extinguished and is thus no longer to be experienced as something that connects with an ego — this finds its sociological . . . counterpart in the constitution of a universal equalisation that places each individual on the *same* level as all others and thereby severs any distinction and comparison upon which the socially influential accentuation of the sense of life . . . results.[33]

In this respect, there is little to choose between the existing limitations of an individualistic society and one organised according to formal socialist principles. This is also the other side of the description of Simmel as the sociologist of differentiation. He is at pains to preserve individual differentiation at all costs.

As a form of social organisation, socialism is seen by Simmel as accentuating the 'tendency towards the complete rationalisation of life, towards its direction by means of a highly unified principle'.[34] Socialism presupposes 'a completely rationalised economic order'.[35] It is,

> directed towards a rationalisation of life, towards control of life's chances and unique elements by the law-like regularities and calculations of reason. At the same time, socialism has affinities with the hollow communistic instincts that . . . still lie in the remote corners of the soul. Socialism's dual motivations have diametrically opposed psychic roots. On the one hand, socialism is the final developmental product of the rationalistic money economy, and on the other, it is the embodiment of the most basic instincts and emotions.[36]

Viewed in this manner, socialism's rationalisation of life is merely an extension of that rationalisation which already exists in the money economy and to which Simmel is so much opposed. Indeed, in one passage at least, Simmel suggests that the current organisation of work may predispose the factory worker to 'think in terms of the socialist form of the state'. Thus, the energy-saving organisation of work, the internal absence of competition, the harmonious co-operation of human energies such as predominate within the individual factory and such as the worker witnesses daily — this suggests that it can be transformed to the whole of human work. Perhaps even more effective still is the concept of machinery. The fact that there are purposive motions and effects that come about with absolute reliability, that the results desired can be obtained completely regardless of personal disturbances . . . the adequate achievement of purposes through an impersonal mechanism — this continually confronts the worker and must therefore prepare for a social ideal in such that the totality is treated like a big machine, all private impulses are excluded and the purposes of the whole will be achieved by means of the working of impersonal completely regulated elements.[37]

Here Simmel clearly sees the model for socialism as lying completely within the capitalist production process. The only problem is its transfer onto a societal level. As such, it does not constitute an alternative form of social organisation but merely an extension of an existing mode of organising production. In other words, socialism offers no qualitative alternative to existing social processes.

Finally, however, Simmel emphasises socialism's 'aesthetic' appeal. This he sees as part of the pervasive influence of 'aesthetic forces' within society. Hence, it is not surprising that some socialist notions have an aesthetic foundation. For instance,

That society as a whole should become a work of art in which every single element attains its meaning by virtue of its contribution to the whole; that a unified plan should rationally determine all of production, instead of the present rhapsodic haphazardness by which the efforts of individuals benefit or harm the whole; that wasteful competition and struggles between individuals should be replaced by an absolute harmony of work — these socialist ideas are undoubtedly directed towards aesthetic interests. [38]

Therefore it is not possible to reduce socialism to a crude material base since 'the social question is not merely an ethical but also an aesthetic one'. In an ironic comment on this statement Simmel declares that this is an aesthetic question

because of the meaning of the immediate sensation of pleasure and displeasure, and not only on account of the beauty of forms. It would seem harder for a typically 'educated' person to overcome the aesthetic discomforts which he experiences during physical contact with the common people, to whom the honourable sweat of work still clings, than to overcome his attachment to crabmeat, lawn tennis, and easy chairs.[39]

This is a good example of what Kracauer refers to as Simmel's reluctance to express his own views — in this case as an 'educated' person — except in the most opaque manner. Elsewhere within this same essay, Simmel seriously suggests that socialism appeals to simple minds. Whereas an individuated society is extremely complex and composed of 'heterogeneous interests and irreconcilable interests', the harmony and symmetry of a socialist society is appealing because 'To understand the social picture here requires a minimum of intellectual effort. This fact in its aesthetic significance would seem to figure decisively in the intellectual appeal of socialism.'[40] Simmel himself, of course, is adept at unravelling the complexities of an individuated society.

There can therefore be little doubt that the aestheticisation of reality which Simmel himself so well describes is, at the same time, an apt description of his own position. The political sphere of life is no exception since its institutions can be organised in such a way as 'to give the individual contingencies of existence a unity and transparency that transposes them into a work of art'. Hence, 'the aesthetic attraction that is aroused by the machine . . . is repeated to a greater extent in the organisation of the factory and . . . the socialist state is supposed to give the widest possible application'[41] of it.

This should not imply, however, that Simmel was particularly enamoured with the society in which he lived. As we have seen, his *Philosophy of Money* at one level provides a critique of a society grounded in a developed money economy that can be seemingly extrapolated into a critique of contemporary capitalism. This recognition of some of the essential tensions and contradictions present in such a society never left Simmel in later years. For instance, in a letter to his friend Hermann Keyserling written in May 1918, we find Simmel relating that

> It would greatly interest me to know the symptoms on the basis of which 'for the past ten years' you have believed in the collapse of Europe. For my part I cannot say the same. Rather, I believed that the dreadful epoch of the machine age and of exclusively capitalistic evaluations was coming to an end and I also believed I could discern signs of a new spirituality that, though weak and without a correct orientation, was nonetheless quite unambiguous.[42]

'The dreadful epoch' (*die entsetzliche Epoche*), however, was to be rescued by 'a new spirituality'. By 1918 he had come to realise that this hope, too, had disappeared. Instead the hope lay with the contemporary youth movement:

In fact, within our present day youth, there exists a passionate revolutionary yearning for a *vita nova*, a determination to struggle for a spiritual form of life that is, neither abstract, theoretical nor aesthetic but can be grasped practically; not an idealistic withdrawal of the self from the world but a cultivation of it even though in a thoroughly idealistic sense; a deadly hatred of all that is bourgeois, of all mechanisation and Americanisation but making use of the forces that these tendencies have nonetheless produced.[43]

This is the response of an intellectual aristocracy with its hatred of the bourgeoisie, and the machine age.[44] Ultimately, it is a cultural critique of capitalism and not a critique of its social and economic foundations. It is a response to a social reality that has been so aestheticised that the only conceivable solution to its problems is a cultural one. But when we turn back to some of Simmel's most penetrating critiques of capitalism – for instance, the analysis of the consequences of the division of labour that are seen by some to anticipate the discovery of Marx's early writings – then we find that what is at issue is not the social, political and economic order of capitalism but the radical separation of subjective and objective culture. Whatever dimensions of a crisis in Wilhelman Germany Simmel may have detected, they increasingly became absorbed into a cultural crisis. The crisis was viewed at a distance from the salon. Perhaps this explains why Heberle, for instance, should conclude that Simmel's

> sociological interpretations, although extremely intelligent and subtle, do not betray a great deal of first hand experience and contact with the great social movements and important societal events of his time. This may partly explain the lack of new original insights into the great social questions of the period.[45]

Symptomatic of this, Heberle argues, is the relative absence of examples and instances from his own contemporary society, for instance, when discussing the labour movement. Instead, the issues that most preoccupy him are those associated with a cultural crisis. And in order to account for this transposition of social and economic issues onto a cultural plane, we must return once more to the form which the aestheticisation of reality takes in Simmel's work.

III

There are three dimensions of the aestheticisation of reality – all of which have already been outlined – that we must consider in order to account for the distinctive nature of Simmel's world view. They are the theory of the alienation of culture, the associated distance from reality that is implied in this process and, connected with the latter, a pervasive perspectivism.

From his *Philosophy of Money* onwards, Simmel maintained a theory of cultural alienation which commenced as a specific societal process and finished as a metaphysical tragic human condition. In *The Philosophy of Money*, Simmel formulates his already established argument to the effect that society is based on social interactions. These interactions in the course of their development replace

> the immediacy of interacting forces with the creation of higher supra-individual formations, which appear as independent representatives of these forces and mediate the relations between individuals. These formations exist in great variety . . . ideal products of human conceptions and valuation, which in our mind now stand beyond the will and actions of the individual as 'pure forms'.[46]

In this context, Simmel has in mind the normative orders of the law and morality as well as political organisations, etc. As such it might merely be seen as an explication of 'objective' social forms. But there is already a further implication that the individual, as the centre of creativity, produces cultural formations which acquire an independent existence and come to confront the individual as something alien. This version of cultural alienation is common to all societies even though it may become more marked in the developed money economy. For instance, money's total indifference to human goals and its facilitation of the reduction of individuals to fragmented functions already suggest that the individual has not merely lost control of one of the purest of social forms but is actually faced by his or her own disintegration as a total personality. Confronted with this fragmentation that now comes to be embedded within individuals themselves, they in turn are unable to act except in order to perform these fragmented functions.

More specifically, when Simmel comes to examine the consequences of the division of labour in contemporary society with its attendant impoverishment of the individual, the actual context is provided by an examination of the crisis of 'contemporary culture' and 'the preponderance of objective over subjective culture that developed during the nineteenth century'. The implication of this is that this objective culture has advanced at the expense of the development of the individual and the gap between objective and subjective culture

> seems to widen steadily. Every day and from all sides, the wealth of objective culture increases, but the individual mind can enrich the

forms and contents of its own development only by distancing itself still further from that culture and developing its own at a much slower pace.[47]

This is, therefore, an argument for our distancing ourselves from the objective material culture in order to preserve our individual personalities. The phenomenal expansion of objective culture thus serves to accentuate 'the enigmatic relationship which prevails between social life and its products on the one hand and the fragmentary life-contents of individuals on the other'. This process of cultural objectification, producing a 'growing estrangement', 'invades even the more intimate aspects of our daily life'.

But the situation is more complex than this apparently one-way process of domination of objective over subjective culture would suggest. The negative side of this domination of objective culture is felt both in money transactions which

> represent the preponderance of objective over subjective mind, as well as the reverse, independent enhancement and autonomous development of the subjective mind. The superior power of the culture of objects over the culture of individuals is the result of the unity and autonomous self-sufficiency that the objective culture has accomplished in modern times. Production . . . seems to be a cosmos with definite and, as it were, logical determinations and developments which *confront the individual in the same way as fate confronts the instability and irregularity of our will*. The formal autonomy, this inner compulsion, which *unifies cultural contents into a moral-image of the natural context*, can be realised only through money.[48]

This objective culture embodied in production and exchange takes on a 'spectral objectivity' that determines human existence in the same manner as fate or as a natural process. The possibilities for intervention by human subjects in what they themselves create and reproduce would seem to be limited, if not closed off altogether.

Yet, paradoxically, this very reification enables the individual to create a sphere of freedom for self-development. Again it is money that makes this possible since, as a mediation between human subject and thing which

> enables man to have, as it were, an abstract existence, a freedom from direct concern with things and from a direct relationship to them, without which our inner nature would not have the same chances of development. If modern man can, under favourable circumstances, secure *an island of subjectivity, a secret, closed-off sphere of privacy* — not in the social but in a deeper metaphysical

sense — for his most personal existence . . . then this is due to the fact that money relieves us to an ever-increasing extent of direct contact with things, while at the same time making it easier for us to dominate them and select from them what we require.[49]

Pushed to its conclusion, this would lead to a situation in which all material life becomes 'increasingly objective and impersonal, so that the remainder that cannot be reified becomes all the more personal, all the more the indisputable property of the self'. In this way, as Lieber has pointed out, it is possible for Simmel to see 'reification, indifference and objectification in actual social structures as possible guarantees for the development and strengthening of a richer inwardness'.[50] It also indicates once more the fundamental significance of distance in his work, a significance that cannot be confined merely to the extensive descriptions of forms of social distance.

For the moment, however, it is important to see how Simmel extends this analysis of the separation of subjective and objective culture into a tragic feature of human existence. It is an interesting instance of his apparent treatment of a feature of the style of life in a contemporary money economy *sub specie momenti* that even in the *Philosophy of Money* has already been transposed onto the level of human fate, that is, it is viewed *sub specie aeternitatis*. In other words, it is an instance of

a general fateful law which, according to Simmel, any culture is unalterably subject to and which he later characterised with the concepts of 'the tragedy of culture' and 'the conflict of culture'. According to Simmel, what is tragic about this conflict that is basic to all cultures, in fact, lies enclosed in the untranscendable tension between subjective and objective culture, between a soul that externalises and an objectified mind.[51]

On this view, any specific socio-historical formation such as capitalism is merely one historical instance of the tragedy that is inherent in culture: the irreconcilable contradiction between the subjective spirit and objective formation.

Not surprisingly, therefore, we find in 'The concept and tragedy of culture' (1911)[52] an account of this separation of subjective and objective culture that has lost any connection with a specific social, historical analysis. In fact, it is now incorporated within a *Lebensphilosophie* that came increasingly to dominate Simmel's later work. This is announced in the introduction to the volume *Philosophische Kultur* (1911) which contains the above essay. The contradiction between subjective and objective culture is now revealed by means of a philosophy that consists of 'a specific intellectual attitude towards the world and life, a functional form and manner of taking up things and dealing with them inwardly'.[53] This kind of philosophising takes up the separation of form and content. It seems to be historically specific in the sense that 'Such a division between function and content, between the living process and its conceptual result signifies a very general direction in the modern mind.'[54] But its modernity is no longer, as it still was in The Philosophy of Money, what is important. Rather, what now interests Simmel is 'the metaphysical significance of historical phenomena' that lies in

> the deep estrangement or animosity which exists between the organic and creative processes of the soul and its contents and products: the vibrating, restless life of the creative soul, which develops toward the infinite contrasts with its fixed and ideally unchanging product, and its uncanny feedback effect, which arrests and indeed rigidifies this liveliness.[55]

Simmel is thus less concerned to give any socially or historically specific detail to this process. He moves further away from any socially specific analysis of modern society that might be extrapolated from his Philosophy of Money.

Indeed, the whole process of alienation and the fragmentation produced by commodity production and the capitalist division of labour are now seen to have their origins in this cultural contradiction. Hence,

> The 'fetishism' which Marx assigned to economic commodities represents only a special case of this general fate of contents of culture. With the increase in culture these centers more and more stand under a paradox. They were originally created by subjects and for subjects: but in their immediate forms of objectivity . . . they follow an immanent logic of development. In so doing, they estrange themselves from their origin as well as from their purpose. *They are impelled not by physical necessities, but by truly cultural ones.*[56]

The 'immanent logic' of commodity fetishism has now become 'truly cultural'. In the same passage, Simmel suggests that it is technology itself that produces the need for excess production as if technology possessed its own logic. Similarly, the now universal 'extreme and total specialisation' produced by the division of labour 'is only a special form of this very general cultural predicament', namely, the separation of subjective and objective culture.

It is no longer the case that things *seem* to be independent of human intervention. For Simmel, they *are* independent:

> Objects, in their development, have a logic of their own — not a conceptual one, nor a natural one, but purely as cultural works of man; bound by their own laws. . . . Man becomes the mere agent of the force by which this logic dominates their development . . . This is the real tragedy of culture.[57]

Herein lies one fundamental reason for the inward retreat of the individual. Confronted with a reified world in which there is no possibility of human action since human beings are 'the mere agent' of the tragedy of culture, a retreat to the intérieur seems the only way to preserve individuality.

Such a response seems all the more likely when reinforced by the progressive fragmentation of human existence. As with the concept of distance in Simmel's work, so too the concept of the fragmentary is not merely a feature of his 'descriptions' of aspects of social life; nor is it merely part of his 'approach' to his subject matter. The manner of presenting the fragmentation of human existence, especially in his later writings, takes on a new metaphysical significance. Whereas we have shown that in his earlier sociological work, Simmel illuminated the fragment of social interaction and revealed its connection with other fragments that together constituted a totality, in his later writings it is not merely aspects of social interaction that are fragments but human beings themselves: 'we are all fragments'. The relationship of the fragments to the totality has become increasingly obscured. We are no longer convinced by the role of the sociologist or philosopher of social life to see through this labyrinth. Rather, caught up within it, we are more and more unable to act within it.

Still later, Simmel maintains that the fragments have become congealed in rigid forms that are opposed to life. Indeed, 'life is always in latent opposition to form'. Even fundamental processes like the mode of production are now taken to be dependent upon 'life'. We find Simmel arguing that

> The economic forces of every epoch develop forms of production which are appropriate to their nature . . . A new mode of production, however, need not have overwhelming energy of its own. Life itself, in its economic dimension . . . provides the dynamic for this whole movement. Life as such is formless, yet incessantly generates forms for itself.[58]

This tension between form and life lacks any social and historical specificity with regard to either pole. The earlier interest in the elucidation of different social forms has given way to a preoccupation with 'form as such'. Simmel argues — in 1918 — that 'we are experiencing a new phase of the old struggle — no longer a struggle of a contemporary form, filled with life, against the old, lifeless one, but a struggle of life against the form *as such*, against the *principle* of form'.[59] Similarly — and in keeping with the *Lebensphilosophie* tradition — the notion of life, equally significant in this eternal dialectic, remains deliberately vague. Simmel notes that,

> The essence of life would be denied if one tried to form an exhaustive conceptual definition. In order for conscious life to be fully self-conscious, it would have to do without concepts altogether, for conceptualisation inevitably brings on the reign of forms; yet concepts are essential to self-consciousness.[60]

Life has become an irrational driving force in history, one that provides its dynamic. On the other hand, and despite its significance, it seems that it cannot be analysed.

This inevitable conflict between life and form and the elevation of the process of fragmentation into a philosophy of life suggests that we cannot confine such concepts to Simmel's sociological writings. Nor can we examine the role of aesthetics in his sociology merely within the framework of the insights derived from the aesthetic realm that are applied to social life. Rather, we have found it necessary to investigate the process of aestheticisation of the very social reality Simmel seeks to describe. It is within this context that we can also understand not merely the concept of distance but also the process of distancing oneself from reality that permeates much of Simmel's work. Many commentators have pointed to the significance of the concept of distance in his sociological work. Few have been prepared to see the process of distancing oneself from reality as its real basis. Further, it is only by examining this process that we can come to understand the pervasive perspectivism in his writings and in his attitude towards social reality.

The starting point for any discussion of the practical consequences of maintaining a distance from reality is not some bland statement to the effect that Simmel was preoccupied with social distance. Instead, we need to look at the extent to which his social theory is predicated upon maintaining one's distance from social reality in order to understand the perspectivism that permeates his work. Perspectivism itself requires that one maintain a distance from reality. It also implies that there is no fixed standpoint from which one can view that social reality.

We have already shown that the process of distancing oneself from reality is important in Simmel's work for a number of reasons. His approach to sociology itself presupposes this distance. It is not grounded in an engagement in the object of study but in a detachment from it. As Becher has argued, Simmel's basic sociological concept is 'the inter-actions of individuals, viewed from a specific distance'.[61] The forms that society takes – individual existence, artistic forms, religious inter-pretations of life – depend upon 'the specific distance or the stand-point from which one observes human life'. Indeed, Becher argues that, in this context and in his early writings, the notion of 'form' itself might be better interpreted as 'perspective'. However, as Simmel developed his philosophical standpoint further, so his sociological conceptions were sharpened and informed by a doctrine of distance. Although this doctrine is more evident in his later philosophy, as Steinhoff argued, it is also present in his sociology. Maria Steinhoff suggests that in the theory of the attitude outlined in his *Hauptproblemen der Philosophie* (1910)[62] the notion of an objective picture of the world is rejected in favour of a variety of different perspectives upon it. In this way,

> Philosophical ideas are *true* as long as they remain within their own sphere; according to the distance from them, the images shift; each is true on its own level. The same is true in sociology. Already in the *Soziologie* (1908) Simmel says at one point: 'It is always a reality that we cannot scientifically apprehend in its immediacy and totality but rather must be taken up from a series of distinctive standpoints and thereby develop a plurality of scientific objects that are inedependent of one another'.[63]

The connection between distance from reality and perspectivism is here already quite explicit. In the *Grundfragen der Soziologie* (1917), the doctrine of distance is even more clearly connected with a theory of cognitive interests. In the first chapter, 'The field of sociology', Simmel argues that the process of abstraction through which we perceive society and social forms rests upon the distance that exists between 'a complex of phenomena and the human mind'. Different pictures of reality are derived from differing amounts of distance from that reality. Further-more – and this is the explicit connection with perspectivism – Simmel maintains that

> At each distance, however, the 'picture' is correct in its particular way and only in this way . . . a view gained at any distance what-ever has its own justification. It cannot be replaced or corrected by any other view emerging at another distance.
> In a similar way, when we look at human life from a certain dis-tance, we see each individual in his precise differentiation from all others. But if we increase our distance, the single individual disappears,

and there emerges, instead, the picture of a 'society' with its own forms and colours. . . . The difference between the two merely consists in the difference between purposes of cognition, and this difference, in turn, corresponds to a difference in distance.[64]

The process of distancing oneself from reality thus lies at the heart of Simmel's sociology.

But as we have already shown, this is not the only dimension of Simmel's social theory in which this process is crucial. Simmel clearly conceives of the relationship between the sociologist and society as if it were that of the art critic observing a work of art. In *The Philosophy of Money*, Simmel examines 'the universal significance of distance' in relation to aesthetic valuation. Distance from objects ensures a degree of objectivity in relation to them since

What really matters, in order to conceive the independent significance of objects, is the distance between them and our impression of them. It is one of the numerous cases in which one has to stand back from the objects . . . in order to get an objective picture of them.[65]

In the aesthetic realm, an object becomes 'an object of contemplation from which we derive pleasure by confronting it with reserve and remoteness, without touching it'.[66] Our appreciation of an object 'becomes aesthetic only as a result of increasing distance, abstraction and sublimation'. It is the 'process of objectification' itself that secures the aesthetic value of an object.

It is, therefore, only a short step from this assertion to the view that objectification can be equated with aesthetic distance. And this is not merely central to grounding the object of sociology but also constitutes an 'attitude' to social reality that Simmel sees as having increased in 'recent times'. This process of increasing distance from social reality is analysed in the light of the consequences of a developed money economy which not only produces social distance but also indifference towards those objects that we have become detached from. Not surprisingly, therefore, the theme of engagement in social reality always plays a subordinate role in Simmel's social theory.

This can be accounted for, in part, by the connection that has already been established between distance and perspective. We have seen that Simmel seldom announces himself in his texts. Instead, as Kracauer put it, he seeks 'to preserve his incognito, often even nervously'. This distance between the author and his own text is further reinforced by Simmel's perspectivism. It is always difficult to pin Simmel down to a single viewpoint, a feature of his work that is probably reinforced by his preference for the essay form which Adorno at least characterises as 'lacking in a standpoint'. There is no fixed standpoint from which Simmel apprehends reality. It can be viewed from many sides and from varying degrees of distance.

The 'many worlds' that Simmel's aesthetic stance provides are not necessarily linked by human action since they have their origin in the particular perspective of the human subject rather than in their practical activity. We can distance ourselves from any one of this variety of worlds and forms. In this context, and with reference to Simmel's later writings, Sibylle Hübner-Funk comments,

> The 'parallelism of worlds' — of science, art, religion, etc. — that emerges in this way in turn has important consequences for everyday life. Thus, for instance, insofar as Simmel regards the real world merely as 'one of many possible' [worlds], the 'general indigencies of action' evaporate. Indeed, Simmel expressly recommends the aesthetic perspective as a means for overcoming the most basic misery of life. In his *Schulpädagogik* he announces that: 'Whoever is capable of seeing things artistically has countless pleasures that raise life to a higher level, is not exposed . . . to many coarse aspects of life to which the aesthetically uneducated are subjected'. This is, astonishingly, written at a time in which the misery of life — in view of the First World War in the years 1915-16 — was so pressingly obvious as seldom before.[67]

The aesthetic perspective, here at least, is given a special status since it protects us from the worst aspects of the world we live in.

In his early writings, too, Simmel saw the aesthetic perspective as reconciling the contradictions in modern life. In his essay on 'Böcklin's landscapes' (1895), for instance, Simmel took as a feature of great art the fact that it performs precisely this function. There he maintains that

> To us modern people, whose life, sensibilities, estimations, and desires have diverged in countless oppositions, who constantly stand between a yes or no, a yes and no, and who conceive of their inner life, just like the external world, in sharply differentiated categories: to us an essential element of any great art appears to be that it reconciles contradictions, undisturbed by the necessity of an either—or.[68]

Again, what this implies is that within the context of Simmel's perspectivism, the aesthetic stance is accorded a privileged position. But even here, this aesthetic perspective is located within individuals. Nor is it located within all individuals, merely the aesthetically educated. Nonetheless, it is perhaps the closest Simmel ever comes to according a higher status to one perspective rather than another.

This perspectivism, however, can only be understood in terms of what is absent from his work. The absence of a genuine historical dimension in Simmel's writings has already been alluded to. On occasion this has been viewed as a positive virtue as when Spykman argues that 'The fact that the historical dimension as an end in itself has entirely disappeared out of Simmel's method, and that he makes a clear distinction between history and science, is perhaps his most valuable contribution.'[69] This judgment fully accords with a broad tradition of American sociology as well as with those more narrowly engaged in the development of a 'formal' sociology. But in Simmel's work, too, the absence of a historical dimension has important real consequences.

The historical sphere is not significant to Simmel because he conceives of the diversity of events as a chaos and because he prefers to conceive of 'the completely dynamic character of the world' in which 'reality is in constant motion'. In order to capture, even for a moment, this world in flux 'Simmel unceasingly changes perspectives'. And each perspective rests upon holding this world at a distance not upon our engagement in it. Any notion of historical praxis is totally alien to him. Transformative action requires engagement and commitment to a standpoint. For Simmel there is no viewpoint that can even begin to grasp the totality of events: 'a viewpoint would be lacking, which our cognition needs, in order to form a picture that would suffice'.[70] If this is the case, then in the light of a conception of the world as in ceaseless flux and ever-changing interactions, where is the resting point for Simmel?

In his later work, it is difficult to avoid the impression that Simmel espouses a perspectivism that readily becomes a thorough-going relativism. Simmel seems to accept Nietzsche's relativist perspective that 'Insofar as the word "knowledge" has any meaning at all, the world is knowable: but it can be *interpreted* differently, behind it lies no meaning but rather countless meanings — "Perspectivism".'[71] Simmel's response to the relativist problematic is to have recourse to a notion of life itself as a dynamic flux that is elevated to an absolute. As Kracauer comments in this context,

> The fact that Simmel makes life the basis of the world seems to transcend his relativism. For him, life becomes an absolute principle out of which all phenomena can be explained and to which the multistructured nature of existence, objective forms and norms just as the subjective interpretations of the diverse must equally be traced back. . . . In his view, in fact, the world can never be fully comprehended starting out from a *single* standpoint.[72]

But this metaphysics of life to which everything is to be traced back is so indefinite, as we have seen, that it, too, is likely to dissolve back into its constituent elements. Individuals, with their various perspectives, remain caught up in the stream of life so that 'All forms and structures then drown us and all that remains is the dull intoxication of the stream of life that flows through the world and us. Thus, life is not only restless, eternal movement, it is, at the same time, more-life [*Mehr-Leben*].'[73] Increasingly, then, Simmel's solution to the perspectivism and relativism of his later work is a philosophy of life that, on many points, converged with Bergson's philosophy.

The central determining role of life, however, is not merely a highly questionable solution to the relativist problematic. Simmel clearly saw intellectual and other movements of his time as actually signalising 'a revolt of life against the forms that violate it'. Yet the other side of this revolt is a strengthening of our cultural alienation since our cultural formations, in turn, come to be determined by 'life' itself. Ludwig Marcuse expressed it as the fact that 'Simmel suffered from the power-lessness of thought [*Ohnmacht des Denkens*] before life'.[74] Never committing himself to any standpoint — except perhaps the aesthetic one which is, by its nature, grounded in detachment — Simmel was left with a reduction of social complexity to a simplified category of life. At this point, distance from reality, perspectivism and relativism converge. Kurt Gassen expresses this convergence in relation to Simmel's relativism:

> Certainly in relation to the problematic dealt with, Simmel often practised a form of *epoche*, a kind of abstention from judgment . . . in his opinion, the taking up of a (value) judgment in favour of *one* position only takes place on the basis of a simplifying disregard for opposed viewpoints. . . . Simmel's *epoche*, his 'relativism' is, accordingly, an expression of his reverence for the enormous diversity and complexity of life.[75]

As someone who 'did not feel himself drawn into the flow of historical development',[76] Simmel withdrew from it. The inward retreat becomes his final political perspective.

On the basis of Simmel's theory of cultural alienation, of distance from reality and his perspectivism and relativism it would not be difficult to construct the central elements of the problematic that a decade later — in a very different context — preoccupied writers like Mannheim on the sociology of knowledge.[77] Even before this discipline had been developed in Germany, Kracauer perceived in Simmel's work one of its key elements when he wrote: 'To reveal the relativity of every standpoint that is taken for an absolute: that is the tragic, highest achievement of the intellect that floats in a void.'[78] The political consequence of this stance is also a detachment, a shrinking from engagement. It is the stance of the man without qualities.

IV

There exist a number of affinities between Simmel and Musil's Man without Qualities that serve to illuminate the practical consequences of Simmel's social theory. But as with the earlier attempt to examine the role of the *flâneur* in relation to Simmel's approach to his object of study, so too with the analogy between Simmel and the Man without Qualities, it is not possible to simply impute the latter's stance to Simmel's work. Nonetheless, the purpose of this final section will be to investigate the parallels between the two figures — the one real, the other imaginary — for the light they throw upon Simmel's writings. In particular, we need to refer to Simmel's wartime writings in order to study the extent to which Simmel followed the path of the Man without Qualities in initially renouncing rational commitment to any standpoint, in other words, failing to engage in rational decisions (*Entscheidungen*), and then finally making an arbitrary decision (*Dezision*) to support the First World War.

The relevance of some of the central themes of *Der Mann ohne Eigenschaften* to an understanding of Simmel's work is not hard to seek. Both Simmel and the novel's hero Ulrich share a commitment to a conscious essayism and to the aestheticisation of reality. This aestheticism seeks to grasp reality from many sides without any commitment to any one of them. In turn, this aestheticised reality is removed from any historically concrete activity. Therefore, any ultimate decisions to be made are likely to be extremely arbitrary. This situation is compounded by the absence of any roots in historical reality. What exist are possibilities without regard to their concrete realisation.

This is hardly the place to take up all the analogies between *The Man without Qualities* and Simmel's later writings. But those themes which bear directly upon Simmel's world view should, at least, be outlined below, especially since many of them have already been touched upon earlier. This is most obviously true of what one commentator on Musil has referred to as the utopias of 'aesthetic life' and 'essayism'.[79]

But the connections between Simmel's work and many of the themes dealt with in Musil's novel are very close in a different sense. Musil artistically and critically reworked the life, attitudes and works of many contemporary figures, often for the purposes of engaging in a critique of ideology. Perhaps the most obvious connection in the novel is between the intellectual industrialist Arnheim and Walther Rathenau. But more pertinent to Simmel's work are many other figures whose stance and works are taken up by Musil. Count Leinsdorf, for example, expresses, amongst other things, the romantic theory of the state espoused by Othmar Spann who, as we have seen, criticised Simmel's concepts of sociology and society. Hans Sepp, the young German nationalist, echoes the views of Ludwig Klages and Oswald Spengler, both critics of Simmel's work. Through Clarisse and other figures in the novel, the work of Nietzsche — a major influence upon Simmel (cf. his *Schopenhauer und Nietzsche*) and many of his contemporaries at the turn of the century — is constantly ironicised. It is not difficult to see in Feuermaul a version of Stefan George with whom Simmel was closely associated. Musil's *Man without Qualities*, then, is populated with a universe of figures who either preoccupied Simmel or who were his contemporaries, even theough they may have been related only tangentially to his own life. More importantly, however, the novel deals with several dimensions of Simmel's 'attitude to life' in a manner that serves to illuminate the consequences of his later philosophy.

In his study of *Der Mann ohne Eigenschaften*, Götz Müller examines the central utopias of Musil's novel, all of which bear directly upon Simmel's attitude to life.[80] The utopia of 'aesthetic life' and of 'essayism' have already been touched upon. An alternative to the aesthetic utopia is the 'utopia of inductive conviction'. All these utopias, like the novel itself, converge not in the 'other condition' which the hero Ulrich seeks but in 'the First World War as a catastrophic "other condition".' How do they illuminate Simmel's writings?

In Simmel's work, the utopia of aesthetic life takes the form of an aestheticisation of reality that rests upon a distance from historical reality and a retreat into its details. Troeltsch describes Simmel's early 'attitude to life' as one in which everything was viewed:

> in living, inwardly fusing, continuous movement and interaction, in a relativity that determined everything through everything else and in the transformative capacity of seeing each thing in terms of every other. At first, he too also stood under the influence of positivism; he sought, by reduction to its smallest elements and then by their coordination, to explain this intricate structure and distinguished himself from it [positivism] only through the complete

openness by which he showed not one but a thousand lines of development whose orders co-exist and are juxtaposed. It is like an Indian summer in which countless vibrant threads that change the light fill the whole air without beginning and end in order, in every conceivable manner, to cross, to mix and to filter it. In his early writings he called it a relativistic pantheism.[81]

Like many of his contemporaries, Troeltsch could only have recourse to images of light and colour, drawn from the artistic realm, in order to describe Simmel's stance. Simmel himself quite explicitly took many of his central concepts from the aesthetic sphere and, like many of his contemporaries, saw artistic experiences as the prototype for creative existence. The sheer bustling diversity and chaos of historical reality could only be grasped by making aesthetic connections between its elements. But this is to juxtapose a creative life — the life of the 'other condition' — against an actual, empirical and historical existence. From the 1890s onwards, as we have seen, Simmel does attribute to the aesthetic realm the capacity for resolving contradictions. Yet insofar as this aesthetic realm rests upon distance from reality and a form of inward retreat, its own historical status becomes problematical. It is a world that lacks genuine activity, each element of which is what Musil describes as a 'happening without anything ever having happened'.[82]

At the centre of his aesthetic realm is the experience of the creative genius. The intensity and quality of what is expressed is dependent upon the subjectivity of the artist, upon his or her inwardness. In *The Philosophy of Money* and elsewhere, Simmel preserves individual creativity from any contamination by material and historical existence. A central aim of his critique of Marx's labour theory of value is to show that it is totally inappropriate to the creative artist. Simmel, who was sometimes termed 'the German Bergson' and who encouraged the translation of Bergson's work (*Evolution créatrice* was translated by his close friend Gertrud Kantorowicz), would have readily concurred with Bergson's characterisation of 'the rare moments of artistic creation' that signify 'this supra-individual life, this supra-consciousness of the *élan vital*'.[83]

But the price paid for this poeticisation of the world is the formation of an 'aesthetic "unreality" as competition with historical reality'. Müller, with reference to Musil's critique of this position, argues that

> The utopia of the other condition threatens to degenerate into a *utopia* of *aesthetic life* and hence into a totally alienated dual life. As a result, the utopia develops into a *coexistence* of two realities, the aesthetic and the empirical–historical.[84]

Co-existence might also imply that these two worlds are equally 'valid', a conclusion hard to avoid in Simmel's case given his perspectivism. Furthermore, what cannot be resolved or united in the real world — as Simmel so often points out — can be unified in an aestheticised reality.

How do we avoid living in an 'imaginary museum' and avoid being a 'person of possibilities' as Musil described his man without qualities?[85] Müller poses the alternatives as follows: 'The genuine alternative . . . to the aesthetic utopia of a life according to art is the practical transformation of reality: the "utopia of inductive conviction or of the given social condition".'[86] With reference to the utopias of essayism and aesthetic life, Musil explicitly states that 'the utopias have arrived at no practical results. The "other condition" provides no guidelines for practical experience.'[87] In other words, the aestheticisation of reality, based as it is upon distance and interior retreat, provides no guidelines for political practice.

It is clear from the preceding outline of some of Simmel's political contributions that he is always reluctant to commit himself to a political stance. This tendency increased as Simmel moved further away from his interest in socialism in the 1890s. Whilst Simmel does, at times, appear to conceive of a socialist society as a possibility, his devaluation of it as resting upon its aesthetic appeal suggests that he never conceived of it as a real alternative. Furthermore, since such a society would reproduce some of the very features of the existing capitalist order, there was no reason to support such an alternative. Yet at the same time, Simmel could analyse the consequences of a capitalist society — for him the developed money economy — in terms of its systematic reproduction of an alienated and reified existence that he was later to see as the result of 'the dreadful epoch' of capitalism. Existing society, however, was tolerable so long as one could maintain one's distance from it, though the interior retreat is itself predicated upon specific concrete social conditions for its own maintenance and reproduction.

Indeed, Simmel could describe precisely this real world of exactitude produced, as he thought, by a mature money economy, from which the individual sought to preserve his 'increasingly solitary ego, the deeply lonely soul'.[88] It is a world that is permeated with indifference; it is a world without historical development. Simmel was acutely aware of both. Even in his early writings, the creation of indifference in all its forms had come to preoccupy him. It culminated in his thoroughgoing analysis of money as the archetype of the 'indifferent means that also reduces ends to total indifference'. In a contribution to *Jugend* in 1897 entitled 'The most indifferent thing', Simmel closes an imaginary conversation with the following passage:

'Everything rests solely upon the individual nuance. You speak of
what is most important and say that you must decide upon it? The
crucial issue? But how long have you actually been living at the end
of this century? Do you still not yet know that what is most important is the most indifferent thing of all?'[89]

This ironic conclusion to 'a moral dilemma' perhaps merely light-
heartedly mirrors Simmel's later analysis of indifference. But it remains
symptomatic of the aestheticisation of reality.

Müller highlights another dimension of Musil's presentation of false
utopias in the juxtaposition of the utopia of exactitude with the utopia
of essayism. The utopia of exactitude is provided by the scientific
world view but occurs more generally in other social relationships:
'The "utopia of exactitude" in the hands of business people and tech-
nicians becomes frozen in ideology . . . The utopia of essayism, in
contrast, aims to make human beings the masters of history.'[90] The
utopia of exactitude appears negatively in Simmel's work as the reification of quantification, as the destruction of individual qualities in
scientism. For Simmel, neither science nor precision could constitute
a utopian perspective. Simmel is totally opposed to the kind of systematic analysis required by science, however much he might have encouraged a somewhat unreflected positivism in his early writings.

The situation is completely different, however, with regard to the
utopia of essayism. Here Simmel shares many of the attitudes of the
Man without Qualities. Musil himself described the Man without
Qualities as a 'theoretician', a 'person without bonds, without a need
for a Yes or a No. A person of the partial solution'.[91] The utopia of
essayism involves 'living hypothetically' since for Ulrich

nothing, no ego, no form, no principle, is safe, everything is in a
process of invisible but never-ceasing transformation. . . . What
better can he do than hold aloof from the world, in that good sense
exemplified by a scientist's attitude towards facts that are trying to
tempt him into over-hastily believing in them? This is why he
hesitates to become anything.[92]

In a more concrete form this hypothesis becomes a conscious essayism
that takes its distinctive attributes from the peculiarity of the essay
which

takes a thing from many sides without comprehending it wholly —
for a thing wholly comprehended instantly loses its bulk and melts
down into a concept . . . [on this basis] he believed he could best
survey and handle the world and his own life. The value of an action

or of a quality, indeed their essence and nature, seemed to him dependent on the circumstances surrounding them, on the ends that they served, in short, on the whole complex — constituted now thus, now otherwise — to which they belonged.[93]

For Simmel, too, the world is seen as in a state of flux. His response is also to hold aloof from it, never committing himself to any aspect of it, except that which preserves the interior retreat. Essayism coincides with perspectivism to produce no single fixed position. As several of his contemporaries commented, Simmel seemed to lack roots. Such a judgment, made by Bloch, Kracauer and others, is made most forcefully by his friend Paul Ernst in a letter to Lukács in 1916 where Ernst suggests that

> Simmel's problem, about which we have indeed often spoken, is the problem of the person who is clever and lacking in instinct. He has no roots; hence in his younger years he developed very unexpectedly and in the years when he should have broadened out he lacked the energy. I do not know whether he himself feels this; in fact, I experience it as a tragic phenomenon and can always really observe him only with the greatest sympathy.[94]

However harsh this judgment, and versions of it are made by other contemporaries, it does indicate that lack of a central core, a lack of commitment that leads Simmel often to hide himself in his works, in essayism, in perspectives.

The various perspectives that Simmel takes up do not constrain us to adopt any one of them. Rather they stand alongside one another without any compelling reason for deciding upon any of them. We can, to use Kracauer's analogy, view the world from the perspective of the frog, not merely from below but also freely moving from one position to another, since they are located within the unceasing flux of life. To the person who lives hypothetically, to the 'person of possibilities' (*Möglichkeitsmensch*) everything could be different. Writing to his friend Hermann Keyserling in 1918, Simmel says of those who inhabit the intellectual milieu they both share that, with some exceptions, 'I have the impression of all of them that: *they can all be different too* — it is ultimately through an accident of the situation and not an inner necessity that they are reactionary or revolutionary, free-minded or catholic, authoritarian or anarchic.'[95] Without real history made by real people, only possibilities and perspectives abound.

Ulrich, the Man without Qualities, actually asks why one does not invent history since 'quite half the definiteness of things could be left out, and it did not make much difference'. With regard to a 'philosophy of the times', Ulrich reflects that

> What one calls an age . . . this broad, unregulated flux of conditions would then amount to approximately as much as a chaotic succession of unsatisfactory and (which taken singly) false attempts at a solution, attempts that might produce the correct and total solution, but only when humanity had learned to combine them all.[96]

But where there exists only a thorough-going perspectivism, a synthesis is no longer possible. A not dissimilar position was detected by Troeltsch in Simmel's philosophy of history. Troeltsch saw Simmel's standpoint as being

> the transformation of history into a somewhat free game of phantasy alongside the always exact but unproductive and never feasible causal research . . . This was the most basic essence of modernity: naturalistic determination and compensation for it by means of the sovereign game of phantasy of the aesthetes. Elsewhere Simmel had characterised it in this manner.[97]

This utopia of exactitude and the utopia of aesthetic life combined to produce a distinctive 'philosophy of the times'. As Troeltsch points out, Simmel himself was aware of this when, in his first major wartime speech of November 1914, he wrote, 'There exists a deep inner connection between too close an attachment to things and too great a distance from them that, with a kind of fear of contact, places us in a vacuum. We knew for a long time that we suffered equally from both of them.'[98] For a short time, at least, Simmel saw the solution to this sickness in an existential commitment to the First World War.

Müller argues that this is also the 'solution' found by the Man without Qualities since 'after the collapse of the aesthetic utopia, the unconscious, if not salvation too, is sought in the experience of the war'.[99] In 1914 Simmel saw the collapse of the aesthetic ideal as if it were a dream: 'The Germany from which we emerged, which we are has sunk like the end of a dream'.[100] In its place must be set 'the renewal of our inner existence' rather than material goals. Nowhere does Simmel reflect upon the substantive origins of the war. Rather the crisis is seen either as cultural or as an individual existential crisis. In Musil's novel, this has its parallel in his outline for the final session of the committee set up to produce a plan for the Austrian Peace Year of 1918 — the Parallel Action. In a dialogue between the German industrialist Arnheim and Diotima, the hostess of the 'salon' attached to this committe, Musil writes:

> Arnheim reminds Diotima: I have already predicted this: Crude
> material interests will gain control of the Parallel Action —
> Diotima in reply: Oh no! It is only the liberation of the soul from
> civilisation that we had made the task of the Parallel Action.[101]

Simmel's response to the outbreak of the war lay in the direction of a
critique of the 'culture' that had produced it. The wartime period
marks the high point of his commitment to a philosophy of life,
even in the end to an existentialism of 'the absolute situation' that
foreshadows a tradition whose ambiguity he did not live to experience.

Conclusion

This study of some aspects of Simmel's social theory has been selective with regard to the themes it has taken up and quite consciously omitted other important aspects of his work. In particular, further re-examination of Simmel's social theory would have to confront Simmel's relationship to Max Weber, whose work has tended to completely overshadow Simmel's, despite the fact that Weber probably owed much to Simmel. This would have to avoid the trap of evaluating Simmel merely as a precursor of Weber and neglecting him as a social theorist in his own right. It would have to investigate both writers' attempts to establish sociology as an independent discipline after both had emerged out of other disciplines, their establishment of a framework for sociology and the development of its basic categories, their respective critiques of Marxism and their, in some ways, parallel development of a pessimistic philosophy of history. All this would belong in a further study.

But rather than take up the wider issue of the reception of Simmel's work — which is, very often, a story of misinterpretation and neglect — the present study has sought to reconstruct his social theory within the context of his contemporary milieux and in the light of contemporary responses to his work. In particular I have attempted to locate some crucial aspects of Simmel's social theory in a distinctive aesthetic stance that can be termed the aestheticisation of reality. Perhaps more problematically, I have tried to suggest that there are some reasons for maintaining that much of Simmel's social theory can be characterised as a form of sociological impressionism.

Yet the attempt to understand anew Simmel's social theory in this way should not merely involve an interpretation of central aspects of his work. Any form of the aestheticisation of reality is not merely a particular stance, vis-à-vis that social reality, it is not merely an interpretation of the world. It also has real consequences that should be reflected upon in any critical response to an author's work. A distance or retreat from social reality has a real foundation in society. It has been especially difficult to extract these origins from so elusive a writer as Simmel, one who could write imaginatively and informatively upon almost any theme without, at the same time, revealing his own person, his own standpoint. Simmel's freedom, like that of the Man without Qualities in the utopia of conscious essayism, is the freedom to grasp 'a thing from many sides' and to reflect its 'meaning as a dependent function' without oneself being 'dependent upon the circumstances'. Kracauer expressed this tragic elusiveness in the following way:

> I see the tragedy of Simmel's intellectual personality as lying in the absence of elementary basic beliefs. He, especially, who is at home in every recess of the heart, and whose finely-spun net never easily let slip any inner emotion, must have recognised from which sources his elusive, many-sidedness emerged, must have been conscious of his rootlessness, as the necessary − and, solely because of this, also tragic − precondition for the distinctive mode of development of his mind.

The 'sources' of his elusiveness are, in fact, reflected in Simmel's own writings. The clues to our interpretation of his social theory are found in his own works even though they are not reflected upon by Simmel.

Nonetheless, the critical interpretation of Simmel's social theory should not lead one to conclude that his is the only theory that is permeated by the weaknesses of an aestheticisation of reality. The reader might also recognise whole traditions of sociology that have and do share this apparent detachment and aesthetic perspective, particularly those that are preoccupied with constructing sociology as a self-enclosed perspective. But as one recent commentator remarks, 'A sociology understood as an end in itself will, in fact, always − sooner or later − finish up in the sphere of aestheticism'. Unlike many of his successors, Simmel was always conscious of his aestheticism even though he may not have been fully aware of its consequences.

Notes

Chapter 1

1. P. E. Schnabel, *Die soziologische Gesamtkonzeption Georg Simmels* (Stuttgart 1974) pp. 40f.
2. N. J. Spykman, *The Social Theory of Georg Simmel* (Chicago 1925; reprinted New York 1966).
3. T. Abel, *Systematic Sociology in Germany* (New York 1929) especially chapter 1.
4. Some of the problems associated with the label 'formal sociology' are discussed in F. H. Tenbruck, 'Formal sociology', in K. H. Wolff (ed.) *Essays on Sociology, Philosophy and Aesthetics by Georg Simmel et al.* (Columbus, Ohio 1959) pp. 61—99. See also chapters 2 and 3 below.
5. Schnabel, *Die soziologische Gesamtkonzeption Georg Simmels.* More recently on the American reception, but less critically, see D. N. Levine, *et al.*, 'Simmel's influence on American sociology', in H. Böhringer and K. Gründer (eds), *Ästhetik und Soziologie um die Jahrhundertwende: Georg Simmel* (Frankfurt 1976) pp. 175—228.
6. K. H. Wolff, *The Sociology of Georg Simmel* (New York 1950). See also K. H. Wolff and R. Bendix (trans.), *Conflict and the Web of Group Affiliations* (New York 1955).
7. See for example T. M. Mills, 'Some hypotheses on small groups from Simmel', *American Journal of Sociology*, vol. 63 (1958) pp. 642—50.
8. T. Caplow, *Two Against One* (Englewood Cliffs, N.J. 1968).
9. L. Coser, *The Functions of Social Conflict* (London 1956).
10. Wolff (ed.), *Essays on Sociology, Philosophy and Aesthetics.*
11. L. A. Coser (ed.), *Georg Simmel* (Englewood Cliffs, N.J. 1965). See also the collection by D. N. Levine (ed.), *Georg Simmel. On Individuality and Social Forms* (Chicago/London 1971).
12. R. H. Weingartner, *Experience and Culture* (Middletown, Conn. 1960).
13. Georg Simmel, *The Philosophy of Money* (trans. T. Bottomore and D. Frisby) (London/Boston 1978).
14. G. Simmel, *The Problems of the Philosophy of History* (trans. G. Oakes) (New York 1977).
15. See Tenbruck, 'Formal sociology'; also F. H. Tenbruck, 'Georg Simmel (1858—1918)', *Kölner Zeitschrift für Soziologie und Sozialpsychologie*, vol. 10 (1958) pp. 587—614.
16. R. Aron, *La philosophie critique de l'histoire* 4th edn (Paris 1969) especially pp. 159—214.
17. R. Aron, *German Sociology* (trans. M. and T. Bottomore) (New York 1956) p. 5. See also M. Susman, *Die geistige Gestalt Georg Simmels* (Tübingen 1959) pp. 14—15.

168   *Sociological Impressionism*

18. An exception is Schnabel, *Die soziologische Gesamtkonzeption Georg Simmels*.
19. T. Parsons, *The Structure of Social Action* (Glencoe, Ill. 1937). Personal communication from the author.
20. P. Lawrence, *Georg Simmel: Sociologist and European* (London 1976) p. 34.
21. G. Simmel, *Soziologie. Untersuchungen über die Formen der Vergesellschaftung* (Berlin 1908).
22. G. Simmel, *Grundfragen der Soziologie (Individuum und Gesellschaft)* (Berlin 1917).
23. See 'Vorwort' to Simmel, *Soziologie*. Even the subtitle, 'Studies in the forms of sociation', should have aroused the suspicion that this was never intended to be a *systematic* work.
24. G. Simmel, *Über sociale Differenzierung. Sociologische und psychologische Untersuchungen* (Leipzig 1890). Some extracts from this early work have been translated in Lawrence, *Georg Simmel*, pp. 95–138.
25. G. Simmel, *Die Probleme der Geschichtsphilosophie. Eine erkenntnistheoretische Studie* (Leipzig 1892). The second edition of 1905 was completely revised and the third edition of 1907 was also enlarged. The second edition has now been translated as *The Problems of the Philosophy of History*, op. cit.
26. G. Simmel, *Philosophie des Geldes* (Leipzig 1900). The second enlarged edition of 1907 has been translated as *The Philosophy of Money*, op. cit.
27. M. Adler, *Georg Simmels Bedeutung für die Geistesgeschichte* (Vienna/Leipzig 1919) p. 6.
28. S. Kracauer, 'Georg Simmel', *Logos*, vol. 9 (1920) p. 308. This is the first chapter of his unpublished study, *Georg Simmel: Ein Beitrag zur Deutung des geistigen Lebens unserer Zeit*, ms., circa 1919–20.
29. H. J. Becher, *Georg Simmel. Die Grundlagen seiner Soziologie* (Stuttgart 1971) p. 14.
30. Simmel, *The Philosophy of Money*, p. 55.
31. Kracauer, *Georg Simmel*, ms., p. 37.
32. Kracauer, 'Georg Simmel', p. 331.
33. Kracauer, *Georg Simmel*, ms., p. 41.
34. Kracauer, 'Georg Simmel', p. 332.
35. For a valuable early discussion of 'form' in Simmel's work see M. Steinhoff, 'Die Form als soziologische Grundkategorie bei Georg Simmel', *Kölner Vierteljahrschefte für Soziologie*, vol. 4 (1925) pp. 214–59. See also F. H. Tenbruck, 'Formal sociology'.
36. Kracauer, *Georg Simmel*, ms., p. 85.
37. M. Frischeisen-Köhler, 'Georg Simmel', *Kantstudien*, vol. 24 (1920) p. 8.
38. G. Simmel, 'Das Problem der Soziologie', *Jahrbuch für Gesetzgebung, Verwaltung und Volkswirtschaft*, vol. 18 (1894) pp. 1301–1307; English translation (K. H. Wolff) of its extended and revised version which appeared in the *Soziologie* (1908) as 'The problem of sociology' in Wolff (ed.), *Essays on Sociology*, pp. 310–36.
39. G. Simmel, 'Exkursus über das Problem: wie ist Gesellschaft möglich?', *Soziologie*, pp. 21–31; English translation (K. H. Wolff) as 'How is society possible?' in Wolff (ed.), *Essays on Sociology*, pp. 337–56.
40. G. Simmel, 'Zur Methodik der Socialwissenschaft', *Jahrbuch für Gesetzgebung, Verwaltung und Volkswirtschaft*, vol. 20 (1896) pp. 227–37.
41. T. Masaryk, 'Simmels Soziologie', *Zeitschrift für Socialwissenschaft*, vol. 12 (1909) pp. 600–7.
42. M. Weber, *Gesammelte Politische Schriften* (ed. J. Winckelmann) 3rd edn (Tübingen 1971) p. 20.

43. M. Landmann, 'Bausteine zur Biographie' in K. Gassen and M. Landmann (eds) *Buch des Dankes an Georg Simmel* (Berlin 1958) pp. 11—33. As will become apparent, I am indebted to this volume as a source of much contemporary material on Simmel's life and for its invaluable bibliography.

44. Susman, *Die geistige Gestalt Georg Simmels*, p. 2.

45. K. Joël, 'Eine Zeitphilosophie', *Neue Deutsche Rundschau*, vol. 12 (1901) p. 814.

46. Susman, *Die geistige Gestalt Georg Simmels*, p. 2.

47. M. Landmann, 'Einleitung' to G. Simmel, *Brücke und Tür* (Stuttgart 1957) p. v.

48. For a discussion of these and other essays upon contemporary social and political life, see chapter 5 below.

49. T. Tagger, 'Georg Simmel', *Die Zukunft*, vol. 89 (1914) p. 36.

50. E. Troeltsch, 'Der historische Entwicklungsbegriff in der modernen Geistes- und Lebensphilosophie', *Historische Zeitschrift*, vol. 124 (1921) p. 446. Somewhat amended, this discussion of Simmel also appears in E. Troeltsch, *Der Historismus und seine Probleme* (Tübingen 1922) esp. pp. 572—95.

51. Kracauer, *Georg Simmel*, ms., p. 147.

52. K. H. Wolff, 'Georg Simmel', *Trying Sociology* (New York/London/Sydney/Toronto 1974) pp. 29—30.

53. Hans Simmel, 'Auszüge aus den Lebenserinnerungen' in Böhringer and Gründer (eds), *Ästhetik und Soziologie um die Jahrhundertwende*, pp. 247—68, especially 247—8.

54. Sabine Lepsius, 'Erinnerungen' in Gassen and Landmann (eds), p. 199.

55. Hans Simmel, 'Auszüge aus den Lebenserinnerungen', p. 249.

56. M. Landmann, 'Georg Simmel: Konturen seines Denkens' in Böhringer and Gründer (eds), *Ästhetik und Soziologie um die Jahrhundertwende*, p. 3. An exception to this neglect of Simmel's early period is the article by H. Böhringer, 'Spuren von spekulativem Atomismus in Simmels formaler Soziologie' that also appears in the same volume, pp. 105—119.

57. G. Simmel, 'Zur Psychologie des Geldes', *Jahrbuch für Gesetzgebung, Verwaltung und Volkswirtschaft*, vol. 13 no. 4 (1889) pp. 1251—64.

58. G. Simmel, 'Über die Grundfragen des Pessimismus in methodischen Hinsicht', *Zeitschrift für Philosophie und philosophische Kritik*, vol. 90 (1887) pp. 237—47.

59. G. Simmel, 'Zur Psychologie der Frauen', *Zeitschrift für Völkerpsychologie und Sprachwissenschaft*, vol. 20 (1890) pp. 6—46.

60. See 'Vorlesungen und Übungen' in Gassen and Landmann (eds), *Buch des Dankes an Georg Simmel*, pp. 345—9.

61. F. Tönnies, 'Simmel G., Ueber soziale Differenzierung', *Jahrbücher für Nationalökonomie und Statistik*, 3rd series, vol. 1 (1891) pp. 269—77.

62. ibid., p. 269.

63. G. Simmel, *Einleitung in die Moralwissenschaft. Eine Kritik der ethischen Grundbegriffe*, 2 vols (Berlin 1892—3). Gassen relates that Simmel referred to this work as the 'philosophical sins of youth' and did not, therefore, permit later editions (after the 2nd of 1904 and the 3rd of 1911) to appear. See Gassen and Landmann (eds), p. 314.

64. Kracauer, *Georg Simmel*, ms., p. 48.

65. See 'Vorlesungen und Übungen' in Gassen and Landmann (eds), pp. 346—8. On socialism see, for instance, G. Simmel, 'Sozialismus und Pessimismus', *Die Zeit*, Vienna, vol. 22 (3 February 1900) as well as references in *The Philosophy of Money*.

66. See the following articles by Simmel: 'Das Geld in der modernen Kultur', *Neue Freie Presse*, Vienna (1896); 'Die Bedeutung des Geldes für das Tempo

des Lebens', *Neue Deutsche Rundschau*, vol. 8 (1897) pp. 111–22; 'Fragmente aus einer "Philosophie des Geldes" ', *Zeitschrift für immanente Philosophie*, vol. 3 (1898); 'Die Rolle des Geldes in den Beziehungen der Geschlechter', *Die Zeit*, Vienna, vol. 14 (15, 22, 29 January 1898); 'Fragmente aus einer "Philosophie des Geldes" ', *Jahrbuch für Gesetzgebung, Verwaltung und Volkswirtschaft*, vol. 23 (1899); 'Zur Philosophie der Arbeit', *Neue Deutsche Rundschau*, vol. 10 (1899) pp. 449–63.

67. G. Simmel, 'Das Problem der Soziologie'; G. Simmel 'Die Selbsterhaltung der sozialen Gruppe. Soziologische Studie', *Jahrbuch für Gesetzgebung, Verwaltung und Volkswirtschaft*, vol. 22 (1898) pp. 589–640.

68. See, for instance, G. Simmel, 'Ein Wort über soziale Freiheit', *Sozialpolitische Zentralblatt*, vol. 2 (1892/3) pp. 333–4; G. Simmel, 'Die Bauenbefreiung in Böhmen', *Allgemeine Zeitung*, Munich, 14/15 August 1894, Supplement; G. Simmel, 'Der Militarismus und die Stellung der Frauen', *Vossische Zeitung*, vols. 21/2, October 1894, Sunday supplement, no. 42 pp. 3–5, no. 43 pp. 2–4; G. Simmel, 'Die Frauenkongress und die Sozialdemokratie', *Die Zukunft*, vol. 17 (1896) pp. 80–4. These and other articles are discussed in chapter 5 below.

69. The attribution of these articles to Simmel was in doubt when Kurt Gassen compiled the bibliography of his writings (cf. K. Gassen, 'Vorbemerkungen' in Gassen and Landmann (eds), p. 312) since they are merely signed 'S.' or 'G.S.' The themes of some of these pieces would itself suggest Simmel's authorship. But further confirmation may be found in Hans Simmel's reminiscences in the course of which he writes:

> My father greatly loved short stories with a thought-provoking background, also wrote some of them himself and often allowed them to be published in the journal *Jugend*. A whole series can be found in the volumes around the turn of the century signed G. S., S. or Fridolin, often under the title 'Snapshots *sub specie aeternitatis*'.

See Hans Simmel, 'Auszüge aus den Lebenserinnerungen', p. 258. Some of these pieces are referred to below.

70. See, for instance, G. Simmel, 'Massenpsychologie', *Die Zeit*, Vienna, vol. 5 (23 November 1895); G. Simmel, 'Stefan George. Eine kunstphilosophische Betrachtung', *Die Zukunft*, vol. 22 (1898) pp. 386–96; G. Simmel, 'Stefan George. Eine kunstphilosophische Studie', *Neue Deutsche Rundschau*, vol. 12 (1901) pp. 207–15; G. Simmel, 'Polymeter', *Die Zeit*, Vienna, vol. 16 (23 July 1898).

71. M. Landmann, 'Bausteine zur Biographie' in Gassen and Landmann (eds), p. 21.

72. Letter to Heinrich Rickert, 19 July 1898 in Gassen and Landmann (eds), p. 95.

73. Letter to Heinrich Rickert, 15 August 1898, in ibid., p. 96.

74. Quoted in Landmann, 'Bausteine zur Biographie', pp. 22–3.

75. ibid., p. 24.

76. Letter to Heinrich Rickert, 24 April 1896, in Gassen and Landmann (eds), p. 92.

77. Letter to Heinrich Rickert, 10 May 1898, in ibid., p. 94.

78. Letter to Heinrich Rickert, 15 August 1898, in ibid., p. 96.

79. For a discussion of the reception of *The Philosophy of Money* see my 'Introduction to the Translation' in *The Philosophy of Money*, especially pp. 5–13.

80. Hans Simmel, 'Auszüge aus den Lebenserinnerungen', p. 265.

81. ibid.

82. See chapter 3 below.

83. Margarete Susman, 'Erinnerungen' in Gassen and Landmann (eds), p. 280.
84. ibid., p. 281.
85. Edith Landmann, 'Erinnerungen' in ibid., p. 210.
86. See W. Benjamin, *Briefe* (ed. G. Scholem and T. W. Adorno) vol. 2 (Frankfurt 1966) pp. 842f.
87. See note 70 above. On the George circle, see also M. Nutz, *Werke und Wertungen im George Kreis* (Bonn 1976) especially pp. 75f. On Simmel's reception of Stefan George's poetry, see G. Freymuth, 'Georg Simmel und Stefan George', *Neue Deutsche Hefte*, vol. 17 no. 3 (1970) pp. 41–50.
88. K. Singer, 'Erinnerungen an Georg Simmel', in Gassen and Landmann (eds) pp. 297–8.
89. Troeltsch, 'Der historische Entwicklungsbegriff', p. 447.
90. Letter to Heinrich Rickert, 28 May 1901, in Gassen and Landmann (eds), p. 100.
91. Troeltsch, 'Der historische Entwicklungsbegriff', p. 423.
92. G. Simmel, *Kant. 16 Vorlesungen, gehalten an der Berliner Universität* (Leipzig 1904).
93. G. Simmel, *Die Probleme der Geschichtsphilosophie*, 2nd edn (Leipzig 1905).
94. G. Simmel, *Kant und Goethe* (Berlin 1906).
95. G. Simmel, *Die Religion* (Frankfurt 1906).
96. G. Simmel, *Schopenhauer und Nietzsche. Ein Vortragszyklus* (Leipzig 1907).
97. Kracauer, *Georg Simmel*, ms., p. 53.
98. Letter to Heinrich Rickert, 4 November 1904, in Gassen and Landmann (eds), p. 101.
99. In particular, see the frequent references to Simmel's work in M. Weber, *Roscher and Knies. The Logical Problems of Historical Economics* (trans. G. Oakes) (New York/London 1975).
100. See G. Simmel 'Der Bildrahmen. Ein ästhetische Versuch', *Der Tag*, Berlin 1902, no. 541; G. Simmel, 'Rodins Plastik und die Geistesrichtung der Gegenwart', *Berliner Tageblatt*, 29 September 1902; G. Simmel, 'Über ästhetische Quantitäten', *Zeitschrift für pädagogische Psychologie, Pathologie und Hygiene*, vol. 5 (1903) pp. 208–12; G. Simmel, 'Venedig', *Der Kunstwart*, vol. 20 (1906/7) 2nd part, pp. 299–303; G. Simmel, 'Das Problem des Stiles', *Dekorative Kunst*, vol. 16 (1908) pp. 307–16.
101. See G. Simmel, 'Über räumliche Projektionen sozialer Formen', *Zeitschrift für Sozialwissenschaft*, vol. 6 (1903) pp. 287–302; G. Simmel, 'Soziologie des Raumes', *Jahrbuch für Gesetzgebung, Verwaltung und Volkswirtschaft*, vol. 27 (1903) pp. 23–71; G. Simmel, 'Soziologie der Konkurrenz', *Neue Deutsche Rundschau*, vol. 14 (1903) pp. 1009–23; G. Simmel, 'Das Ende des Streits', *Die Neue Rundschau*, vol. 16 (1905) pp. 746–53; G. Simmel, 'Zur Soziologie der Armut', *Archiv für Sozialwissenschaft*, vol. 22 (1906) pp. 1–30; G. Simmel, 'Dankbarkeit. Ein soziologische Versuch', *Morgen*, vol. 1 (1907) pp. 593–8; G. Simmel, 'Zur Philosophie der Herrschaft. Bruchstücke aus einer Soziologie', *Jahrbuch für Gesetzgebung, Verwaltung und Volkswirtschaft*, vol. 31 (1907) pp. 439–71; G. Simmel, 'Zur Soziologie des Adels. Fragmente aus einer Formenlehre der Gesellschaft', *Frankfurter Zeitung*, 27 December 1907; G. Simmel, 'Soziologie der Sinne', *Die Neue Rundschau*, vol. 18 (1907) pp. 1025–36; G. Simmel, 'Soziologie der Über- und Unterordnung', *Archiv für Sozialwissenschaft*, vol. 24 (1907) pp. 477–546; G. Simmel, 'Der Brief. Aus einer Soziologie des Geheimnisses', *Österreichische Rundschau*, vol. 15 (1908) pp. 334–6; G. Simmel, 'Der Mensch als Feind. Zwei Fragmente aus einer Soziologie', *Morgen*, vol. 2

(1908) pp. 55–60; G. Simmel, 'Psychologie des Schmuckes', *Morgen*, vol. 2 (1908) pp. 454–9; G. Simmel, 'Über das Wesen der Sozial-Psychologie' *Archiv für Sozialwissenschaft*, vol. 26 (1908) pp. 285–91.

102. Aside from some of the brief appendices to various chapters, the two chapters that had not already appeared between 1903 and 1908 in some form or other are chapters 2, 'The quantitative determination of the group' (pp. 32–100), and 6, 'The web of group affiliations' (pp. 305–44), of G. Simmel, *Soziologie*, 5th edn (Berlin 1968).

103. Tenbruck, 'Georg Simmel', pp. 592–3.

104. Quoted in Gassen and Landmann (eds) p. 25.

105. ibid., p. 26.

106. ibid.

107. Letter to Max Weber, 18 March 1908, in ibid., pp. 237–8.

108. ibid., p. 108.

109. M. Weber, 'Georg Simmel as Sociologist' (trans. D. Levine) *Social Research*, vol. 39 (1972) p. 159.

110. Letter to Max Weber, 15 December 1909, in Gassen and Landmann (eds), pp. 129–30. My emphasis.

111. G. Simmel, 'Soziologie der Geselligkeit', *Verhandlungen des Ersten Deutschen Soziologentages* (Tübingen 1911) pp. 1–16.

112. Letter to Max Weber, 15 June 1911, in Gassen and Landmann (eds), p. 131.

113. G. Simmel, *Hauptprobleme der Philosophie* (Leipzig 1910).

114. G. Simmel, *Philosophische Kultur. Gesammelte Essais* (Leipzig 1911).

115. G. Simmel, *Goethe* (Leipzig 1913).

116. G. Simmel, 'Soziologie der Mahlzeit', *Berliner Tageblatt*, 10 October 1910.

117. G. Simmel, 'Über Takt. Soziologie der Geselligkeit', *Frankfurter Zeitung*, 22 October 1912.

118. G. Simmel, 'Weibliche Kultur', *Archiv für Sozialwissenschaft*, vol. 33 (1911) pp. 1–36.

119. See G. Simmel, 'Die Kunst Rodins und das Bewegungsmotiv in der Plastik', *Nord und Süd*, vol. 129 (1909) pp. 189–96; for example, on Goethe see G. Simmel, 'Goethes Individualismus', *Logos*, vol. 3 (1912) pp. 251–74; G. Simmel, 'Philosophie der Landschaft', *Die Guldenkammer*, vol. 3 (1912/13) pp. 634–44; G. Simmel, 'Vom Wesen der Philosophie', *Frankfurter Zeitung*, 6 February 1910; G. Simmel, 'Der Begriff und Tragödie der Kultur', *Logos*, vol. 2 (1911/12) pp. 1–25; G. Simmel, 'Das Individuelle Gesetz', *Logos*, vol. 4 (1913) pp. 117–160.

120. Letter to Hermann Keyserling, 30 March 1911, in G. Simmel, *Das Individuelle Gesetz* (ed. M. Landmann) (Frankfurt 1968) p. 241.

121. Kracauer, *Georg Simmel*, ms., p. 75.

122. Letter to Edmund Husserl, 19 February 1911, in Gassen and Landmann (eds), p. 87.

123. Hans Simmel, 'Auszüge aus den Lebenserinnerungen', p. 266.

124. P. Honigsheim, 'Erinnerungen an Simmel' in Gassen and Landmann (eds), p. 266.

125. Letter to Adolf von Harnack, 3 January 1914, in Gassen and Landmann (eds) p. 82.

126. Quoted in M. Landmann, 'Bausteine zur Biographie' in ibid., p. 31.

127. Letter to Heinrich Rickert, 28 January 1914, in ibid., pp. 111–12.

128. Letter to Hermann Keyserling, 22 April 1914, in G. Simmel, *Das Individuelle Gesetz*, p. 242.

129. M. Landmann, 'Ernst Bloch über Simmel', in Böhringer and Gründer (eds), *Ästhetik und Soziologie um die Jahrhundertwende*, p. 271.

130. See H. Lübbe, *Politische Philosophie in Deutschland* (Basle/Stuttgart

1963) part 4, 'Die philosophischen Ideen von 1914', especially pp. 219ff. See also chapter 5 below.

131. Letter to Heinrich Rickert, 26 December 1915, in Gassen and Landmann (eds) pp. 114—15.

132. Letter to Heinrich Rickert, 13 December 1915, in ibid., p. 114.

133. Letter to Heinrich Rickert, 26 December 1916, in ibid., p. 117.

134. G. Simmel, *Das Problem der historischen Zeit* (Berlin 1916); see also G. Simmel, 'Die historische Formung', *Logos*, vol. 7 (1917/18) pp. 113—52.

135. Simmel, *Grundfragen der Soziologie*.

136. G. Simmel, *Rembrandt. Ein kunstphilosophische Versuch* (Leipzig 1916).

137. G. Simmel, *Der Krieg und die geistigen Entscheidungen. Reden und Aufsätze*, Munich/Leipzig 1916).

138. G. Simmel, *Der Konflikt in der modernen Kultur* (Munich/Leipzig 1918).

139. G. Simmel, *Lebensanschauung. Vier metaphysische-Kapitel* (Munich/Leipzig 1918).

140. Letter to Hermann Keyserling, 25 March 1918, in Simmel, *Das Individuelle Gesetz*, p. 243.

141. Letter to Marianne Weber, 4 July 1918, in Gassen and Landmann (eds) p. 135.

Chapter 2

1. The quotation at the start of this chapter comes from a letter to Althoff to whom Simmel sent a copy of his essay 'The problem of sociology'. See M. Landmann, 'Bausteine zur Biographie' in Gassen and Landmann (eds), *Buch des Dankes an Georg Simmel*, p. 24.

2. These figures are given in M. Landmann, 'Bausteine zur Biographie', in ibid., p. 21. Karl Joël, *'Georg Simmel'*, *Die Neue Rundschau*, vol. 30 (1919) p. 244.

3. See 'Vorlesungen und Übungen' in Gassen and Landmann (eds), pp. 345—9.

4. G. Simmel, *Die Probleme der Geschichtsphilosophie* (Leipzig 1892).

5. G. Simmel, *Die Probleme der Geschichtsphilosophie*, 2nd edn (Leipzig 1905). This is now in translation as G. Simmel, *The Problems of the Philosophy of History*, (trans. G. Oakes) (New York 1977). There exists a host of references to this revised edition in M. Weber, *Roscher and Knies: The Logical Problems of Historical Economics*, (trans. G. Oakes) (New York/London 1975).

6. G. Simmel, 'Das Problem der Soziologie', *Jahrbuch für Gesetzgebung, Verwaltung und Volkswirtschaft*, vol. 18 (1894) pp. 271—7.

7. G. Simmel, 'Das Problem der Soziologie', in *Soziologie*, 5th edn (Berlin 1968) pp. 1—21. This is translated in Wolff (ed.), *Essay on Sociology, Philosophy and Aesthetics*, pp. 310—36.

8. F. Tenbruck, 'Georg Simmel', *Kölner Zeitschrift für Soziologie und Sozialpsychologie*, vol. 10 (1958) p. 593.

9. Simmel, *Grundfragen der Soziologie*.

10. G. Simmel, 'Das Gebiet der Soziologie' in ibid., pp. 5—31. See G. Simmel, 'The field of sociology', in K. H. Wolff (ed.), *The Sociology of Georg Simmel* (New York 1950) pp. 3—25. The Anglo-American reception of Simmel's work suffers from the absence of any chronological sense of his development and from the lack of a translation of the whole of his *Soziologie* even though most of the essays have now been translated in various places.

11. Interestingly, Simmel's 'How is society possible?' is one of the few pieces in the *Soziologie* that is not a reprint or reworking of an earlier essay. Its significance is discussed below.

12. Notably, G. Simmel, 'Massenpsychologie', *Die Zeit* (Vienna), vol. 5 (23 November 1895) and G. Simmel, 'Ueber Massenverbrechen', *Die Zeit*, vol. 13 (2 October 1897).

13. M. Steinhoff, 'Die Form als soziologische Grundkategorie bei Georg Simmel', *Kölner Vierteljahrshefte für Soziologie*, vol. 4 (1925) pp. 216–17.

14. G. Simmel, *Über sociale Differenzierung* (Leipzig 1890). The work was never reprinted possibly because Simmel thought he had advanced beyond the views set out in the first chapters: 'Einleitung Zur Erkenntnistheorie der Socialwissenschaft', pp. 1–20.

15. M. Frischeisen-Köhler, 'Georg Simmel', *Kantstudien*, vol. 24 (1920) p. 2.

16. On Simmel's early writings, see H. Böhringer, 'Spuren von spekulativem Atomismus in Simmels formaler Soziologie', in Böhringer and Gründer (eds), *Aesthetik und Soziologie um die Jahrhundertwende: Georg Simmel* pp. 105–17.

17. Notably in Tenbruck 'Georg Simmel'. Also U. Gerhardt, 'Immanenz und Widerspruch', *Zeitschrift für philosophische Forschung*, vol. 25 (1971) pp. 276–92.

18. See, for instance, Dilthey's remarks in W. Dilthey, *Einleitung in die Geisteswissenschaften*, 2nd edn (Leipzig/Berlin 1923) which contain a critique of sociology in its Comtean and Spencerian variant in its first edition of 1883. In his notes towards a new edition around 1904–6, Dilthey specifically excepts Simmel's sociology from such a critique (cf. pp. 420–3).

19. Dilthey, *Einleitung in die Geisteswissenschaften*, p. 37. See also his 'Uber das Studium der Geschichte der Wissenschaften vom Menschen, der Gessellschaft und dem Staat' (1875) in W. Dilthey, *Gesammelte Schriften*, vol. 5 (Leipzig/Berlin 1924) pp. 31–73.

20. Simmel, *Über sociale Differenzierung*, p. 2.

21. ibid., p. 3.

22. ibid., p. 4.

23. ibid., p. 5.

24. ibid., p. 7.

25. ibid.

26. The problem of social complexity has been dealt with more recently in German sociology by Luhmann. See, for example, N. Luhmann, 'Systematische Argumentationen. Eine Entgegnung auf Jürgen Habermas' in J. Habermas and N. Luhmann, *Theorie der Gesellschaft oder Sozialtechnologie — Was leistet die Systemforschung?* (Frankfurt 1971) especially pp. 292–315.

27. Simmel, *Über sociale Differenzierung*, p. 9.

28. ibid., p. 10.

29. ibid., p. 11.

30. ibid., pp. 12–13.

31. ibid., p. 13.

32. ibid.

33. ibid., p. 14.

34. Steinhoff, 'Die Form als soziologische Grundkategorie bei Georg Simmel', pp. 228–29.

35. Simmel, 'Das Problem der Soziologie'.

36. ibid., p. 271.

37. ibid., p. 272.

38. ibid.

39. ibid., p. 273.

40. ibid., p. 275.
41. ibid.
42. ibid.
43. See R. A. Makkreel, *Dilthey. Philosopher of the Human Studies* (Princeton 1975) especially pp. 205f.
44. Simmel, 'Das Problem der Soziologie', p. 276.
45. See W. Windelband, 'Geschichte und Naturwissenschaft' in *Präludien*, vol. 2 (Tübingnen 1924).
46. G. Simmel, 'Zur Methodik der Socialwissenschaft', *Jahrbuch für Gesetzgebung, Verwaltung und Volkswirtschaft*, vol. 20 (1896) pp. 227–37. In the Terman discussion of Simmel this review has been widely neglected.
47. R. Stammler, *Wirtschaft und Recht nach der materialistischen Geschichtsauffassung* (Leipzig 1896). Weber's subsequent review of this important work was of the second revised edition of 1906. See M. Weber, 'R. Stammler's "Überwindung" der materialistischen Geschichtsauffassung', *Archiv für Sozialwissenschaft und Sozialpolitik*, vol. 24, 1907; reprinted in M. Weber, *Gesammelte Aufsätze zur Wissenschaftstheorie*, 3rd edn (Tübingen 1968) pp. 291–359.
48. M. Weber, *Critique of Stammler* (trans. G. Oakes) (New York 1976).
49. Simmel, 'Zur Methodik der Socialwissenschaft', p. 227.
50. ibid., p. 230.
51. ibid.
52. ibid., p. 232.
53. ibid.
54. ibid., pp. 232–3.
55. ibid., p. 235.
56. ibid., p. 237.
57. See K. Schrader-Klebert, 'Der Begriffe der Gesellschaft als regulative Idee. Zur transcendentalen Begrundung der Soziologie bei Georg Simmel', *Soziale Welt*, vol. 19, pp. 97–118.
58. G. Simmel, 'Zur Soziologie der Familie I', *Königliche priviligierte Berliner Zeitung*, (*Vossische Zeitung*), 30 June 1895, Sonntagsbeilage 26.
59. ibid.
60. G. Simmel, 'Massenpsychologie', *Die Zeit*, vol. 5 (23 November 1895).
61. ibid.
62. G. Simmel, 'Ueber Massenverbrechen', *Die Zeit*, vol. 13 (2 October 1897).
63. ibid.
64. G. Simmel, 'Die Selbsterhaltung der sozialen Gruppe', *Jahrbuch für Gesetzgebung, Verwaltung und Volkswirtschaft*, vol. 22 (1898) pp. 589–640. In its revised version it appeared as chapter 8 of Simmel, *Soziologie*, pp. 375–90.
65. See, for instance, G. Simmel, 'Über räumliche Projektionen sozialer Formen', *Zeitschrift für Sozialwissenschaft*, vol. 6 (1903) pp. 287–302; G. Simmel, 'Soziologie der Konkurrenz', *Neue Deutsche Rundschau*, vol. 14 (1903) pp. 1009–23; G. Simmel, 'Die Soziologie der Religion', *Neue Deutsche Rundschau*, vol. 9 (1898) pp. 111–123.
66. Simmel, 'Die Selbsterhaltung der sozialen Gruppe', pp. 235–6.
67. ibid., p. 236. My emphasis.
68. ibid.
69. ibid., p. 238.
70. ibid.
71. ibid.
72. ibid., p. 239.
73. ibid., p. 286.

176   *Sociological Impressionism*

74. Quoted in K. H. Wolff (trans. and ed.) *The Sociology of Georg Simmel* (New York 1950) p. xxvi. My emphasis.
75. ibid., p. xxvi.
76. ibid., p. xxxiii.
77. F. Tönnies, 'Ueber sozial Differenzierung', *Jahrbücher für Nationalökonomie und Statistik*, 3rd Series, I (1891) pp. 269—77.
78. Quoted in S. Lukes, *Emile Durkheim* (London 1973) n. 72, pp. 404—5.
79. E. Durkheim, 'Sociology and its scientific field' in K. H. Wolff (ed.) *Essays on Sociology and Philosophy by Emile Durkheim et al.* (Columbus 1960) pp. 354—75.
80. ibid., p. 356.
81. ibid., p. 357.
82. ibid., p. 358.
83. ibid., p. 359.
84. Simmel, *The Philosophy of Money*, p. 100.
85. Durkheim, 'Sociology and its scientific field', p. 362.
86. Notably in O. Spann, *Wirtschaft und Gesellschaft* (Dresden 1907); reprinted in O. Spann, *Frühe Schriften in Auswahl* (Graz 1974) especially pp. 223—60.
87. M. Weber, 'Georg Simmel as Sociologist', *Social Research*, vol. 39 (1972) pp. 155—163. The reference to Spann's work is n. 5, p. 162. My emphasis.
88. ibid., pp. 161—2.
89. ibid., p. 162.
90. ibid.
91. ibid., p. 163.
92. D. Koigen, 'Sociologische Theorien', *Archiv für Sozialwissenschaft und Socialpolitik*, vol. 31 (1910) pp. 908—24.
93. ibid., p. 909.
94. ibid., p. 924.
95. T. Masaryk, 'Simmels Soziologie', *Zeitschrift für Socialwissenschaft*, vol. 12 (1909) pp. 600—7.
96. ibid., p. 601.
97. A. Vierkandt, 'Literaturbericht zur Kultur- und Gesellschaftslehre für die Jahre 1907 und 1908', *Archiv für die gesamte Psychologie*, vol. 17, 'Literatur' (1910) pp. 57—138.
98. ibid., p. 61.
99. ibid.
100. ibid., pp. 61—3.
101. Simmel, *Soziologie*, p. 635.
102. E. Troeltsch, 'Der historische Entwicklungsbegriff in der modernen Geistes- und Lebensphilosophie', *Historische Zeitsehrift*, vol. 124 (1921) p. 421.
103. G. Simmel, 'Anfang einer unvollendeten Selbstdarstellung', in Gassen and Landmann (eds) pp. 9—10.
104. ibid., p. 9; my emphasis.
105. M. Steinhoff, 'Die Form als soziologische Grundkategorie bei Georg Simmel', *Kölner Vierteljahrschefte für Soziologie*, vol. 4 (1925) pp. 215—59.
106. F. H. Tenbruck, 'Formal sociology' in Wolff (ed.) *Essays on Sociology, Philosophy and Aesthetics by Georg Simmel et al.* pp. 61—99; also Tenbruck, 'Georg Simmel'.
107. H. J. Becher, *Georg Simmel: Die Grundlagen seiner Soziologie* (Stuttgart 1971).
108. K. Schrader-Klebert, 'Der Begriff der Gesellschaft als regulative Idee', *Soziale Welt*, vol. 19 (1968) pp. 97—118.
109. Tenbruck, 'Formal sociology', p. 75.
110. Steinhoff, 'Die Form als soziologische Kategorie bei Georg Simmel', p. 231.

111. ibid., p. 242.
112. ibid., p. 250.
113. Tenbruck, 'Formal sociology', p. 85.
114. Becher, *Georg Simmel*. Becher's central argument is that 'the concept of interaction is in fact a central or, perhaps better, key concept in Simmel's sociology' (p. 1).
115. Simmel, 'Anfang einer unvollendeten Selbstdarstellung', p. 9.
116. Becher, *Georg Simmel*, p. 17.
117. ibid.
118. ibid., pp. 30—1.
119. ibid., p. 32.
120. ibid., p. 51.
121. In his essay 'How is society possible?', Simmel refers several times to phenomenology. The whole enterprise can be taken to be a phenomenological rather than a Kantian grounding of society. This is the direction of O'Neill's article 'How is society possible?' in J. O'Neill, *Sociology as a Skin Trade* (London 1972) pp. 167—76.
122. Schrader-Klebert, 'Der Begriff der Gesellschaft als regulative Idee' p. 105.
123. This important essay appears in the *Soziologie* after 'The Problem of Sociology' but merely as a kind of appendix to the chapter: see 'Exkurs über das Problem: wie ist Gesellschaft möglich?' in G. Simmel, *Soziologie, op. cit.*, pp. 21—30. 'How is Society Possible?' is translated in Wolff (ed.), *Essays on Sociology, Philosophy and Aesthetics* pp. 337—56.
124. Simmel, 'How is society possible?', p. 338.
125. ibid., pp. 343—4. Translation slightly amended.
126. ibid., p. 345.
127. ibid., p. 353. Translation slightly amended.
128. Schrader-Klebert, 'Der Begriff der Gesellschaft als regulative Idee', p. 116.
129. ibid., p. 118; my emphasis.

Chapter 3

1. G. Simmel, *Über sociale Differenzierung. Sociologische und psychologische Untersuchungen* (Leipzig 1890) especially pp. 1—9.
2. G. Simmel, *The Philosophy of Money*, (trans. T. Bottomore and D. Frisby) (London/Boston 1978) pp. 53—6, especially 55—6.
3. See, for example, T. G. Masaryk, 'Simmels Soziologie', *Zeitschrift für Socialwissenschaft*, vol. 12 (1909) pp. 600—7, especially 600—3; A. Vierkandt, 'Literaturbericht zur Kultur- und Gesellschaftslehre für die Jahre 1907 und 1908', *Archiv für die gesamte Psychologie*, vol. 17, pp. 57—138, especially pp. 60f.
4. G. Simmel, *Grundfragen der Soziologie (Individuum und Gesellschaft)* (Berlin 1917). The volume contains four chapters on the scope of sociology, the social and individual level, sociability and individual and society in eighteenth and nineteenth century views of life.
5. G. Simmel, 'Zur Methodik der Socialwissenschaft', *Jahrbuch für Gesetzgebung, Verwaltung und Volkswirtschaft*, vol. 20 (1896) pp. 227—37, especially p. 236.
6. G. Simmel, *Einleitung in die Moralwissenschaft. Eine Kritik der ethischen Grundbegriffe*, 2 vols (Berlin 1892—3). The comment on this volume was made to Kurt Gassen; cf. Gassen and Landmann (eds), *Buch des Dankes an Georg Simmel*, p. 314.

7. For the earlier versions of the *Soziologie* volume, see chapter 1 above, n. 101.
8. I have discussed the construction of *The Philosophy of Money* in my 'Intro-duction to the Translation' in Simmel, *The Philosophy of Money*, pp. 1—49. For the essay outlines that contribute to this volume see p. 37, n. 3.
9. M. Frischeisen-Köhler, 'Georg Simmel', *Kantstudien*, vol. 24 (1920) p. 7.
10. T. W. Adorno, 'Der Essay als Form', *Noten zur Literatur*, vol. 1 (Frankfurt 1958) p. 10.
11. L. von Wiese, *Allgemeine Soziologie als Lehre von den Beziehungen und Beziehungsgebilden der Menschen* (Munich/Leipzig 1924).
12. Frischeisen-Köhler, 'Georg Simmel', pp. 6—7.
13. G. Lukács, 'On the Nature and Form of the Essay', *Soul and Form* (trans. A. Bostock) (London 1974) pp. 1—18.
14. Adorno, 'Der Essay als Form'.
15. Lukács, 'On the Nature and Form of the Essay', p. 17.
16. Adorno, 'Der Essay als Form', pp. 22—3.
17. ibid., pp. 26—7.
18. Kracauer, *Georg Simmel*, ms., p. 41.
19. Adorno, 'Der Essay als Form', pp. 37—8.
20. Kracauer, *Georg Simmel*, ms., p. 41.
21. ibid., p. 43.
22. A. Koppel, 'Für und wider Karl Marx. Prolegomena zu einer Biographie', *Volkswirtschaftliche Abhandlungen der Badischen Hochschulen*, vol. 8 no. 1 (Karlsruhe 1905) p. 19. Despite the somewhat misleading title, Koppel's comparison of Marx and Simmel contains some valuable insights into the latter's social theory.
23. Kracauer, *Georg Simmel*, ms., pp. 44—5.
24. The concept of the *flâneur* is developed in W. Benjamin, *Charles Baudelaire: A Lyric Poet in the Era of High Capitalism*, (trans. H. Zohn) (London 1973) especially pp. 35—66. More recently, the material on Baudelaire has been reworked following the Benjamin tradition in D. Oehler, *Pariser Bilder 1. (1830—1848). Antibourgeoise Ästhetik bei Baudelaire, Daumier und Heine* (Frankfurt 1979) especially pp. 119ff.
25. G. Simmel, *Philosophische Kultur. Gesammelte Essais* (Leipzig 1911).
26. M. Landmann (ed.), *Brücke und Tür* (Stuttgart 1957).
27. See G. Simmel, 'Dante's Psychologie', *Zeitschrift für Völkerpsychologie und Sprachwissenschaft*, vol. 15 (1884) pp. 18—69.
28. See G. Simmel, 'Zur Psychologie des Geldes', *Jahrbuch für Gesetzgebung, Verwaltung und Volkswirtschaft*, vol. 13 (1889) pp. 1—14.
29. See Frischeisen-Köhler, 'Georg Simmel', p. 52, and M. Adler, *Georg Simmels Bedeutung für die Geistesgeschidik* (Vienna/Leipzig 1919) pp. 25f. The connections between Hegel and Simmel are examined more fully in P. Christian, *Einheit und Zwiespalt. Zum hegelianisierenden Denken in der Philosophie und Soziologie Georg Simmels*, dissertation, Heidelberg University 1977.
30. H. -J. Lieber, 'Kulturkritik und Gesellschaftstheorie im Denken Georg Simmels', in *Kulturkritik und Lebensphilosophie* (Darmstadt 1974) p. 77.
31. For further comparison of Hegel and Simmel on the treatment of money see B. Liebrucks, 'Über den logischen Ort des Geldes', in *Erkenntnis und Dialektik* (Hague 1972) pp. 265—301.
32. G. Simmel, 'Brücke und Tür', in Landmann (ed.), *Brücke und Tür*, p. 1.
33. Quoted in a letter by Paul Ernst to Georg Lukács in 1916 in K. A. Kutzbach (ed.), *Paul Ernst und Georg Lukács* (Emsdetten Westf., 1974) p. 85.
34. A. Vierkandt, 'Einige neuere Werke zur Kultur- und Gesellschaftslehre', *Zeitschrift für Socialwissenschaft*, vol. 4 (1901) pp. 640—1.
35. Frischeisen-Köhler, 'Georg Simmel', p. 6.

36. W. Benjamin, 'The Work of Art in the Age of Mechanical Reproduction', in *Illuminations* (trans. H. Zohn) (New York 1969) pp. 218—9.

37. ibid., p. 224. We might add here that Simmel does not blindly take up the notion of the autonomy of the work of art. In his essay on 'The problems of style' (1908), he explicitly takes up the difference between reproducible art and crafts or handicrafts [*Kunstgewerbe*] and art [*Kunst*]. Whereas the essence of handicrafts lies in the fact that they 'exist many times over', 'the essence of the work of art, in contrast, is uniqueness'. See G. Simmel, 'Das Problem des Stiles', *Dekorative Kunst*, vol. 11 no. 7 (1908) pp. 307—16, especially p. 309.

38. Quoted in W. Benjamin, *Charles Baudelaire*, p. 36.

39. ibid., p. 37.

40. ibid., p. 54.

41. Kracauer, *Georg Simmel*, ms., pp. 45—6.

42. J. Freund, 'German Sociology in the Time of Max Weber', in T. Bottomore and R. Nisbet (eds.), *A History of Sociological Analysis* (London 1979) p. 158.

43. W. Benjamin, *Charles Baudelaire*, p. 57.

44. ibid., p. 106.

45. Simmel, *The Philosophy of Money*, p. 474.

46. Koppel, 'Für und wieder Karl Marx', p. 20.

47. Kracauer, *Georg Simmel*, ms., p. 93.

48. Simmel, *The Philosophy of Money*, p. 55.

49. ibid., p. 56.

50. Kracauer, *Georg Simmel*, ms., p. 52.

51. S. Hübner-Funk, 'Ästhetizismus und Soziologie bei Georg Simmel', in H. Böhringer and K. Gründer (eds.), *Äesthetik und Soziologie um die Jahrhundertwende: Georg Simmel* (Frankfurt 1976) p. 55.

52. Simmel, *Soziologie*, Leipzig 1908, p. 31.

53. G. Simmel, 'Soziologische Aesthetik', *Die Zukunft*, vol. 17 (1896) p. 205.

54. Quoted in W. Benjamin, *Charles Baudelaire*, p. 82.

55. E. Troeltsch, *Der Historismus und seine Probleme* (Tübingen 1922) p. 593.

56. L. A. Coser, 'The stranger in the academy', in L. A. Coser (ed.) *Georg Simmel* (Englewood Cliffs, N.J. 1965) pp. 29—42.

57. W. Benjamin, *Charles Baudelaire*, p. 170.

58. G. Simmel, 'The Stranger', in D. N. Levine (ed.), *Georg Simmel. On Individuality and Social Forms* (Chicago/London 1971) p. 143.

59. ibid., p. 145.

60. Hübner-Funk, 'Ästhetik und Soziologie bei Georg Simmel', p. 46.

61. D. N. Levine, 'The structure of Simmel's social thought', in K. Wolff (ed.), *Essays on Sociology, Philosophy and Aesthetics: Georg Simmel* (New York 1965) p. 23.

62. M. S. Davis, 'Georg Simmel and the Aesthetics of Social Reality', *Social Forces*, vol. 51 (1973) p. 320.

63. Hübner-Funk, 'Ästhetik und Soziologie bei Georg Simmel', pp. 68—9.

64. ibid., p. 47.

65. ibid., p. 50.

66. ibid., p. 49.

67. ibid.

68. R. Goldscheid, 'Jahresbericht über Erscheinungen der Soziologie in den Jahren 1899—1904', *Archiv für systematische Philosophie*, vol. 10 (1904) pp. 411—12.

69. Hübner-Funk, 'Äesthetik und Soziologie bei Georg Simmel', p. 51.

70. L. von Wiese, 'Simmel's formal method' trans. M. Nicolaus), in L. Coser

(ed.), *Georg Simmel* (Englewood Cliffs 1965) pp. 55—6.

71. ibid., pp. 56—7.

72. Simmel, 'Soziologische Aesthetik', p. 78. This passage is very similar to the later treatment in his *Philosophy of Money*, pp. 474—5.

73. Simmel, *The Philosophy of Money*, p. 477.

74. Simmel, 'Soziologische Aesthetik', p. 73.

75. ibid., p. 74.

76. Simmel, *The Philosophy of Money*, p. 174.

77. See chapter 5 below.

78. R. Hamann and J. Hermand, *Impressionismus. Epochen deutscher Kultur von 1870 bis zur Gegenwart*, vol. 3 (Frankfurt 1977) p. 108.

79. G. Simmel, 'Dantes Psychologie', *Zeitschrift für Völkerpsychologie und Sprachwissenschaft*, vol. 15 (1886) pp. 18—69; G. Simmel, 'Michaelangelo als Dichter', *Vossische Zeitung* (8 September 1889) pp. 6—9; G. Simmel, 'Rembrandt als Erzieher', *Vossische Zeitung* (1 June 1890) pp. 7—10; G. Simmel, 'Das Abendmal Lionardo da Vincis', *Der Tag* (1905); G. Simmel, 'Michaelangelo', *Logos*, vol. 1 (1910/11) pp. 207—27; G. Simmel, 'Rembrandts religiöse Kunst', *Frankfurter Zeitung* (30 June, 1 July 1914); G. Simmel, 'Rembrandt und die Schönheit', *Vorsische Zeitung* (25 December 1914); G. Simmel, 'Rembrandtstudie', *Logos*, vol. 5 (1914/15) pp. 1—32; G. Simmel, 'Von Tode in der Kunst', *Frankfurter Zeitung*, 2 April 1915).

80. G. Simmel, 'Gerhart Hauptmanns "Weber" ', *Sozialpolitisches Zeutralblatt*, vol. 2 (1892/3); G. Simmel, 'Böcklins Landschaften', *Die Zukunft*, vol. 12 (1895) pp. 272—7; G. Simmel, 'Stefan George. Eine kunstphilosophische Betrachtung', *Die Zukunft*, vol. 22 (1989) pp. 386—96; G. Simmel, 'Polymeter', *Die Zeit*, Vienna (23 July 1898); G. Simmel, 'Stephan George. Eine kunstphilosophische Studie', *Neue Deutsche Rundschau*, vol. 12 (1901) pp. 207—15; G. Simmel, 'Rodins Plastik und die Geistesrichtung der Gegenwart', *Berliner Tageblatt* (29 September 1902); G. Simmel, 'Die Kunst Rodins und das Bewegungsmotiv in der Plastik', *Nord und Süd*, vol. 129 (1909) pp. 189—96; G. Simmel, 'Der Siebente Ring', *Münchner Neueste Nachrichten* (11 July 1909); G. Simmel, 'Erinnerung an Rodin', *Vossische Zeitung* (27 November 1917).

81. G. Lukács, 'Georg Simmel', in Gassen and Landmann (eds), p. 175.

82. Lukács, *Soul and Form*, p. 83.

83. Kracauer, *Georg Simmel*, p. 51.

84. See H. Böhringer, 'Spuren von spekulativem Atomismus in Simmels formaler Soziologie', in Böhringer and Gründer (eds), *Ästhetik und Soziologie um die Jahrhundertwende*, pp. 105—14.

85. G. Simmel, 'Soziologische Aesthetik', *Die Zukunft*, vol. 17 (1896) pp. 213—14.

86. ibid., p. 215.

87. ibid., p. 216.

88. E. Utitz, 'Georg Simmel und die Philosophie der Kunst', *Zeitschrift für Ästhetik und allgemeine Kunstwissenschaft*, vol. 14 (1920) p. 6.

89. G. Lukács, 'Georg Simmel' in Gassen and Landmann (eds), p. 172.

90. ibid., p. 173.

91. ibid.

92. ibid., p. 174.

93. ibid.

94. ibid., p. 175.

95. ibid.

96. ibid., p. 176.

97. Günther Jacoby quoted by K. Gassen in Gassen and Landmann (eds), p. 303.
98. K. Mannheim, 'German Sociology (1918–1933)', in K. Mannheim, *Essays on Sociology and Social Psychology* (London 1953) p. 217.
99. Lukács, 'Georg Simmel', p. 175.
100. Kracauer, *Georg Simmel*, p. 139.
101. W. Benjamin, 'Zentralpark', in *Illuminationen* (Frankfurt 1955) p. 262.
102. Kracauer, *Georg Simmel*, p. 37.
103. This essay is translated by Bendix as 'The Web of Group Affiliations' in G. Simmel, *Conflict and The Web of Group Affiliations* (New York 1955).
104. Kracauer, 'Georg Simmel', *Logos*, vol. 9 (1920) p. 314.
105. ibid.
106. ibid., p. 315.
107. Simmel, *The Philosophy of Money*, p. 174.
108. ibid., p. 175.
109. Kracauer, 'Georg Simmel', p. 316.
110. Kracauer, *Georg Simmel*, ms., p. 92.
111. Hamann and Hermand, *Impressionismus*, p. 86.
112. G. Simmel, *Philosophische Kultur* (Leipzig 1911) p. 8.
113. Hamann and Hermand, *Impressionismus*, p. 86.
114. Kracauer, *Georg Simmel*, ms., p. 126.
115. ibid., p. 124.
116. Margarete Susman in Gassen and Landmann (eds), p. 286.
117. K. Gassen in ibid., p. 303.
118. E. Bloch, 'Weisen des "Vielleicht" bei Simmel' in E. Bloch, *Philosophische Aufsätze zur objektiven Phantasie* (Frankfurt 1969) p. 57.
119. Hamann and Hermand, *Impressionismus*, p. 86.
120. Bloch, 'Weisen des "Vielleicht" bei Simmel', p. 58.
121. H. Böhringer, 'Spuren von spekulativem Atomismus in Simmels formaler Soziologie' in Böhringer and Gründer (eds), *Ästhetik und Soziologie um die Jahrhundertwende*, p. 110.
122. Frischeisen-Köhler, 'Georg Simmel', p. 26.
123. G. Simmel, 'The Crisis of Culture' in P. Lawrence, *Georg Simmel: Sociologist and European* (London 1976) p. 257.
124. R. Heberle, 'Simmel's Method', in Coser (ed.), *Georg Simmel*, p. 121.
125. Kracauer, *Georg Simmel*, ms., p. 137.

Chapter 4

1. Benjamin, *Charles Baudelaire*, p. 132. Benjamin also wrote a brief study of photography in W. Benjamin, 'Kleine Geschichte der Photographie' in *Angelus Novus* (Frankfurt 1966) pp. 229–47.
2. Kracauer, *Georg Simmel*, ms., p. 92.
3. G. Lukács, 'On the Nature and Form of the Essay' in *Soul and Form*, p. 9.
4. T. W. Adorno, 'Der Essay als Form' in *Noten zur Literatur I*, p. 25.
5. Hamann and Hermand, *Impressionismus*, p. 86.
6. G. Lukács, 'Georg Simmel' in Gassen and Landmann (eds), p. 172.
7. G. Simmel, 'Böcklins Landschaften', *Die Zukunft*, vol. 12 (1895) pp. 272–7.
8. ibid., p. 272.
9. ibid., p. 273.
10. F. Tenbruck, 'Georg Simmel', *Kölner Zeitschrift für Soziologie*, vol. 10 (1959) pp. 592–3.

11. G. Simmel, *The Philosophy of Money*, p. 54.
12. ibid.
13. ibid., p. 55.
14. G. Simmel to Hermann Keyserling, 31 October 1908, in M. Landmann (ed.) *Georg Simmel. Das individuelle Gesetz* (Frankfurt 1968) p. 239.
15. G. Simmel, 'Zur Psychologie des Geldes', *Jahrbuch für Gesetzgebung, Verwaltung und Volkswirtschaft*, vol. 13, no. 4 (1889) pp. 1251–64.
16. Simmel, 'Zur Psychologie des Geldes', p. 1258.
17. ibid., p. 1264.
18. Kracauer, 'Georg Simmel', *Logos*, vol. 9 (1920) p. 320.
19. ibid., p. 322.
20. E. Bloch, *Geist der Utopie*, 2nd edn, (Frankfurt 1964) p. 93.
21. G. Schmoller, 'Simmels Philosophie des Geldes', *Jahrbuch für Gesetzgebung, Verwaltung und Volkswirtschaft*, vol. 25 no. 3 (1901) p. 814.
22. Kracauer, 'Georg Simmel', p. 330.
23. Schrader-Klebert, 'Der Begriff der Gesellschaft als regulative Idee', p. 97, n. 5.
24. Simmel, *The Philosophy of Money*, p. 53.
25. ibid., pp. 55–6.
26. ibid., p. 54.
27. ibid., p. 56.
28. H. -J. Lieber, *Kulturkritik und Lebensphilosophie* (Darmstadt 1974) p. 71.
29. ibid., pp. 69–70.
30. Quoted in Gassen and Landmann (eds), p. 94.
31. Simmel, *The Philosophy of Money*, p. 84.
32. H. Blumenberg, 'Geld oder Leben' in Böhringer and Gründer (eds), *Ästhetik und Soziologie um die Jahrhundertwende*, p. 125.
33. Simmel, *The Philosophy of Money*, p. 84.
34. ibid.
35. ibid., pp. 83–4; my emphasis.
36. ibid., p. 83.
37. ibid., p. 89.
38. ibid., p. 90.
39. ibid., p. 82.
40. ibid., p. 101.
41. In K. Marx, *The Poverty of Philosophy* (New York 1963) p. 180.
42. Simmel, *The Philosophy of Money*, p. 174.
43. ibid., p. 129.
44. ibid., p. 175.
45. ibid., p. 119.
46. ibid.
47. ibid., p. 117.
48. A. Arato, 'The neo-idealist defense of subjectivity', *Telos*, no. 21 (1974) p. 154.
49. K. Mannheim, 'Eine soziologische Theorie der Kultur und ihrer Erkennbarkeit', unpublished ms., p. 9.
50. ibid.
51. G. Simmel, *The Philosophy of Money*, pp. 178–9.
52. ibid., pp. 409–28.
53. H. Brinkmann, *Methode und Geschichte. Die Analyse der Entfremdung in Georg Simmels 'Philosophie des Geldes'* (Giessen 1974) p. 82.
54. Simmel, *The Philosophy of Money*, p. 413.
55. G. Simmel, 'Geld allein macht nicht Glücklich', *Jugend*, vol. 6, I (1901) p. 300.
56. G. Simmel, 'Berliner Gewerbe-Ausstellung', *Die Zeit*, vol. 8 (25 July 1896).

57. G. Masur, *Imperial Britain* (London 1971) p. 126.
58. Simmel, 'Berliner Gewerbe-Ausstellung'.
59. ibid.
60. ibid.
61. Benjamin, *Charles Baudelaire*, p. 165.
62. Simmel, 'Berliner Gewerbe-Ausstellung'.
63. ibid.
64. ibid.
65. Benjamin, *Charles Baudelaire*, p. 165.
66. See G. Simmel, 'Zur Psychologie der Mode', *Die Zeit*, vol. 5 (12 October 1895); G. Simmel, 'Soziologie der Konkurrenz', *Neue Deutsche Rundschau*, vol. 14 (1903); G. Simmel, *Philosophie der Mode* (Berlin 1905); G. Simmel, 'Das Problem des Stiles', *Dekorative Kunst*, vol. 16 (1908) pp. 307—16.
67. H. -J. Lieber, *Kulturkritik und Lebensphilosophie*, p. 74.
68. ibid., p. 75.
69. A. Arato, 'The neo-idealist defense of subjectivity', p. 153.
70. Simmel, *The Philosophy of Money*, p. 335; my emphasis.
71. ibid., p. 296.
72. ibid., pp. 352—3.
73. ibid., p. 454.
74. ibid.
75. ibid., pp. 455—6.
76. ibid., p. 456.
77. ibid., p. 457.
78. ibid., p. 458.
79. ibid.; my emphasis.
80. ibid., p. 459.
81. ibid., p. 461.
82. ibid., p. 461.
83. ibid., p. 462.
84. ibid., p. 463.
85. Simmel, 'Das Problem des Stiles'.
86. ibid., p. 314.
87. ibid., p. 313.
88. Simmel, *The Philosophy of Money*, p. 469.
89. ibid., p. 484.
90. Benjamin, *Charles Baudelaire*, p. 166.
91. T. W. Adorno, *Kierkegaard*, 3rd edn (Frankfurt 1966) p. 87.
92. Simmel, *The Philosophy of Money*, pp. 510—11.
93. ibid., pp. 494—5.

Chapter 5

1. K. Joël, 'Eine Zeitphilosophie', *Neue Deutsche Rundschau*, vol. 12 (1901) pp. 812—26.
2. ibid., p. 812.
3. P. Ernst, 'Philosophie des Geldes', *Die Zukunft*, vol. 35 (1900) p. 377.
4. Kracauer, *Georg Simmel*, ms., pp. 137 and 106.
5. P. Fechter, 'Erinnerungen an Simmel', in Gassen and Landmann (eds), *Buch des Dankes an Georg Simmel*, p. 159.
6. F. Wolters, 'Erinnerungen an Simmel', p. 195.
7. H. G. Gadamer, *Truth and Method* (London 1975) p. 57.

8. On Weber's contemporary social and political analysis, see W. Mommsen, *Max Weber und die deutsche Politik: 1890—1920*, (Tübingen 1959); W. Mommsen, *The Age of Bureaucracy* (Oxford 1974); D. Beetham, *Max Weber and the Theory of Modern Politics*, (London 1974); W. Schluchter, 'Das Wilhelminische Deutschland in der Sicht eines Soziologen: Max Webers Kritik am Kaiserreich', in *Rationalität in Perspektive: Studien zu Max Weber* (Tübingen 1979).

9. G. Simmel, 'Deutschlands innere Wandlung' in *Der Krieg und die geistigen Entscheidungen* (Munich/Leipzig 1917) p. 26.

10. ibid., pp. 24—5.

11. Becher, *Georg Simmel*, pp. 23—4.

12. Simmel, *Einleitung in die Moralphilosophie*, vol. 2, pp. 359—60.

13. Simmel, *The Philosophy of Money*, p. 484.

14. G. Simmel, 'Anfang einer unvollendeten Selbstdarstellung' in Gassen and Landmann (eds), p. 9.

15. H. Simmel, 'Auszüge aus den Lebenserinnerungen' in Böhringer and Gründer (eds), *Ästhetik und Soziologie um die Jahrhundertwende: Georg Simmel*, p. 260.

16. See S. Lozinskij, 'Simmels Briefe zur jüdischen Frage', in Böhringer and Gründer (eds), pp. 240—3. Also H. Liebeschütz, *Von Georg Simmel zu Franz Rosenzweig: Studien zum jüdischen Denken im deutschen Kulturbereich* (Tübingen 1970) pp. 103—40.

17. G. Simmel, 'Ein Wort über soziale Freiheit', *Sozialpolitische Centralblatt*, vol. 1 (1892) pp. 333—5.

18. T. Zeldin, *France 1848—1945: Politics and Anger* (Oxford 1979) chapter 8.

19. Simmel, 'Ein Wort über soziale Freiheit', p. 334.

20. ibid.

21. Simmel, 'Soziale Medizin', *Die Zeit* (Vienna) vol. 10 (13 February 1897). Translated in J. Casparis and A. C. Higgins, 'Georg Simmel on Social Medicine', *Social Forces*, vol. 47 no. 3 (1968) pp. 330—4.

22. ibid., p. 332.

23. ibid., p. 334.

24. ibid.

25. G. Simmel, 'Der Frauenkongress und die Sozialdemokratie', *Die Zukunft*, vol. 17 (1896) pp. 80—4.

26. ibid., p. 81.

27. ibid., p. 82. These 'socialist' measures are, of course, associated with Bismarck's social policy.

28. ibid., p. 84.

29. ibid.

30. See G. Simmel, 'Das individuelle Gesetz', *Logos*, vol. 4 (1913). A much enlarged version also appears in G. Simmel, *Lebensanschauung* (Munich/Leipzig 1918).

31. A. Koppel, *Für und wider Karl Marx* (Karlsruhe 1905) pp. 89—90.

32. G. Simmel, 'Sozialismus und Pessimismus', *Die Zeit*, vol. 22 (3 February 1900).

33. Simmel, 'Sozialismus und Pessimismus'.

34. G. Simmel, 'Parerga zur Sozialphilosophie', *Jahrbuch für Gesetzgebung, Verwaltung und Volkswirtschaft*, vol. 18 (1894) p. 263.

35. G. Simmel, 'Zur Philosophie der Arbeit', *Neue deutsche Rundschau*, vol. 10 (1899) p. 462.

36. Simmel, *The Philosophy of Money*, p. 346.

37. ibid., pp. 263—4.

38. G. Simmel, 'Sociological Aesthetics', in K. P. Etzkorn (trans.) *Georg Simmel*.

The Conflict in Modern Culture and Other Essays (New York 1968) p. 74; translation amended.
39. Simmel, 'Sociological Aesthetics', p. 80.
40. ibid., p. 75.
41. Simmel, *The Philosophy of Money*, p. 493.
42. Letter to Count Hermann Keyserling, 18 May 1918, in M. Landmann (ed.), *Georg Simmel. Das individuelle Gesetz* (Frankfurt 1968) p. 246.
43. ibid.
44. In his review of *The Philosophy of Money*, Gustav Schmoller suggested that 'The conventional socialists will scent an aristocrat in him'. See G. Schmoller, 'Simmels Philosophie des Geldes', *Jahrbuch für Gesetzgebung, Verwaltung und Volkswirtschaft*, vol. 25 no. 3 (1901) p. 816.
45. R. Heberle, 'Simmel's method' in L. A. Coser (ed.), *Georg Simmel*, (Englewood Cliffs, N.J. 1965) p. 120.
46. Simmel, *The Philosophy of Money*, p. 174.
47. ibid., p. 449.
48. ibid., p. 469; my emphasis.
49. ibid.
50. H. -J. Lieber, *Kulturkritik und Lebensphilosophie* (Darmstadt 1974) p. 17.
51. ibid.
52. G. Simmel, 'Der Begriff und die Tragödie der Kultur' in *Philosophische Kultur* (Leipzig 1911); translated in Etzkorn, *Georg Simmel*, pp. 27—46.
53. G. Simmel, 'Einleitung', *Philosophische Kultur*, p. 7.
54. ibid.
55. Simmel, 'The concept and tragedy of culture', p. 31.
56. ibid., p. 42; my emphasis.
57. ibid., p. 43; amended translation.
58. G. Simmel, *Der Konflikt der modernen Kultur. Ein Vortrag* (Munich/Leipzig 1918); translated in Etzkorn, *Georg Simmel*, pp. 11—26, especially p. 12.
59. ibid.
60. ibid., p. 26.
61. Becher, *Georg Simmel*, p. 74.
62. G. Simmel, *Hauptproblemen der Philosophie* (Berlin 1910).
63. Steinhoff, 'Die Form als soziologische Grundkategorie bei Georg Simmel', p. 225.
64. G. Simmel, 'The field of sociology' in Wolff (trans. and ed.) *The Sociology of Georg Simmel*, pp. 7—8.
65. Simmel, *The Philosophy of Money*, p. 71.
66. ibid., p. 73.
67. S. Hübner-Funk, 'Ästhetizismus und Soziologie bei Georg Simmel', in Böhringer and Gründer (eds), *Ästhetik und Soziologie um die Jahrhundertwende*, p. 51.
68. G. Simmel, 'Böcklins Landschaften', *Die Zukunft*, vol. 12 (1895) p. 275.
69. N. J. Spykman, *The Social Theory of Georg Simmel* (Chicago 1925; reprinted New York 1965) pp. 270—1.
70. Kracauer, *Georg Simmel*, ms., p. 43.
71. F. Nietzsche, *Werke IV*, (ed. K. Schlechta) (Frankfurt/Berlin/Vienna 1972) p. 903.
72. Kracauer, *Georg Simmel*, ms., p. 103.
73. ibid., p. 75.
74. L. Marcuse, 'Erinnerungen an Simmel' in Gassen and Landmann (eds) p. 189.
75. K. Gassen, 'Erinnerungen an Simmel', in Gassen and Landmann (eds), pp. 305—6.
76. Kracauer, *Georg Simmel*, ms., p. 89.

77. See my *The Alienated Mind: The Emergence of the Sociology of Knowledge in Germany 1918—33* (London 1981).

78. Kracauer, *Georg Simmel*, ms., p. 115.

79. G. Müller, *Ideologiekritik und Metasprache — in Robert Musils Roman 'Der Mann ohne Eigenschaften'* (Munich/Salzburg 1972). I have relied heavily upon Müller's interpretation. For another account see H. Böhme, *Anomie und Entfremdung* (Kronberg/Ts., 1974).

80. ibid., pp. 59—88.

81. E. Troeltsch, 'Der historische Entwicklungsbegriff in der modernen Geistes — und Lebensphilosophie', *Historische Zeitschrift*, vol. 124 (1921) p. 422.

82. R. Musil, *Gesammelte Werke*, (ed. A. Frisé), vol. 4 (Reinbeck bei Hamburg 1978) p. 1237.

83. Quoted in Müller, *Ideologiekritik und Metasprache*, p. 61 n. 46.

84. ibid., p. 65.

85. On the historicist implications see K.-O. Apel, *Towards a Transformation of Philosophy* (trans. G. Adey and D. Frisby) (London/Boston 1980) pp. 59f.

86. Müller, *Ideologie Kritik und Metasprache*, p. 69.

87. R. Musil, *Der Mann ohne Eigenschaften* (ed. A. Frisé) (Reisbeck bei Hamburg 1970) p. 1579.

88. M. Susman, *Die geistige Gestalt Georg Simmels* (Tübingen 1959) p. 16.

89. G. Simmel, 'Das Gleichgiltigste. Ein Moralische Dilemma', *Jugend*, vol. 2, II (1897) p. 775.

90. Müller, *Ideologiekritik und Metasprache*, p. 87.

91. Quoted in ibid., p. 85.

92. R. Musil, *The Man without Qualities*, (trans. E. Wilkins and E. Kaiser) (London 1968) vol. 1, pp. 314—15. Unfortunately the whole of the original now assembled, together with posthumous fragments, has yet to be translated.

93. ibid., p. 315.

94. Paul Ernst in a letter to Georg Lukács, 23 March 1916 in K. A. Kutzbach (ed.) *Paul Ernst und Georg Lukács. Dokumente einer Freundschaft* (Emsdetten, Westf. 1974) p. 85.

95. Letter to Count Hermann Keyserling, 5 July 1918, in Landmann (ed.) *Georg Simmel. Das Individuelle Gesetz*, p. 249.

96. Musil, *The Man without Qualities*, vol. 2, pp. 70—1.

97. Troeltsch, 'Der historische Entwicklungsbegriff', p. 431.

98. Simmel, 'Deutschlands innere Wandlung', p. 25.

99. Müller, *Ideologiekritik und Metasprache*, p. 78.

100. G. Simmel, 'Deutschlands innere Wandlung', p. 9.

101. Musil, *Der Mann ohne Eigenschaften*, p. 1574.

Bibliographical Note

There is an excellent comprehensive bibliography of Georg Simmel's works together with a bibliography of books and articles on Simmel up to 1958 by Kurt Gassen in K. Gassen and M. Landmann (eds), *Buch des Dankes an Georg Simmel* (Berlin 1958) pp. 311—65. This may be supplemented by H.-M Sass's 'Nachträge zur Bibliographie Georg Simmel' in H. Böhringer and K. Gründer (eds), *Ästhetik und Soziologie um die Jahrhundertwende: Georg Simmel* (Frankfurt 1976) pp. 277—82, which brings the bibliography up to 1975. For the period up to 1958, the English reader should consult the following book edited by Kurt Wolff: *Essays on Sociology, Philosophy and Aesthetics by Georg Simmel et al.* (Columbus, Ohio 1959; New York 1965) pp. 357—81.

In addition, mention should be made of the following recent translations:

P. Lawrence (ed. and introd.) *Georg Simmel: Sociologist and European* (London 1976).

G. Simmel *The Problems of the Philosophy of History* (trans. and ed. G. Oakes) (New York 1977)

G. Simmel *The Philosophy of Money* (trans. T. Bottomore and D. Frisby, with an introduction by D. Frisby) (London/Boston 1978)

On Simmel's work the following should also be consulted:

P. E. Schnabel *Die soziologische Gesamtkonzeption Georg Simmels* (Stuttgart 1974)

P. E. Schnabel 'Georg Simmel' in D. Kasler (ed.) *Klassiker des soziologischen Denkens*, vol. 1 (Munich 1976) pp. 267—311.

Index of Names